Innovation Commons

Innovation Commons

The Origin of Economic Growth

JASON POTTS

OXFORD
UNIVERSITY PRESS

OXFORD
UNIVERSITY PRESS

Oxford University Press is a department of the University of Oxford. It furthers the University's objective of excellence in research, scholarship, and education by publishing worldwide. Oxford is a registered trade mark of Oxford University Press in the UK and certain other countries.

Published in the United States of America by Oxford University Press
198 Madison Avenue, New York, NY 10016, United States of America.

Library of Congress Cataloging-in-Publication Data
Names: Potts, Jason, 1972– author.
Title: Innovation commons : the origin of economic growth / Jason Potts.
Description: New York, NY : Oxford University Press, [2019] |
Includes bibliographical references and index.
Identifiers: LCCN 2018045757 | ISBN 9780190937492 (hardcover : alk. paper) |
ISBN 9780190937508 (pbk. : alk. paper)
Subjects: LCSH: Technological innovations—Economic aspects. |
Diffusion of innovations. | Cooperation.
Classification: LCC HC79.T4 P677 2019 | DDC 338/.064—dc23
LC record available at https://lccn.loc.gov/2018045757

1 3 5 7 9 8 6 4 2

Paperback printed by Sheridan Books, Inc., United States of America
Hardback printed by Bridgeport National Bindery, Inc., United States of America

CONTENTS

ILLUSTRATIONS

Figures

Tables

PREFACE: AGAINST PROMETHEUS

Prometheus the Titan loved humans, and for them he stole fire from Zeus and the other gods. Zeus was outraged and punished Prometheus for eternity. But because of Prometheus's heroic sacrifice, human beings now had fire and new powers of their own.

The Prometheus myth remains potent in modern innovation economics. In the Athenian-Schumpeterian translation, the lone heroic entrepreneur wrests knowledge away—innovates, as we say now—but must pay for this impudence against the natural order of things. And in the modern telling, the power of the gods has been largely replaced by the power of government. And instead of eagles feasting on livers, now it's IP lawyers and taxes. But mutatis mutandis you see the same story at work.

It begins in Vienna at the turn of the twentieth century, when a young Joseph Schumpeter (1911) locates the wellspring of market capitalism in the heroic venturing of the entrepreneur. Soon, America's chief engineer (Bush 1945) will declare that science is the endless frontier, and America's top economist (Arrow 1962a,b) will explain that without government there is no science. So innovation policy will come to pass, and as it spreads throughout the world, it will be understood of the new technologies—these new ideas and innovations that drive and power the wealth of nations—that they come from the gods, or from god-like individuals: from government, or from heroic inventors and entrepreneurs.

The Prometheus myth is powerful because it identifies—in the heroic individual entrepreneur who disrupts markets, and in the powerful benevolent government that fixes market failures—the *primus movens* of the market economy. It tells you where to look to find the causes of change in the prospects an economy. Look to the gods and their messengers. Look to entrepreneurs and to entrepreneurial firms. Look to government and its innovation policy.

The Prometheus myth fetishizes heroic genius and power. What it less easily admits is that a bunch of human mortals, alone in the universe but for each other, could pool and share insights and experiences, could pass ideas from mind to mind, could between themselves work together to eventually figure out fire. It misses the insight that we innovate together.

ACKNOWLEDGMENTS

I wish to thank the Australian Research Council for support with the Future Fellowship grant (FT120100509). I would like to thank colleagues and PhD students—my own happy little innovation commons—including Sinclair Davidson, John Hartley, Trent MacDonald, Prateek Goorha, Vijay Mohan, Darcy Allen, Aaron Lane, Christopher Berg, Duncan Law, Stuart Thomas, Mady Tyson, Mikayla Novak, John Foster, Kurt Dopfer, Peter Earl, Stuart Cunningham, and others who have worked on the theory of innovation commons, and have contributed and shaped the ideas in this book. I would also specifically like to thank seminar participants at conferences and workshops at Arizona State University, the Conference for the International Society of the Commons (Edmonton), "Bioeconomics of Cooperation and Conflict in the Family" (Sydney), the Public Choice Society, the International Joseph A. Schumpeter Society, the School of Economics at New York University, ShanghaiTech University, and RMIT University. And of course Ellie Rennie, who wanted me to make utterly clear, once and for all, so as to end these ridiculous rumors, that she is not Satoshi Nakamoto.

1

We Innovate Together

Modern market capitalism is an institutional system that grows and evolves through a process of innovation. New ideas enter through entrepreneurial firms and develop in competitive markets, causing industrial dynamics. The institutions of the innovation system are firms, markets, and governments, and thereby, so it would seem, the origin of innovation must logically begin with entrepreneurial action in firms, markets, or governments. Indeed, it was Joseph Schumpeter who insisted that the general theory of economic dynamics should start thus: "In the beginning is the entrepreneur . . ."

Yet the true origin of innovation, as I will argue in this book, is an economic process that actually starts prior to the entrepreneur in the *innovation commons*, which is the economic institution that guides the innovation process from a nascent technical idea to conditions sufficient both for entrepreneurial action in firms and markets and then for innovation policy.

An innovation commons is a system of rules for cooperation to facilitate pooling of information in order to maximize the likelihood of opportunity discovery. An innovation commons is a governance institution to incentivize cooperation to pool distributed information, knowledge, and other inputs into innovation under conditions of high uncertainty. The purpose of an innovation commons is to facilitate the entrepreneurial discovery of an economic opportunity. In other words, the true origin of innovation is not entrepreneurial creativity or imagination per se, but the creation of a common-pool resource *from which entrepreneurs can draw* to discover opportunities. An innovation commons is an institution to incentivize cooperation to create the fundamental resource that is the true origin of innovation.

The theory of innovation begins not with Schumpeter, but rather with Elinor Ostrom's governance model of the commons operating in Friedrich Hayek's world of distributed knowledge and information under uncertainty. When the economic value or worth of a new technological prospect is shrouded in uncertainty—which arises because information is distributed or is only experimentally obtained—a *commons* can be an economically efficient governance institution. Specifically, a commons is efficient compared to the creation of alternative economic institutions that involve extensive contracting and networks, private property rights and price signals, or public goods (i.e., firms, markets, and governments).

This book will present the theory of the innovation commons, which argues that innovation begins with institutions to govern the cooperative pooling of innovation resources (including, especially, information) under conditions of uncertainty to facilitate entrepreneurial discovery of opportunity. This new framework for analysis of the origin of innovation draws on evolutionary theory of cooperation and institutional theory of the commons and carries important implications for our understanding of the origin of firms and industries, and for the design of innovation policy.

1.1 The Origin of Innovation

Innovation is the economic process by which new ideas for value creation are originated within, adopted into, and retained by the economic system. Innovation is a process of entrepreneurial action working through investment by firms and disruption in markets. Economic innovation is the origin of prosperity, wealth, and ultimately human flourishing. But what is the origin of innovation itself? In the standard economic model—both neoclassical and Schumpeterian—innovation is a combination of human creativity, imagination, entrepreneurship, and investment.

Indeed, modern economic theory explains the origin of wealth much like the modern scientific account of the origin of life: a bunch of very unlikely things all had to come together, but once the process got going, it became, under a driving evolutionary logic, an inevitable and cumulative dynamical process. Just as life evolves, so do cultures, societies, and economies by the same process of variation, selection, and replication. The classical economists taught us this, although it was the post-Darwinian social theorists and economists such as Menger, Marx, Veblen, Mises, and Schumpeter who laid the foundations of this modern understanding of the market economy as an evolutionary process (Nelson and Winter 1982; Hodgson 1993).

So what causes economic growth? The things that come together to drive economic growth are the factors in any macroeconomic growth equation, namely:

$$Y = f\{\text{natural resources, labor, capital, technology, institutions, } \ldots\}$$

Modern economics drops natural resources and labor from this set, focusing on different forms of *capital*—mostly physical (Solow 1956) and human capital (Lucas 1988), but also more exotic forms such as social capital—all as consequences of *investment*, which then also extends to technology through R &

D investment (Romer 1990). This pushes the question back to why investment in knowledge and capital works to cause growth, and here explanation shifts to the effective *institutions* that incentivize capital investment (North 1990, 2005; Acemoglu and Robinson 2012).

However, if good institutions are so important, we might wonder why they arrived so late in the human story, in the northwest corner of a dark and cold Europe in the 1700s and not sooner, or in another part of the world. Recently, McCloskey (2006, 2010, 2016) and Mokyr (2002, 2009, 2016b) have argued that this was because of a moral revolution among a knowledge elite as an outgrowth of the Enlightenment.

The macro theory of the origin of wealth makes a comprehensive, compelling, and coherent story. It explains how human society figured out how to create and grow knowledge, put it to valuable use, and systematically build on that advance. It explains global growth, as others were able to copy it, expanding the universe of economic cooperation, creating feedback for the growth of knowledge processes. A moral revolution begat an institutional revolution begat an industrial revolution, and here we are now, with abundant food, clothing, and leisure, self-driving trucks and self-parking cars, on the verge of bioengineering the human germ-line, and seriously discussing how we're going to get to Mars and what we might do with quantum computing.

What is striking about how we became rich, or on the path to becoming so, is that while markets and competition are very much in the foreground, and essential to the warp and weft of modern economic life, this is ultimately a story of the triumph of human cooperation.[1] We *Homo sapiens* are, as Bowles and Gintis (2013) explain, a highly cooperative species, and we are so because we evolved that way (Nowak 2011; Turchin 2015). It's our niche; we cooperate better than any other animal.

But—and a very important *but*—we are not a collectivist animal. We are most unlike the social insects, those paragons of self-sacrificing cooperation. We are not instinctively cooperative in the universal altruistic (or socialist) sense. Rather, we humans are a "groupish" or "demic" animal (Dunbar 2005; Hartley and Potts 2014). We cooperate readily with our in-group, less so with the out-group, an evolved consequence of multilevel selection (Wilson and Wilson 2007). The genius of our moral and institutional revolutions, and the institutions of trade and exchange, is how they greatly expanded the functional definition of the in-group (Seabright 2004). We are intensely cooperative in groups, and those cooperative groups compete with other cooperative groups, a process that has shaped human evolution. This same process powers societal, institutional, and economic evolution.

This book will emphasize a particular use of cooperation that is instrumental to economic progress, namely cooperation to produce new knowledge and to discover new economic opportunities. This use of cooperation in what I will call the innovation commons differs from the more generalized forms of cooperation analyzed in, for example, prisoner's dilemma or stag hunt games, where the coordination problem is associated with commitment to a known or expected outcome, which is to say that the "game" of new knowledge discovery and its uses is profoundly open and uncertain. It's hard to credibly commit to a cooperative endeavor when you don't quite know what it is that you're doing, or how it will turn out, or even what your role in it will be. Innovation begins, I will argue, with an institutional solution to the problem of cooperation under extreme uncertainty.[2]

Modern evolutionary economics, certainly since Schumpeter or Marshall, and as developed in Penrose (1959) and Cyert and March (1963) and exemplified in Nelson and Winter (1982), did an end run around this problem by casting cooperation in the search for new knowledge in terms of the organization of the innovating firm. It's an entirely valid and enormously fruitful working assumption, and it plainly captured the significant role of the industrial organization of research and development that came of age through the twentieth century (Bush 1945; Nelson 1959; de Sola Price 1963; Eisenberg and Nelson 2002), and which was in turn the basis for the subsequent extension of this concept of the metacooperative structures known as innovation systems (Freeman 1987; Nelson 1993). But the upshot of this sequence of intellectual development of the economics of innovation, broadly known as evolutionary or neo-Schumpeterian economics, was a model in which the creative entrepreneur was subsumed into the innovating firm, and the innovating firm then subsumed into the innovation system. Cooperation disappears beneath the surface of this framework, contained within the institutions that coordinate competitive markets, organize innovating firms, and design innovation systems.

So why, then, are some times and places, or societies and cultures, so fertile with innovative possibility, and others not? In the evolutionary account of economic growth and development, the central explanatory factor is the growth of knowledge (Popper 1972; Loasby 1999; Ziman 2000; Harvey and Metcalfe 2004), or in its narrower economic sense, the evolution of technology (Rosenberg 1982; Arthur 2009). In the preceding account, it is because those times and places had effective institutions for innovation, which in turn enabled innovating organizations to prosper through effective investment and entrepreneurship. And that must indeed be the case, and so evolutionary economics has made substantial contributions to our understanding of economic dynamics by unpacking the nature of these institutions, organizations, and investments, and the entrepreneurs who populate these domains. We now know a great deal about the characteristics of an innovative economy and the industrial dynamics of new technology.

Yet we still don't really know how this all gets started. We're still mostly students of Schumpeter's dictum: "In the beginning is the entrepreneur . . ."

Origins are the hardest part of any inquiry into dynamics. Evolutionary theory itself, manifestly, is not a theory of origins, but only a theory of what happens once a process of variation in population under differential selective pressure gets started. (Note that the working assumption is that origins are random chance, i.e., a mutation, a random recombination.) The analogue should be obvious: the entrepreneur is the mutation, creatively imparting variety into the economic system, upon which the evolutionary forces of differential market selection then work. That's Schumpeter's theory of economic development (McCraw 2009; Dekker 2016). Entrepreneurial creative genius, in the Schumpeterian hypothesis, is the origin of economic evolution.[3]

My argument, however, is that cooperation is how it all gets started. Or specifically, that *creative genius is necessary but not sufficient* to engender economic evolution, and that the market opportunities exploited by entrepreneurial action, which are the apparent origin of the innovation trajectory (Schumpeter 1939; Dosi 1982; Perez 2002), which is in turn the dynamic unit of economic evolution (Dopfer and Potts 2008), actually originate in a prior phase of economic coordination that I call the innovation commons.

Entrepreneurial action is the proximate but not the ultimate cause of an innovation trajectory, and therefore of economic evolution. The true origin of economic evolution occurs one step further back, in the commons.

An innovation commons is in this sense an emergent institution, characterized by the formation of a cooperative group, under conditions of extreme uncertainty, toward the mutual purpose of opportunity discovery about a nascent technology or new idea. An innovation commons may well be heavily populated by creative geniuses. It is in this respect entirely consistent with the upper-tail human capital theory of the growth of knowledge (Mokyr 2016; Shleifer 2016). But the more salient observation is that it is usually populated with enthusiasts and skilled amateurs—or in the vernacular, with *hobbyists* and *hackers*—who are at the forefront of developing and exploring the new technology, whether by happenstance or by intention, and in so doing have accumulated information and knowledge about the new idea.

We innovate together. We do this not because we are brilliant, lovely, and humble people, each of us committed to the well-being of our community and our descendants. Perhaps some of us are; and you, dear reader, surely are: but that's not why we have succeeded thusly. Rather, we have done so because innovation is hard, even when you're a creative genius. Innovation is hard because information is distributed and even the sharpest among us only see part of the picture. So any mechanism that pools that information thereby creates an advantage to those who can access that pool. The smart people want to be in the pool. But, and this is where the economics kicks in, pooling creates a social dilemma, a point that Garret Hardin (1968) saw was infinitely and universally tragic, but that Elinor Ostrom (1990) realized could be, and routinely in fact was, overcome by human ingenuity. We invent institutions to govern cooperation.

Modern innovation economics follows Hardin, who espoused a rigorous logical position about the instability of cooperation in collective action (e.g., Arrow 1962b; cf. Olson 1965). However, in this book I will argue that Ostrom had it right for natural resource commons, and as she and her colleagues subsequently pointed out, this is also true for knowledge commons (Hess and Ostrom 2006; Madison et al. 2010a; Frischmann et al. 2014).

Modern Schumpeterian innovation economics largely bypassed this insight by locating the problem within the space of the innovating firm, by definition a hierarchical organizational structure that is governed by contract. This was buttressed within a framework of intellectual property rights over ideas, protecting the innovating firm from market failure due to the tragedy of the commons. In this firm-centered view, invention is necessary but not sufficient, and innovation drives economic development. Innovation was essentially a story of production costs and the competitive returns to R & D. In the modern Schumpeterian view, then, the innovation problem is an organizational and coordination problem resolved within firms and markets. There is no space for the commons here because there is no role for such cooperation in the story. The origin of innovation, the *primum movens*, is the entrepreneurial insight that emerges, fully formed, as a conjecture of prospective value waiting to be tested by the market process.

This model resonates, particularly in business schools, and is of course true in many practical respects: entrepreneurs propose and markets test, in an ongoing evolutionary Popperian dialectic. But as an analytic perspective, this process is always ex post.

My starting point in this book, instead, is to consider what this looks like ex ante (Shackle 1972). In the fog of uncertainty associated with a new idea or technology, where it is unclear what exact prospect the idea has (at the time of writing, pertinent examples are blockchain technology, civilian drone technology, CRISPR, and AI), where many people are knowledgeable, but everyone is aware that they only have insight into part of the puzzle—and furthermore where all of us are never quite sure what part we have insight into—a practical solution to the innovation problem is to pool information and knowledge.

To form a group is to seek to combine those parts, and to do so, as it were, from behind a veil of ignorance about the value of the contributed parts, the purpose of which is to reveal and discover the latent entrepreneurial opportunity. But this group that seeks to cooperate as such is not yet a firm. It is not a hierarchical and contract-bound organization. It has no leader, or at least no residual claimant. Uncertainty is too high for that to happen. And if you could somehow see how to form a firm—and so to persuade investors to finance and employees to join—so as to make financial and labor contracts, then ipso facto, you have revealed a bubble of probabilistic mutual expectation. Good. No need for an innovation commons. You can proceed straight to an efficient market institutional solution. The context of the innovation commons is the uncertain space before that entrepreneurial insight occurs. It is when there is an idea, a prospect, a promise, a hope, and in most cases a passionate sense of value prospect, a reason that something is good and that society would benefit from more of it, but as yet no obvious way, as it were, to monetize it or to reveal a profitable opportunity.

Value creation is complex. It is not enough that something new is clever and good. It also has to be of value within the immediate situational complex of information and possibility, which is to say within the economic system and its constraints and prospects as they currently exist. That is a much more difficult problem, indeed, a far harder problem than assessing whether a new technology or idea is clever and good. An innovation commons is an institutional resolution to this harder problem through the expedient of ad hoc group formation under spontaneous institutional governance.

The origin of innovation is cooperation under uncertainty, which requires governance. We cooperate at the point of very early enthusiasm about a new idea or technology. And we do so under the harsh competitive shadow of a market economy with entrepreneurial initiative and innovating firms, because in the beginning no one knows, and everyone benefits from access to other people's knowledge in order to figure out what it is that they themselves know. Entrepreneurial discovery is misleadingly represented as a kind of insightful genius. This is a factor, to be sure. But mostly it is a process of information assembly and construction (Sarasvathy 2008, as well as judgment about the quality and meaning of information that arrives from distributed components (Foss and Klein 2012). The pointed question here is what is the most effective *institution* for the required assembly, for the productive process that results in entrepreneurial discovery that reveals the opportunity, the apparent origin of the innovation trajectory? I will argue that in many circumstances the most effective institution is the innovation commons, which is the true origin of innovation.

1.2 The Commons in the Innovation Commons

What sort of economic good is innovation? The modern answer—first elaborated by Ken Arrow (1962a, 1962b) in the context of the economics of information and imperfect competition, which became the foundation of new growth theory (Romer 1990)—is that new information, being nonrivalrous and nonexcludable, has properties of a public good. Markets do not efficiently supply public goods, only private goods.[4]

Social welfare maximization therefore requires innovation either (a) to be artificially made into a private good, for example using intellectual property rights; or (b) to be publicly provided. That analytic toggling between private goods and public goods (with market or government solutions) is the Weltanschauung of modern innovation theory and policy: innovation is something individuals do and, when that fails, is something the state fixes. But there are other possibilities besides private and public goods. Innovation might also be a common-pool resource, from the commons.

What Is a Commons?

A *commons* is a type of property regime or classification of economic goods in terms of excludability and rivalry, where a good in the commons—also known as a *common-pool resource*—has the conjoint properties of rivalrousness and nonexcludability, in contrast to private, public, and club goods, as in figure 1.1.[5]

A commons may be classified in one of four types of economic goods ordered by dimensions of rivalrousness[6] and excludability (Ostrom and Ostrom 1999): private goods (rivalrous, excludable); public goods (nonrivalrous, nonexcludable); club goods[7] (nonrivalrous, up to a congestion point, excludable); and common-pool resources (rivalrous, nonexcludable).

A commons is a *communal property regime* over a shared resource in which each stakeholder has an equal interest.[8] However, communal or shared property is not the same as public property, as Ostrom (1990) and colleagues carefully and painstakingly analyzed and reported. Rather, a commons is a form of property *governed by rules* that are created and enforced by the relevant *community* associated with the resource. As Frischmann (2012, 8) observes, a "commons is an institutionalized community practice, a form of community management or governance." In this definition, the "basic characteristic that distinguishes commons from noncommons is institutionalized sharing of resources among members of a community" (Madison et al. 2010b, 841).

	Excludable	Non-excludable
Rivalrous	Private goods	Common goods
Non-rivalrous	Club goods	Public goods

Figure 1.1 Economic goods

As a form of property or a class of economic good, "the commons" is often portrayed as atavistic, relatively weak, and unsophisticated (but harked back to romantically, for its communitarian goodness), and prone to social dilemmas (i.e., collective action problems), or what Hardin (1968) famously called the "tragedy of the commons" (see also Gordon 1954; Olson 1965) referring to the tendency of an open-access resource to be subject to free riding to the point of exploitation, exhaustion, and collapse.

Now, it certainly is true that common-pool resources are the oldest institutional form of property, prior to modern nation-states and public goods provisions, and prior to modern notions of private property and goods produced by private firms and traded in markets. Where, once upon a simpler time, most resources were communitarian and in the commons, the past few global centuries have seen both the *enclosure* of these into private goods with the rise of the market, and the *appropriation* of their domain as public goods with the rise of the state (Scott 1998). Furthermore, it is also true that the commons, lacking the credible threat of violence a nation-state can bring to enforce private property rights and to compel taxation for public goods, must rely on emergent cooperative behavior and communitarian goodwill (Bowles and Gintis 2011). This tends to constrain the domain of the commons to ad hoc tribe-sized communities with effective self-governance, and only those that, for some reason, have fallen outside the reach of market or government institutional provision—the badlands and "shatter-zones," as James Scott (2009) put it.

So it is not entirely misleading to portray the commons as an old and somewhat unstable institutional technology, lacking the scale and efficiency of modern government-supported institutions. From this perspective, it would perhaps seem perverse to seek to foist the commons off on readers as a better solution to the innovation problem than modern solutions based in private intellectual property, tax credits and investment incentives, and the full gamut of well-planned, state-based innovation policy (Martin and Scott 2000).

The basic problem that a commons addresses is the governance of a collective resource that would otherwise collapse due to individual self-interest, whether by taking more than one's share of the benefit of the resource, or by contributing less than one's share to the cost of the resource. In game theory, this is a prisoner's dilemma, and the rational play is to defect, or not to cooperate. Yet Elinor Ostrom (1990), working with many others (Dietz et al. 2003; Aligica and Boettke 2009; Ostrom et al. 2012), showed that under identifiably specific but still quite general conditions (Wilson et al. 2013), rational people were able to come together and cooperate, over and over again. Ostrom traced this not to the unique loveliness of these people, but rather to the quality of the particular institutions of the commons that they were able to create to solve the social dilemmas inherent in creating and managing a common-pool resource. The surprising idea here is not just that the commons works—we already knew that to be true, albeit for relatively small-scale and simple resources, such as grazing pastures or watersheds—but that the commons can work *better* than more ostensibly modern and sophisticated solutions such as firms (i.e., where resources are professionally managed under high-powered incentives), markets (i.e., where resources are privately held), and governments (i.e., where resources are either government regulated or publicly owned).

It was Ostrom's combination of exhaustive fieldwork knitting together thousands of case studies of common-pool resources in practice, with laboratory experimental work on prisoner's dilemma games in an evolutionary setting that enabled communication, coordination, and punishment, all seen through the theoretical lens of polycentric governance, that furnished an explanation for why the commons, when it worked, could work very well (Ostrom 1990, 1999a, 2000, 2010; Poteete et al. 2010; Earl and Potts 2011). The answer, in essence, is that the commons can make effective use of local information when a community is able to make and enforce its own governance rules, an observation that built on the ideas of Hayek (1945) and Vincent Ostrom et al. (1961) (Aligica and Tarko 2012).

What Ostrom discovered was that while the particular resources that a commons sought to govern could differ substantially, as could the types of communities seeking to create or exploit these resources, the underlying rules for governing the commons were remarkably consistent. Ostrom (1990) summarized these rules in eight "design principles" (Cox et al. 2010; Wilson et al. 2013):

Principle 1: Well-defined boundaries

Principle 2: Congruence between appropriation and provision rules and local conditions

Principle 3: Collective-choice arrangements

Principle 4: Monitoring

Principle 5: Graduated sanctions

Principle 6: Conflict-resolution mechanisms

Principle 7: Minimum recognition of rights

Principle 8: Nested enterprises

These principles describe the qualities of the rules and governance that tend to be found in successful commons, which is to say that commons that fail often lack one or more of these features. (We will discuss this topic in detail in chapter 6.) But underneath these effective design rules was a deeper logic about why they worked. The problem with the one-shot prisoner's dilemma analysis of collective action (Olson 1965) is that it excludes the possibility of communication and coordination, and then of subsequent monitoring and enforcement. In essence, it excludes the possibility that a community could figure out a way to work together, that is, to supply its own private governance.

What Ostrom's (1990) research showed was that when a community could arrive at effective rules for governance to coordinate actions and overcome the free-riding problem, that institutional solution tended to produce better-quality outcomes at lower economic costs—because of lower *transaction costs* (even where there was a trade-off with loss of production economies of scale)—than alternative institutional systems involving private property or public regulation or ownership.

Even after Ostrom shared the Nobel Prize in Economics with Oliver Williamson in 2009, this seemingly counterintuitive, but remarkably important, finding still struggles to penetrate mainstream thinking about the generalized efficiency of both markets and government solutions to economic problems. Ostrom et al. (2007) explicitly use the language of seeking to go "beyond panaceas," of always seeking simple solutions to complex problems, as a close cousin of Harold Demsetz's "nirvana fallacy," which is the tendency to compare actual situations with perfect theoretical solutions. Ostrom's point is that once we get beyond panaceas and stop falling for the nirvana fallacy, the commons can be a surprisingly efficient and robust institutional solution to shared resource problems of appropriation and provisioning.

Ostrom's (1990) early work was based around natural resource commons, in the areas of fisheries, forests, grazing systems, wildlife, water resources, irrigation systems, agriculture, land tenure and use, and particularly those found in developing nations. She also studied very long-lived commons, such as alpine grazing pastures in Switzerland and irrigation systems in Spain, that had continuously operated for hundreds of years. This work has been extended by colleagues and other researchers to global commons such as climate change, air pollution, and transboundary disputes. In the past two decades, in contrast with the original focus on agricultural and natural resource commons, a growing body of work has emerged on "new commons" (Hess 2008). Among the topics of these studies are *urban commons*, for example in apartment buildings, parking spaces, playgrounds (Foster 2011); *sharing economies* (Benkler 2006; Hamari et al. 2015; Sundararajun 2016; Munger 2018); and *infrastructure commons* (Rose 2008; Frischmann 2012).

At the core of the "new commons" work is a significant focus on information as a resource, both in production and in consumption. This resource has been examined in the cultural commons (Schultz 2006; Madison et al. 2010; Hess 2012); the knowledge commons (Ostrom and Hess 2007; Frischmann et al. 2014); the internet, digital, and intellectual property commons (Benkler 2006;

Lessig 2004a; Boyle 2008; Raustiala and Sprigman 2006); the scientific and data commons, particularly genomic data and repositories for open science (David 1998, 2001; Nelson 2004; Harvey and McMeekin 2007, 2009; Nielsen 2011).

What Type of Commons Is an Innovation Commons?

The innovation commons fits this broader research program as a key instance of a new knowledge commons (Allen and Potts 2016). A *commons* refers jointly to a resource that is available to a community and to the institutions that govern the appropriation and provisioning of this resource among the community. An *innovation commons* is one where the resources are inputs into innovation. In a natural resource commons, such as a fishery, it is reasonably obvious what the resource refers to, in this case fish, or perhaps more accurately to access to fishing territories. But what exactly is the resource in an innovation commons? It's rather abstract to say that "innovation" is in the innovation commons, so what specific resources are in there?

In an innovation commons the shared resources would logically be "resources for innovation." But that can refer to many different things, including physical resources, access to other people and their ideas and experiments, and information. The first point is that it is not obvious whether the innovation commons is a site of production or consumption. Many scholars argue that knowledge commons differ from more conventional natural resource commons, such as grazing pastures or fisheries, and indeed from most other common-pool resources, in predominantly being sites of production rather than consumption (or access, use, or subtraction) (Benkler 2006; Madison et al. 2010; Frischmann et al. 2014).

In an innovation commons, input resources are pooled for common use, and these resources are at least partially subtractable or subject to congestion. In a hackerspace, for example, much equipment is pooled as a common resource (Kostakis et al. 2014). Technical expertise, as human capital, is often also pooled. In a patent pool, intellectual property is placed in the commons (Lerner and Tirole 2004). In these ways, an innovation commons is like a natural resource commons. However, there are other pooled inputs into the innovation commons with very different properties, in particular what Hayek (1945: 519) called "*the knowledge of the particular circumstances of time and place*" that accumulates in a commons.[9] This knowledge can be read by those in the commons as a map of the opportunity and its costs and benefits that attach to whatever new idea or technology defines the innovation commons. This information resource also pools and circulates in the commons and is a reason why many are in the innovation commons; no such comparable feature exists in a natural resource commons.

It is instructive to think about the rival and nonrivalrousness and excludability of the key resource in an innovation commons. Recall that a common-pool resource is a good that is rivalrous but nonexcludable (as in figure 1.1). However, the economic purpose of an innovation commons is to pool innovation resources, including information, to produce information about an entrepreneurial opportunity. Information is nonrivalrous, and if the production context is nonexcludable, that would seem to describe a public good, or if excludability can be achieved, a club good (or toll good). However, my central argument is that the valuable resource in the innovation commons is information about the entrepreneurial opportunity, and that opportunity is highly rivalrous from the perspective of expected benefit. To the extent that you exploit the opportunity—whether as market profit, reputational propriety, hierarchic status, power gained through monopoly (e.g., an intellectual property filing or a market territory beachhead established), and so on—there are fewer rents for me to capture. A simple example is academic publishing, where the scientific and scholarly commons furnishes information input into a scientific discovery (Dasgupta and David 1994; David 2004; Nelson 2004), but the Mertonian norms of priority award the property rights in the claim to whoever is first to publish. The claim to priority is rivalrous, while the inputs to that claim are nonrivalrous. This is to say that the rivalrous exploitable opportunity revealed by the emergent (nonrivalrous) information is the true resource in the commons.

A directly related complicating factor is that innovation commons will therefore tend to be temporary and persist only under special circumstances. The reason has to do with the value of the key resource in the commons. To the extent that an innovation commons is a knowledge commons, as a repository of technical information (Frischmann et al. 2014), and there is persisting value of that information owing to a continuous flow of new seekers of that knowledge, then such a well-governed commons would be expected to be persistent. But if that information is being pooled strategically to gather the many parts of a puzzle together in an institutionally efficient way, then at some point that information is going to reveal its message, and that message will be exploited by whoever can most effectively capitalize on it, and the commons will collapse to some other institutional or organizational form. This is the sense in which the information is entropic, and the opportunity revealed by the information is a rivalrous good.

In an innovation commons the resource does not usually preexist the commons. It might not even be clear what the resource is. It is more often an intention to create something rather than an actual thing, and therefore the resource in the commons will refer to all of the things that can make that creation possible. Most often the goal is a targeted technology or body of practical knowledge that can only be created by combining resources that are distributed among several, and possibly a great many, people, all of which are inputs into that creative process.

An innovation commons is thus a potential resource of uncertain value, rather than a known resource of known value. And while it may be clear who the "innovation commoners" are by their participation, they themselves may not have a clear idea of what resources they are contributing to the common pool, or of the resources' value at the time they are contributed. These fuzzy, uncertain features are the normal, natural properties of an innovation commons.

This fuzziness gives a clue to the nature of the key resource in the commons. An innovation commons is born of fundamental *uncertainty* about the prospect of a technical opportunity.[10] This uncertainty presents a collective action problem, the need to pool distributed and specialized information, which can be efficiently done in the commons. But once the pooling of information is realized, the functional rationale for the commons collapses, and so most likely the commons also. Innovation commons are temporary for the very same reason they exist: uncertainty engenders their creation, and resolution of that uncertainty instigates their collapse.

The key resource in an innovation commons is not innovation. An innovation commons does not produce innovation. Rather, it furnishes inputs into innovation, much of which is in the form of information, and this information has value in proportion to its ability to reduce uncertainty for entrepreneurial action.

Common Pooling and Peer Production in an Innovation Commons

An innovation commons is a somewhat unusual species of commons. The nature of the resource in the commons is actually produced in it by *pooling* disparate and distributed bits of information, none of which have clear or distinct value until combined with other bits of information. This is manifestly an instance of *peer production*, in the sense advanced by Benkler (2006) and Bollier (2013), because of the distributed nature of the information that must come together, as well as the ex ante and ex post egalitarian nature of that operation. A commons is not a hierarchy: all are equal within it, although each brings different knowledge. This arrangement is sometimes presented as an ethical ideal from the communitarian perspective, but it is a simple consequence of the uncertain value of the individual bits of information and the need to structure cooperation from behind a veil of uncertainty.

A further unusual feature of an innovation commons is that what it produces is sometimes not clear. This is distinctly unlike peer production in contexts, such as open-source software (Lerner and Tirole 2002; Osterloh and Rota 2007; von Krogh et al. 2012), where what is being produced is known in advance (e.g., a UNIX-like operating system, a user-produced encyclopedia, etc.). Furthermore, with peer production the value of what is being produced is usually apparent to most participants, who know what they contribute and what they expect to get out of the project, even when these costs and benefits are tacit and multidimensional (Gächter et al. 2010). Yet this awareness may be lacking in the innovation commons.

An innovation commons is, in this sense, a common *pooling* of resources, rather than a common-pool resource. The resources that constitute the value of the innovation commons have little value until they are in the commons and combine with other bits of distributed information and knowledge. The value of access to the commons thus *increases* with the number of other agents in the commons, unlike a congestible, natural resource commons. This information and knowledge is often embodied in experiments and bits of kit or demonstrators that help others see ideas and conceptualize possibilities (Vincenti 1990). An innovation commons is thus similar to a data commons such as those in the big-data sciences of genomics or astronomy (Harvey and McMeekin 2009; Nielsen 2011; Frischmann et al. 2014, chs. 4–6). The value of the innovation commons comes from the value of the pool of information it gathers and the inferences that can be made from that total set. Individuals, as potential entrepreneurs, can discover new information or the meaning of the information they already have, in a way that would be costly or impossible in the absence of the common-pooling institution.

An innovation commons can be construed as part of the sociopolitical project of "commoning" (e.g., Bollier 2014; Kostakis and Bauwens 2014), which sees social value in the promotion of cooperative institutions for the peer production of resources that can be consumed collectively. This work often critiques the political philosophy of neoliberalism and the practical efficacy of market economy solutions through promotion of an alternative institutional model, "social provisioning." Proponents of peer production in the commons emphasize its full-cost efficiency in comparison to institutions based around private ownership and profit-seeking firms (e.g., Benkler 2006). Shirky (2008) and Leadbeater (2008) explicitly extend this analysis to the peer production of innovation. Its efficiency is attributed to better technology that has made new forms of organization feasible and unleashed innate human cooperative instincts (Bowles and Gintis 2011), a new institutional watershed in the possibilities of organization of economic production.

An innovation commons can certainly be understood from this "commoning" perspective. Indeed, in politically libertarian technologies such as cryptocurrencies and privacy protocols, or explicitly communitarian technologies such as platforms for free-cycling or ride-sharing, this new ethos is unmistakable (Munger 2018). But the crucial point I want to emphasize is that it is not necessary to explain the instrumental logic of the innovation commons. Specifically, an innovation commons is not identical with a peer production commons for a very important reason: an innovation commons is usually temporary because what it produces is not usually a thing, such as a product that meets a provisioning need. Rather, it peer-produces information to enable entrepreneurs, who are among the peers, to act individually and cooperatively to reduce uncertainty and reveal the outlines of an opportunity. Once that information is produced, the rationale for the existence of the commons weakens.[11]

1.3 Clunkers and Homebrew

If you were in the Bay Area of Northern California in the early 1970s, stood in just the right spot, and tuned in to what was going on around you, you would have witnessed the R & D origins of at least two new global technology industries.

One of them, the result of which can be found in most homes today and is especially popular among young males, was gathering in Cupertino in what is now known as Silicon Valley. A motley crew of young engineer-hippie types started to hack together parts from old machines to create something new and fun and never seen before, which they tried out on themselves. They called themselves the Morrow Dirt Club, aka the Cupertino Riders.[12] It was 1972 and they'd just invented the mountain bike.

Some 60 miles north of Cupertino, at Mount Tamalpais in Marin County, the Lakespur Canyon Gang was also laying claim to inventing the new sport of mountain biking.[13] These early bicycles were called "clunkers" because they were cobbled together from secondhand and heavy-duty parts from other bikes, including the brake drums from tandem bicycles and the brake levers and balloon tires from motorbikes. Off-road clunker riding soon turned into clunker racing (or cyclo-cross, as they first called it, riding all-terrain bicycles, or ATBs), as the community grew from a handful to 50 or so in a few years (Kelly 1979). The emergence of mountain biking is an instance of what innovation scholars call user-driven innovation (von Hippel 1986; Lüthje et al. 2005). The mountain bike was not invented by one person, but by a community that tried things out to see what worked. Buenstorf (2003, 61), who has studied the innovation economy of mountain biking, explains it like this: "Races were the primary 'research labs' of early mountain bike development."

Actually, most new sports start like this, with amateur enthusiasts hacking together new sporting equipment, trying out new moves, and sharing information in a community-shaped "research environment." Snowboarding, skateboarding, beach-break surfing, big-wave surfing, and windsurfing all started and developed this way (Shah 2000, 2006; Franke and Shah 2003). Sporting goods firms that produce, develop, and retail equipment—boards, bikes, rigs, and clothing—organize events, and sell media content have tended to emerge from this initial community of users, enthusiasts, hobbyists, and hackers (Shah and Tripsas 2007). The modern sport of skateboarding emerged from a tight group of riders called the Zephyr skate team, portrayed in the iconic 2001 Stacy Peralta documentary *Dogtown and Z-Boys*, as they taught themselves new acrobatic tricks they imported from the surf community and perfected in the curved bowls of the drought-emptied swimming pools of Southern California. By the mid-1970s they had created a new sport that spread across the United States and then across the world. That's innovation too.

"The innovation and spread of the mountain bike," says Guido Buenstorf (2003, 68), an evolutionary economist, "cannot be understood unless the group setting of its clunker origins is considered." These gritty, hippie, teenaged-themed, sweat-and-beer-flavored origin stories are perhaps easy enough to ignore when it's just sports, "extreme sports" no less. It's right there in the name that they're not representative. But at the core of these origin stories are high-functioning communities of mutually motivated enthusiasts, and it is these groups that represent the true nature of the early stages of innovation. Innovation begins as a *group* activity, and the secret to innovation is to understand how these groups form and the forces that bind them together. The economics of innovation begins with inquiry into the economics of collective action and transaction costs.

Another name for this is "collective invention," a term coined by the economist and technology historian Robert Allen (1983) to describe the institutional governance of innovation processes in the blast furnaces of the Cleveland district in Britain at the height of iron production. Nuvolari (2004), another technology historian, detailed this same mechanism of collective invention in the development of Cornish Pumping Engines in the coal mines of the early Industrial Revolution (see also Frenken and Nuvolari 2004). Meyer (2003) adds further examples of steel production in the United States in the late nineteenth century and open-source software in the late twentieth century (see also Nuvolari 2005; Osterloh and Rota 2007). So it's not just sports. It's the Industrial Revolution and the computer revolution too.

In the early 1970s, not so far from Cupertino, another group of young enthusiasts gathered every two weeks at Stanford University to pool ideas and share resources. They called themselves the Homebrew Computer Club and met in the auditorium of the Stanford Linear Accelerator Center. Afterward they went for beers at The Oasis in Menlo Park. They were exploring what could be done with the cheap, powerful microprocessors (computers on a chip) that were newly available as off-the-shelf hardware (Freiberger and Swaine 1984; Meyer 2003). One of the innovations they developed was the software industry. Another was the personal computer industry. Microsoft and Apple emerged from Homebrew,[14] along with dozens of other start-up technology companies.[15] The combined value of what came out of that little club is easily over a trillion dollars. That's trillion, with a *t*. It all seems so obvious now, but back then the Homebrew club was an efficient institutional solution to the fundamental problem of distributed knowledge and technological uncertainty. This problem was resolved by creating a knowledge commons (i.e. the "club") to reduce the transaction costs of pooling and sharing knowledge, lowering the costs of innovation.[16]

Homebrew club members were all early amateur enthusiasts who were *users* and builders of the new microprocessor kits (hobbyists), but in doing so they were also learning about what they could do (experimentalists), and modifying the kit to do new things (hacking). The club provided fast and high-quality feedback for inventors, as many club members had advanced degrees in electrical engineering and were experienced computer programmers. But they were also engaging in their own experiments and developments, and benefited from seeing what others were able to do (or not do). The club was in principle open to anyone, and certainly anyone could read the newsletter, but in practice there were rules. There was a fierce culture of sharing, and an implicit understanding that if you built something, you had to share it with the club. This is precisely what made the club valuable to its members, but, in turn, to gain access you had to have something to share. To participate, you had to contribute.[17] The club and its newsletters during the random-access period, when people would find others who were interested in what they were making, exchanging information and swapping code—an early digital Tinder—was at heart an emergent community that pooled distributed knowledge. In doing so, it gathered the information necessary to reduce technological uncertainty and reveal the shape of entrepreneurial opportunities. Indeed, once the clouds of uncertainty lifted, revealing the outline of the entrepreneurial opportunities, the hobbyists transformed into entrepreneurs, and off they went.

1.4 The Republic of Letters

The industrial enlightenment[18] begat the Industrial Revolution, which begat modern economic growth, or the Great Enrichment (McCloskey 2016). But what begat the industrial enlightenment?

Mokyr (2016b) argues that it was a virtual community of scholars who called themselves *Respublica Literaria*, the Republic of Letters. This community was in many ways like the Homebrew Computer Club, except that it existed from roughly 1680 to 1720 over all of western Europe, was virtual in that its members almost never met each other,[19] and conducted business in Latin. But its aims were similar, and the means by which it achieved them would have been innately familiar to the Homebrewers.

The Republic of Letters was an emergent institution to share and disseminate knowledge from the amateur enthusiasts of the day, what we would now call scientists. It gave rise to subsequent organizations such as the British Royal

Society. Rather than a newsletter, the Republic of Letters set up correspondence clearing houses to disseminate private communications. Yet as Mokyr (2016a, 31) explains: "It managed to create and enforce a substantial number of rules that amounted to the emergence of open science in Europe."[20] These rules emphasized norms of the "knowledge club" (Potts et al. 2016; Hartley and Potts 2014) through a Mertonian ethos of universalism, communalism (with respect to placing knowledge in the commons), disinterestedness in the pursuit of truth, and organized skepticism (*nullius in verba*).

The Republic of Letters was not just the simultaneous existence of a trans-European bunch of gentlemen scholars, that is, individuals communicating with each other. This was crucially a *self-governing community*, a group of people who arrived at an effective institutional solution to a fundamental economic problem in the production of knowledge. And while the time and place and clothes and language and subject matter and cultural and political milieu were different, it was the same institutional solution arrived at centuries later in Northern California. The institutions that enable a group with a common interest to form into a self-governing community involved in the production of a common-pool resource were first clearly spelled out by Ostrom (1990) in her work on natural resource commons, and the subsequent extension to knowledge commons (Ostrom and Hess 2007; Frischmann et al. 2014). By studying thousands of instances of the microinstitutional structure of common-pool resources, Ostrom discovered eight design rules that tend to be present in the governance of successful commons, the principles previously enumerated in this chapter.

Ostrom's eight design rules work together to solve a *collective action problem* (also known as a "social dilemma"), inherent in the economics of joint production and consumption. The problem is this: the production of new knowledge benefits from the coproduction of complementary knowledge. And while each bit of knowledge is costly to produce, it improves in quality when it is given critical, honest, and disinterested assessment and moreover can build on other recently produced knowledge. The problem is that while everyone benefits if everyone cooperates by sharing and contributing, individuals have an incentive to maximize what they take from the knowledge pool and minimize what they contribute, whether because of the private costs of contributing or the option value of retaining secret knowledge. But if everyone makes that calculation, the knowledge commons collapses, reverting to the long-run equilibria of autarkic knowledge production.

The Republic of Letters was a radical social innovation that built on the prior idea of improvement itself as a social process.[21] The Republic of Letters solved this institutional problem through specific, but often implicit, rules regarding reputational property rights on knowledge placed in the commons, creating strong incentives through signaling (Merton 1973; Dasgupta and David 1994; David 2004). The result was a spontaneous network of common interests that functioned as a self-governing community of innovation deeply committed to open science in propositional knowledge. However, the network was less committed to prescriptive knowledge or technology that could be efficiently protected, whether through secrecy or government-sanctioned and government-enforced monopoly privilege (Mokyr 2002).[22] In other words, like Homebrew, a knowledge commons worked well up to the point where individuals could effectively use the collective pool of knowledge to figure out an exploitable and commercial opportunity. In both cases, this led to what we will later call the "fundamental transformation."

Across the Atlantic in prerevolutionary America, a similar knowledge commons developed around the singular person of Benjamin Franklin (Lyons 2013). Franklin was dedicated to the quest for useful knowledge to benefit the newly forming American society. Franklin has been personified as an inventor of the archetypical solitary genius type—experimentally flying kites in lightning storms, a revolution in experimental physics, and inventing in 1741 the baffled or "Franklin" stove, a revolution in home heating. Yet he saw the quest for such useful knowledge as a collective pursuit, the product of collaborative exchange of information, ideas, and observations. Franklin strove to promote and where necessary create the institutions that would facilitate such sharing. Franklin, for instance, founded the nonprofit Library Company of Philadelphia in 1731, the world's first lending library, as an offshoot of his Leather Apron Club, a mutual improvement society that he founded in 1727 when just 21 years old. The purpose of the society was to debate questions of morals and politics, to discuss natural philosophy, and to exchange knowledge of business affairs. It was a forerunner of a subsequent society Franklin would create in 1743—the American Philosophical Society—dedicated to the furtherance of useful knowledge, and not incidentally America's first national institution.

Such societies were not just for importing knowledge from Europe, but also for finding the most effective uses for such knowledge in newly developing industries, disseminating that knowledge among new colonies and new industry pioneers, and discovering and exploiting new opportunities.[23] In other words, they managed not just technological dissemination and uncertainty, but also market uncertainty and entrepreneurial discovery. Such societies were part of a private sector industrial policy to solve problems through knowledge coordination and opportunity discovery (Bakhshi et al. 2011).

A century or so later, much the same process played out in microcosm in the fertile valleys of the new colony of New South Wales, in what wasn't yet Australia. In 1788, a bunch of hobbyists and viticultural experimentalists planted the first grapes in what later become the Hunter Valley wine region, still Australia's oldest continually producing wine region, and the locus of Australia's modern wine industry. But back then, before there was a recognizable industry and before the famous estates were established around the perfection of the big reds, there was a self-governing community pooling and sharing knowledge in order to overcome technological uncertainty and to discover market opportunities.

McIntyre et al. (2013) used archival records to document a cooperative institutional culture in the Hunter Region that continues to the present. They document sharing of plant stock and printed instructions, and of practical advice in viticulture and viniculture when such knowledge was sparse and still experimental in the Australian climate. None of those pioneers knew entirely what they were doing, yet everyone acquired fragments of knowledge through trial and error, even if it wasn't always clear how that knowledge could be assembled into successful production of wine. These historians emphasize the subtle institutional rules that emerged to govern this effective sharing of information. They also note in passing that the NSW Department of Mines and Agriculture began publishing its *Gazette* and appointed its first viticultural expert in 1890. In other words, public science and industry policy came long *after* the entrepreneurial originators had developed the industry in the innovation commons, through collaborative experimentation and pooling of knowledge.

The point of these disparate examples is to show that private sector self-governance in the very early stage of innovation is the rule, not the exception. And the patterns look the same: namely a new technology, resource, or invention is worthless until you can figure out who it is of value to and how. And this involves adding a lot more information, information that is invariably distributed. To understand its value, you need to combine distributed knowledge and do so in an institutionally efficient way. Under certain circumstances, but particularly when technological and market uncertainty is high, a commons can be an efficient institutional structure for the economic organization of the early phase of innovation.

1.5 Why Groups, Why Cooperation, Why Open?

The origin of new industries and the development of new technologies almost always begins with a group of enthusiasts sharing knowledge in order to get to the point where entrepreneurship is possible. Soon enough, if the innovation commons functions effectively, it will collapse and the innovation trajectory will continue through the conventional Schumpeterian evolutionary pathways of entrepreneurial rivalry between firms, creative destruction in markets, and government support.

But why does this group of enthusiasts need to work together in the first place? Why does it need to be a group? And why do they need to share? Why does contracting or exchange fail? Or more specifically, why do these institutional forms (contracts, firms, markets, governments) tend to fail early on in the innovation process, when we know plainly and unambiguously that these same institutional forms do succeed later on? What is different about the very beginning of innovation that seems to require a wholly different institutional arrangement?

Transaction costs in the coordination of knowledge and other innovation resources are part of the problem, and so too is fundamental uncertainty about the prospective value of the innovation, the shape of the entrepreneurial opportunity, and the expected value of the resources and factors of production involved. But transaction costs and uncertainty alone do not explain what is going on here, because these are key parts of the subsequent phases of innovation. The real issue is *distributed, specialized knowledge*.

In the very early stages of an innovation process, the relevant information, knowledge, and resources that need to be combined to reveal the shape of the entrepreneurial opportunity are *distributed* among several, and possibly many, people. That all necessary innovation resources are concentrated in one person is improbable because of *specialization*.

The innovation process is often modeled as *search* over a high-dimensional landscape. This type of model is analytically convenient because searching is a behavior single agents can do, with the choice variables being how much they search and the cost of search.[24] In both neoclassical and evolutionary economics, this is the standard way to model R & D in an innovating firm, as an allocation of resources to searching. Yet it may be that the process of discovery in the very early stages of innovation is not best represented as searching, but rather as a different type of coordination to discover a valuable set of connections (i.e., a structure of knowledge complementarity) among complementary bits of specialized knowledge, without a prior sense of what those bits that need to come together actually are.

A useful model for this is what Michael Kremer (1993b) called an O-ring production function. Assume there are n bits of knowledge (with each bit of knowledge in a separate person) and that all n bits need to come together in a particular way to reveal an entrepreneurial opportunity. So the minimum viable discovery group needs to be at least n people. But because no one in the group knows which n bits of information are essential, the minimum effective size of the group will be $> n$. An O-ring production function has the form $y = q^n n$, where y is the innovation, n is the number of bits of knowledge that must be combined (or tasks in a production process), and q is an index of the quality of each of those bits of knowledge (Kremer 1993b; Jones 2010; Jones 2012). Unlike standard (Cobb-Douglas) production functions, O-ring production functions do not trade off quantity and quality in a production process. You can't substitute poor quality in one step with greater quantity in another step. If you miss one step, such that $q_i = 0$ for that bit of knowledge or task, then the whole equation goes to zero, irrespective of what happens in the other parts. If the O-ring fails, then irrespective of how well the other parts perform, the space shuttle explodes. If one of the *n* parts fails, nothing is created.

Early stage innovation may well be like this, which is to say that an innovation originates with the discovery of critical strategic complementarities or connections between elements of knowledge. A certain set of things, that is, pieces of knowledge, will have to come together in a particular way, and if one part is missing, wrong, or deficient, nothing of value is produced. There is no prospect of substituting for a missing or poor-quality factor, as is always possible in a Cobb-Douglas production function (e.g., if labor is expensive, you can substitute more capital).

An O-ring approach to the economics of early stage innovation helps explain why the critical institutional function is to create a *group* of sufficient size and quality that it contains all the necessary *n* bits of knowledge and other strategically complementary resources. Moreover, this institution needs to assemble this group prior to knowing what those bits of knowledge are, how many there are, their eventual worth in the parts, and the value of the whole. And this all needs to be assembled behind a veil of ignorance about these eventual outcomes in a way that minimizes the transaction costs of doing so. This set of requirements invariably means a structure that is as close as possible to a hierarchically flat and relatively egalitarian *community* governed by a constitution of shared rules, shared understandings, and shared intentions, thereby minimizing the (expensive) use of force or contract.

Economists have long puzzled over the success of the "open": open-source software (Lerner and Tirole 2005), open innovation (Chesbrough 2003a), open-access publishing, open science (Nielsen 2011), among other domains of the open model. In the context of innovation, this closely relates to long neglect of the efficacy of "user-led" innovation (von Hippel 1987), along with low-level skepticism about why the user model works. The basic puzzle from the conventional economic perspective is that the individual incentives never seem strong enough for open models to work (without positing some other hidden motivations), and that user incentives seem much weaker than competition-honed and profit-directed producer incentives to R & D. But the efficacy of open innovation and user innovation makes more sense when we realize that they are not efficient due to the shape or strength of individual incentives (e.g., to invest in R & D), but because open and user structures are institutional contexts that create powerful group-forming and community-making mechanisms.[25]

The motive force here is neither private individual incentives nor altruistic cooperation, but *shared intentionality* harnessed to *surplus resources* to form a transaction cost-minimizing *innovation commons*. An innovation commons is a way of producing a common-pool resource—new knowledge and the discovery of entrepreneurial opportunity—but it is not well characterized as investment, as an allocation of scarce capital with a clear expectation of return. Rather, the resources that are allocated to the innovation commons are in some sense surplus, undervalued, of uncertain value, or attain value only when placed in the context of other resources held within a community of peers. Technology enthusiasm, for instance, is a commonly underutilized form of capital, and can accumulate undervalued surpluses that can be profitably redirected in the low-transaction cost environment of an innovation commons.

An innovation commons is an institutional structure for casting distributed knowledge into the origin of innovation by using community governance—a crucible for melting down uncertainty and shards of technological prospect into pure entrepreneurial insight and opportunity. The apparent proximate origin of innovation is the entrepreneurial insight (Gaglio and Katz 2001). But that, I argue, is the outcome of a sequence of events and processes that begins well before the insight. The ultimate origin of innovation is coping with uncertainty in knowledge discovery through group formation, which is a cooperative action that, because of the hazards inherent in cooperation, requires rules for governance. These are the rules of the innovation commons.

The fundamental innovation problem is not that of dealing with market failure. There are no markets in the very beginning. It is also not that of dealing with government failure, because if markets haven't yet failed, then government responses are not yet part of the story. The real issue, prior to all of this, is figuring out the opportunity space, and that requires cooperation. Fortunately, cooperation is also an economic problem, one that is solved with governance, not government. In the beginning, the innovation problem is a governance problem that, once addressed, solves a discovery problem.

1.6 Overview of Book

This introduction has outlined the main arguments in this book, and the next eight substantive chapters and plus conclusion will develop them, particularly at the analytic and theoretical level. I also draw implications for the research agenda of evolutionary and innovation economics and for innovation policy.

Chapters 2 and 3 locate my argument in the broader context of Schumpeterian, evolutionary, Austrian, and what Peter Boettke calls "mainline economics," with a contextualization of the innovation problem as both a *knowledge problem* and a *coordination problem*, and therefore as a governance problem solved with institutions. I make a big deal about this across two chapters because I believe it is a new foundation for thinking about the economics of innovation (Potts 2014, 2018; Potts and Hartley 2015; Allen and Potts 2016; Davidson and Potts 2016a), arguing that we can usefully approach the innovation problem from the New Institutional perspective, and particularly using the work of Elinor Ostrom, in combination with the analytic frameworks of Deirdre McCloskey, F. A. Hayek, and Oliver Williamson.

Chapters 4 and 5 are the theoretical core of the book, explaining how innovation commons work: how they pool information and what specific problems they solve in order to discover entrepreneurial opportunities. Chapter 6 then explores the basic institutional similarities between innovation commons (as a species of knowledge commons) and the rules of commons that Ostrom discovered.

Chapters 7, 8, and 9 explore implications of this new conceptual and analytical view. In chapter 7 I consider a life-cycle view of an innovation trajectory in which innovation commons evolve into industry associations. Chapter 8 examines the implications of this book's perspective on the origin of innovation for innovation policy. Chapter 9 draws out a particular formulation of this origin perspective as a new framework for innovation policy based around permissionless innovation.

I conclude by placing innovation commons in a broader sweep of economic history in order to emphasize the institutional origin of innovation as an outcome of cooperative pooling of information and knowledge.

Notes

1. Adam Smith, of course, made this point long ago, building his theory of the wealth of nations (Smith 1776) on the moral sentiment of sympathy, or "fellow feeling" (Smith 1759).
2. "The engineers were optimistic about the future of the technology but did not know for sure how it would develop. The future nature of products, production processes, and markets was not clear or commonly known. Visions of that future varied and at least some were wrong. This is *technological uncertainty*" (Meyer 2003, 15).
3. An analogue is the Austrian notion that entrepreneurial alertness is the origin of the market process (Kirzner 1973).
4. These are the fundamental theorems of welfare economics.
5. Club goods (also known as *toll goods*) were first defined by James Buchanan (1965) as *local* public goods. The idea was that a group of people could create a shared resource if they were able to exclude noncontributors. The canonical example is a fenced local public swimming pool.
6. Ostrom and Ostrom (1999) use the term *subtractable* (in joint consumption) rather than *rival*. The term *rivalrous*, probably due to Romer (1990), has become the preferred term in the literature.
7. On the theory of clubs, see Buchanan (1965) and Sandler and Tschirhart (1980). As Nordhaus (2015) observes, "The major conditions for a successful club include the following: (i) that there is a public-good-type resource that can be shared (whether the benefits from a military alliance or the enjoyment of a golf course); (ii) that the cooperative arrangement, including the dues, is beneficial for each of the members; (iii) that non-members can be excluded or penalized at relatively low cost to members; and (iv) that the membership is stable in the sense that no one wants to leave." In this sense, a club and a well-governed commons have substantial overlap when analyzed as organizations.
8. A *common-pool resource* refers to a natural or human-made resource where one person's use subtracts from another's use (it is rivalrous) and where it is often necessary, but difficult

and costly, to exclude those outside the group from using the resource (Ostrom and Ostrom 1999). *Common property* is a formal or informal property regime that allocates a bundle of rights to a group. Such rights may include ownership, management, use, exclusion, and access to a shared resource.

9. The full context of Hayek's (1945) point is worth elucidating to show how the same argument also applies to innovation: "Today it is almost heresy to suggest that scientific knowledge is not the sum of all knowledge. But a little reflection will show that there is beyond question a body of very important but unorganized knowledge that cannot possibly be called scientific in the sense of knowledge of general rules: *the knowledge of the particular circumstances of time and place*. It is with respect to this that practically every individual has some advantage over all others because he possesses unique information of which beneficial use might be made, but of which use can be made only if the decisions depending on it are left to him or are made with his active coöperation."
10. Note that this fundamental focus on uncertainty is also plainly read in the foundational analyses of the economic problem of innovation in Arrow (1959, 1962b) and Hirschman and Lindblom (1965).
11. At this point of collapse (what we call "the fundamental transformation") the commons will often transmogrify into a different sort of institution, a collective action organization and political lobby such as an industry association, a point we will return to in chapter 7.
12. http://mmbhof.org/the-cupertino-riders/.
13. http://mmbhof.org/mtn-bike-hall-of-fame/history/.
14. Or rather Microsoft emerged *because of* Homebrew, not from Homebrew, in respect of Bill Gates's infamous open letter in the June 1975 Homebrew Computer Club newsletter accusing the hobbyists of stealing his software (the DOS code for Altair BASIC—the Altair 8800 was the first do-it-yourself personal computer, and the common interest of many of the Homebrew club members). But that copying made the Microsoft product sufficiently popular that it became the de facto standard adopted by industry (e.g., National Semiconductor).
15. Steve Wozniak says 21 companies. http://www.atariarchives.org/deli/homebrew_and_how_the_apple.php.
16. AnnaLee Saxenian (1994) describes the economic geography of innovation on the interaction between technology development and social networks in Silicon Valley.
17. Kealey and Ricketts (2014) call this situation a "contribution good," suggesting that science can be modeled as a contribution good (rather than a public good). Here the comparison is with private good, but the point remains that the basic mechanism is one that incentivizes private cooperation to create a public benefit.
18. "Industrial enlightenment" is a term introduced by (Mokyr 2002, 2009). It refers to the eighteenth-century "culmination of a transnational movement toward the creation, dissemination and application of experimental philosophy (as contemporaries referred to what we would call science) to the useful arts" (Mokyr 2016a, 30).
19. "It was a network of individuals connected by letters, books pamphlets and rare but intense personal visits. The common denominator of members was . . . their Baconian belief that this knowledge may in the end be of service to mankind as a whole" (Mokyr 2016, 33).
20. On the emergence of the institutions of open science in enlightenment Europe, see David (1998, 2004, 2008).
21. See Slack (2014) on the invention of improvement in seventeenth-century England.
22. The Statute of Monopolies (the first expression of patent law) was passed by the English Parliament in 1624.
23. See, for instance, Benjamin Franklin's "A Proposal for Promoting Useful Knowledge among the British Plantations in America" http://nationalhumanitiescenter.org/pds/becomingamer/ideas/text4/amerphilsociety.pdf (Lyons 2013).
24. This is represented in Stigler's (1961) model of the economics of information.
25. See Hartley and Potts (2014) on the evolutionary theory of group-making culture, and on the application of this cultural science to innovation see Potts and Hartley (2015).

2

The Innovation Problem

In a book about the economics of innovation, it's appropriate to start by examining *the economic problem of innovation*, that is, the innovation problem.

Innovation is an economic problem. But it's easy to make it not an economic problem. To wit: assume there is a creative imaginative person with a clever idea. The idea is good, so he or she starts a firm. This is the Schumpeterian moment when the creative destruction begins.

Did you see how there is no economic problem until we get to the point where the firm is started and it seeks capital in financial markets, seeks people in labor markets, tries to sell things in product markets, and so on. The economic problem only reveals itself once we're in the space of entrepreneurial firms acting in markets. But at the beginning there was no economic problem, just a creative, imaginative entrepreneur with a great idea. The creativity was free. The imagination was free. The idea just appeared. The entrepreneur was always there. This suggests a neurological, psychological, sociocultural, managerial, socioevolutionary, or even random explanation, but this very first part is not usually considered to require an economic explanation. The economic problem of innovation only appears once the entrepreneur is ready for business.

However, my argument is that the economic problem of innovation starts well before the entrepreneurs, firms, and venture capital appear on stage in what is usually taken to be act 1 of the Schumpeterian drama. So where does it start?

2.1 Trade and New Knowledge Explain Growth

An economy works something like this: a bunch of resources are distributed over people. Some have more, some fewer, although some have exactly the same amount—which might be zero—in some dimensions. But generally, what each person has or has access to is different. This is true of all scarce resources in the world, including people's capacities for thinking and acting. An economy is a distributed engine fueled by difference. Now, from this starting point, each person acts in a way that she expects will make her better off without making anyone else worse off. (Why that last bit? To rule out coercion and force, but also because *Homo sapiens economicus* is a supercooperative species, and economics is the study of large-scale cooperation, mostly with strangers [Dopfer 2004; Seabright 2004; Bowles and Gintis 2013; Nowak 2011].)

As all successful societies have known, long before Adam Smith wrote it down, the best way to mutually achieve that goal is for each person to seek out opportunities for gain through voluntary trade in *markets*, which are a foundational technology of civilization. These can be markets for goods or markets for reputations. Samuel Bowles (2004, 449) expressed it as part of an epic evolutionary adventure:

> Pursuing good ideas with practical applications is a costly and uncertain project, much like hunting large game. Success is rare, but its fruits are immensely valuable. A new drug or software application is not so different in this respect from an antelope. It is not surprising that the system of prestige and norms in some parts of the modern information-intensive economy in many ways parallel the culture of the foraging band.

Trade creates wealth by enabling people to exchange the things they value less for things they value more—a mutually enriching process because different people value things differently—but also because it drives *specialization*, which is what gives an economy structure. As specialization evolves, this increasingly complex structure creates further opportunities for trade, and so economies evolve and the wealth of nations grows.

Economics is the study of this market process as the basic mechanics of how economies grow. To a first approximation, most of what economists have been doing since Adam Smith's pithy formulation amounts to refinements and elaborations on this basic understanding of human nature, resource distributions, and the market mechanism. But something else is needed to make sense of the wealth of nations: namely ideas and knowledge, or more specifically new ideas and new knowledge. An economy is made of resources and things, but an economy is also, at the same time, made of ideas and knowledge.

That somewhat gnomic ontological claim—that an economy is made of both things and ideas—is crucial to modern economics because it establishes that economies don't actually grow but evolve. Wealth and income grow, but economies evolve. When the *things* in an economy change, the classical microtheory explanation is that we reallocated those things, produced more things (transformed some things into other things, which is really a type of exchange) (Kirzner 1973), or consumed some things (transforming things into utility, or waste). But the type of economic change we are concerned with here is a different sort, namely the process by which *the economy* changes (as opposed to change in the things in the economy). When the economy changes, it is because *ideas* and *knowledge* change. This process, for each idea carried as knowledge, is called innovation and is the process by which an economy evolves.

This is all in Joseph Schumpeter.[1] Evolutionary economics began when we realized this dynamic process was how economies change. Much of what evolutionary economists have been doing since 1942 is developing population and replicator-dynamic models of knowledge-based innovating firms with institutional dynamics.

Innovation is the evolutionary process by which economies develop through space and time: it is the origination, adoption, and retention of new ideas in the economic system. These changes in ideas and knowledge subsequently cause reallocations and changes in resources and their organization, leading to changes in firms, markets, industries, and regions, as well as commodities, households, jobs, and lifestyles. Some of these new ideas are technologies. Others are new sources of supply, new production processes, or new business models. Some technologies are physical, as rules for organizing matter-energy. Other technologies are social, as rules for organizing and coordinating people (these we call institutions). Innovation changes the knowledge base of the economy.[2]

Innovation changes what we do and how we do it—namely the structure and content of the economy—in ways that create new value. That is why the study of innovation is fundamental to the study of economic growth and to explaining the wealth of nations. Beyond exchange in markets and production in households and firms, innovation is the core process that explains the overarching thing that economists seek to understand, namely why some people and places are rich, while others are poor.

This observation—that market exchange *and innovation* are necessary to explain economic growth and development—is the core of the Schumpeterian paradigm.[3] From that point, the modern evolutionary economic research program is constructed around models of consumers, entrepreneurs, and knowledge-based firms that form complex innovation trajectories, industrial dynamics, networks, and innovation systems, all in the evolutionary context of institutions and under the constitutional provisions and overarching management of governments.

There are two classes of explanation for the wealth of nations: the Adam Smith story based on exchange in markets and the Joseph Schumpeter story based on innovation in markets. In the modern formulation of growth theory—although not in Smith or Schumpeter, as McCloskey (2016) and Loasby (1999) elucidate—there lurks an idealized model of the market process, called the theory of *perfect competition*, with associated notions of rational agents (i.e., zero cognitive costs), complete information (i.e., zero search costs), incentive compatible coordinating institutions (i.e., zero transaction costs, optimal mechanism design), and so on.[4] Perfect competition in economics is like the frictionless surface in physics—a theoretical device to model fundamental force, and to predict the eventual equilibrium of the system.

The role for economic policy is calibrated with respect to departures from these perfectly competitive conditions, as in *market failure*, when the private incentives to consumption or investment depart from the socially optimal levels, or *coordination failure* in the provision of public goods. In essence, the role for government arises when the market is less than perfect, which is often. In other words, technological innovation—which is plainly understood to drive economic growth and human prosperity—is not a matter of smart people, but of smart investment, or more specifically it is an investment problem for society. This is an allocation problem. It's about directing the proper level of resources to tinkerers and geniuses, as well as creating enough slack in the system (Penrose 1959). The risk, however, is that if we leave it to creative geniuses themselves, we might allocate too few resources to create new knowledge. If that happens, then we're all worse off, from a social perspective, because there will be a suboptimal investment in innovation.

Now "we" are of course a fine and mighty nation with deep furrows of native talent, so the problem is not whether "we" have enough geniuses—although, needless to say, further investment in education will surely help. Rather, the problem in situ is the optimal allocation of scarce resources, whether by incentives or transfers, to those creative geniuses. We invest resources to produce new technology. At the margin, further invested resources produce more new technologies. The question is: are we investing enough? Or, more pointedly: are the incentives and supports strong enough such that our innovative knowledge economy is somewhere in the neighborhood of a Pareto equilibrium?

What is going on here is that a particular problem, namely the origin of new technologies and innovation—which was itself diagnosed by Schumpeter at the beginning of the twentieth century as the core long-run economic growth and development—is set up in such a way that the policy diagnosis inevitably breaks on the side of public involvement. This is achieved by lining up two seemingly uncomplicated elements of textbook economic theory: namely "market failure" and "public goods." Specifically, the investment problem in new knowledge—that is, the innovation problem—is said to experience market failure.

The market failure is due to special properties associated with the economics of information. The heart of the matter is that new information (such as the production of new technology) has distinct public good-like properties. When I invent a new idea for my own use, you can also use it without inhibiting my use: as an economic good, a new idea is what economists call *nonrivalrous*, possessing a property that ideas have and sandwiches, say, don't. Furthermore, unless I take measures to stop you, the idea will be free for you to copy: which is what economists call being *nonexcludable*. Public goods are nonrivalrous and nonexcludable, and these properties jointly cause new ideas to experience so-called market failure. New ideas, as knowledge, are nonrivalrous. However, crucially, the market value of opportunity is indeed rivalrous: if you exploit it, there is less for me.

But in this simple information-focused view (but not the opportunity-focused view), a new technology is a privately produced public good. A new idea is nonrivalrous. From a social welfare perspective, market incentives will therefore induce too little private investment to produce the economic good. The market has failed, as an institution, to deliver the socially correct level of the particular economic good.[5] That's the diagnosis: too little private investment, given market incentives, compared to a social optimum.[6]

And the treatment? It follows that where markets fail, ipso facto, we must expect government action to correct that failure. How? There are legislatively created monopolies called "intellectual property." There are direct public spending programs directed to client firms in the vicinity of a favored technology called "industry policy." There are mechanisms that work through the corporate tax system to publicly reimburse favored types of spending, traveling under the heading of "innovation policy." And there are direct government programs, subsets of what former US president Dwight Eisenhower called the *military-industrial-academic complex*.[7]

Government response to market failure in the production of new knowledge does not consist of a single intervention but of a vast suite of programs. Some are more market facing (e.g., intellectual property and R & D tax credits), some are mixed (e.g., industry policy, infrastructure support, protective regulation, or trade policy), and others proceed in the traditional manner of direct government planning and spending (e.g., public science, special industry support, or direct purchasing). Whether the elements within this suite are market-facing mechanisms, bureaucratically administered operations, legislative enactments, or the outcomes of political bargains, and irrespective of what particular matrix or system by which they are combined, they are all, ultimately, government solutions to market failure.

The same argument, mutatis mutandis, is used in the context of innovation policy, where the role of government is to deal with the economic problems of innovation that exist because of departures from what we can call perfect innovation. What is *perfect innovation*? It's a concept that is mostly implicit among innovation economists, but it's worth spelling out: it's the analogue of perfect competition with respect to the origination, adoption, and retention of a new idea in the economy.

With perfect innovation, creativity is free and new ideas are available at the real interest rate. This is because finding new ideas competes at the margin with exploiting existing ideas. No agent fails to see an idea, or to apprehend its market value, or to figure out whom to contract with to produce the new product, as well as how to realize value—that is, perfect rationality, zero search costs, zero transaction costs, complete markets. With perfect innovation, the market for ideas is just another complete market (cf. Coase 1974 and Gans and Stern 2010). The role of government in the economic context of innovation—what I'll call the scope of innovation policy—begins when innovation is less than perfect, which is also common.

Allowing broad-brush simplifications: just as economic policy addresses market failure—defined as departures from perfect competition—innovation policy addresses innovation failure, defined as departures from perfect innovation. Yet innovation economics is not usually framed in this way, as the theory of perfect innovation, with innovation policy organized around instances of departure from perfect innovation. Rather, a slightly different language is used in terms of the "innovation problem," which expresses the "economic problem" of the allocation of scarce resources to the production of valuable new knowledge (i.e., innovation) in the context of perfect competition. Now because *perfect competition* is a well-known concept and *perfect innovation* is not, I'm going to proceed with the language of "innovation problem"—but the point I want to make clear is that these two concepts are equivalent.

2.2 The Innovation Problem as Economic Problem

In 1932, Lionel Robbins, a young professor at the London School of Economics, published *The Nature and Significance of Economic Science*. He defined economics as "the science which studies human behavior as a relationship between ends and scarce means which have alternative uses," (Robbins 1932, 16) thus arguing for a positivistic approach to economics. He succeeded, supplying what was to become the textbook definition of "the economic problem" as the optimal allocation of known resources to competing ends, aka the allocation problem.

In 1945 another young LSE professor, Friedrich Hayek, published in the *American Economic Review* a new definition of the economic problem, not as the allocation of scarce resources but rather as the coordination of distributed knowledge. Hayek wasn't arguing with Robbins, but with the contemporary market socialists, yet the point he made about the price mechanism and the distribution of knowledge has—like Robbins's textbook staple—become a fundamental redefinition of the economic problem that builds on knowledge rather than resources, aka the "knowledge problem." In "The Use of Knowledge in Society" Hayek (1945, 519) explained:

> The economic problem of society is thus not merely a problem of how to allocate "given" resources—if "given" is taken to mean given to a single mind which deliberately solves the problem set by these "data." It is rather a problem of how to secure the best use of resources known to

> any of the members of society, for ends whose relative importance only these individuals know. It is a problem of the utilization of knowledge which is not given to anyone in its totality.

These two modern views of "the economic problem"—Robbins's allocation of scarce resources (allocation problem) and Hayek's coordination of distributed knowledge (knowledge problem)—have a parallel in the economic problem of innovation, or the "innovation problem." You can see the innovation problem as an allocation problem, and you can see the innovation problem as a knowledge problem. Yet it's both an allocation problem and a knowledge problem. We need to separate these different economic problems out in order to identify when we're dealing with an allocation problem and when we're dealing with a knowledge problem.

An overarching thesis of this book is that modern innovation economics—and the contemporary definition of the innovation problem—has almost exclusively adopted an allocation problem definition, eschewing the knowledge problem definition, and has carried this framing over to innovation policy too.

The Schumpeter-Nelson-Arrow Version of the Innovation Problem

The modern view of the economics of innovation begins with Joseph Schumpeter, who formulated a dynamic theory of capitalism as an evolutionary process of endogenous change. The disruptive entrepreneur is the prime mover, and innovation is the dynamic process of creative destruction in firms, markets, and industries that drives economic evolution (Dopfer 2012). For Schumpeter, stationary capitalism is a contradiction in terms: "The same process of industrial mutation . . . incessantly revolutionizes the economic structure from within, incessantly destroying the old one, incessantly creating a new one" (Schumpeter 1943, 83). "This process of Creative Destruction" was for Schumpeter "the essential fact about capitalism." It is instructive to observe that Schumpeter's framework has aspects of both microtheoretical argument (the entrepreneur, in Schumpeter 1912) and also macrotheoretical argument (the dynamics of capitalism, socialism, and democracy, and the process of creative destruction, in Schumpeter 1942). Connecting these two was his historical theoretical work on technology-driven business cycles (in Schumpeter 1939). Dopfer (2012) argues that we should understand Schumpeter's work as the origin of *meso* economics (Dopfer et al. 2004; Dopfer and Potts 2008). For Schumpeter, then, innovation was how an economy changed and developed from within. The economic problem for Schumpeter was innovation itself.

The modern conception of the innovation problem as a Robbinsean economic problem—that is, as the optimal allocation of scarce resources, namely innovation inputs, to the production of new knowledge in order to maximize a social welfare function—was first developed by Nelson (1959) in the *Journal of Political Economy* in an article entitled "The Simple Economics of Basic Scientific Research," which outlined the social-welfare-maximizing case for public science as a Pigovian externality. This was developed more rigorously by Ken Arrow (1962b) in "Economic Welfare and the Allocation of Resources for Invention," the paper that established the innovation problem as a particular form of economic problem, and which elaborated Nelson's classic welfare economics approach into an argument based on the economics of information and uncertainty.[8] Arrow showed a generalized market failure in the incentives to private investment in the production of information—that is, new ideas, or R & D. The implication was profound and immediate: from the perspective of economic efficiency, innovation could not be left to the market; government needed to get involved.

Nelson and Arrow were colleagues at the RAND corporation, a US military think tank in Santa Monica, and both were concerned with the same economic problem of the optimal level of spending that a nation should devote to R & D. Both realized the same basic point, that if left to the market, a suboptimal level of R & D investment would follow, which they explained as due to the peculiar properties of the economic good being produced, namely new information. Innovation economics implied an active role for innovation policy. Richard Nelson's and Ken Arrow's work subsequently developed in different directions, becoming distinct schools of thought.[9] However, the conjoint Nelson-Arrow diagnosis of the innovation problem is the foundation of modern innovation policy throughout the world.[10]

In the Nelson-Arrow diagnosis, innovation occurs in markets—specifically in innovating firms under Schumpeterian competition—but this will not produce an optimal outcome from a social welfare perspective. These firms will invest too little, because of the market incentives they face, and in particular due to problems associated with appropriation of ideas by other firms, and by the chilling effect of uncertainty on the ability of firms to estimate the market value of these new ideas. There is a powerful role for government to furnish support for these innovating firms, correcting the incentive problems in markets by creating artificial rents or transfers. The sum of these activities—ranging across intellectual property, R & D tax credits, public science, targeted industry protection and indirect subsidy, targeted public procurement (e.g., in defense spending), and so on—is innovation policy. From the long-term perspective, innovation policy is the core of economic growth policy.[11]

Innovation is not an economic problem because new knowledge drives economic growth and development, as Schumpeter explained, and hence has value. Rather, innovation is an economic problem because it has value because it is costly and scarce, which is to say that the resources committed to it have alternative uses. That's the Robbinsean definition at work. Innovation has an opportunity cost.

If the economic problem is the allocation of scarce resources, then the micro version of the innovation problem is what resources to allocate to new knowledge discovery and adaptation for use, that is, to innovation. The economic problem of innovation then is due to the special properties of the production of new information in markets—indivisibilities, nonconvexities, uncertainty (Arrow 1962b)—that cause innovation to experience market failure. A competitive market only weakly incentivizes the discovery of new knowledge (Nelson 1959; Martin and Scott 2000; Gans et al. 2002). From the social welfare perspective, this outcome can be improved (Usher 1964; Romano 1989). Market failure in private investment in R & D requires government intervention to ensure a socially optimal level of investment in innovation through such mechanisms as intellectual property, R & D tax credits, public spending on innovation inputs and outputs.

The macro version adds an intertemporal aggregate production function to ask what fraction of goods produced today should be reinvested for future consumption. Here the innovation problem is subsumed into the growth problem, yet it is still an allocation problem, although now as an intertemporal optimization problem over society's resources. Furthermore, at the macro level, innovation is costly not only in the resources used to innovate (investment in future consumption), but also in dealing with the disruptive consequences and costs of innovation that propagate through markets, including collapse of existing economic activities, loss of jobs and bankruptcy of firms, and devaluation of extant resources, capital, and skills (Schumpeter 1942; Juma 2016). Which is simply to say that Schumpeterian innovation has costs and benefits, and these have distributional consequences, potentially requiring a further round of reallocation of societal resources in order to maximize social welfare (or to minimize disruptive political consequences).

Modern innovation economics separates into two distinct schools with respect to these micro and macro innovation problems: broadly an evolutionary school, and a neoclassical/institutional school (Verspagen and Werker 2003). In the evolutionary school, the focus is the study of industrial dynamics as Schumpeterian competition (Nelson and Winter 1982; Dopfer 2012). The neoclassical school turns this same insight back into welfare and information economics, observing that innovation is incompatible with perfect competition (Arrow 1962b; Romer 1990). These are methodologically distinct approaches, yet both consistently view innovation through the lens of competitive markets.

For evolutionary economists, who view competition as a process, entrepreneurial innovation is a powerful but inherently wasteful form of competition. For neoclassical economists, who view competition as an outcome, the innovation problem stems from market failure under perfect competition. Evolutionary economists insist that evolutionary competition in market capitalism is statically inefficient but dynamically efficient. For neoclassical economists, Pigovian-type interventions are necessary to induce efficient levels of investment in innovation. But in both schools, the innovation problem is an optimal investment problem (i.e., an allocation problem, in the context of a production function for innovation) between rivalrous firms in competitive markets within the market institutions of capitalism. In sum: new knowledge is not free, markets fail, and firms compete through innovation. Competition through innovation is socially valuable—driving technological change (i.e., output) and multifactor productivity growth (i.e., real incomes)—but innovation consumes resources, cannot be left to the market, and is a disruptive process. In these standard analytical perspectives, innovation is an economic problem of market failure (suboptimal allocation of resources) requiring government attention to produce a socially improved outcome.

The Hayek Version of the Innovation Problem

But there is also another economic problem that innovation brings: the problem of *discovery of value*, which is a knowledge problem. Call this the "Hayek version" of the innovation problem.

For any new idea or technology, before entrepreneurial action can occur, questions need to be answered: What is this best used for? Who will use it? How will they use it, and in combination with what? What are the range of uses? Who will be able to make this and where? What costs are involved in producing and delivering this? What business models will work best? What constraints to development will emerge? How will these problems be solved? What unintended effects will this have? And so on. This information is what distinguishes an invention from a potential innovation, and needs to be assembled for the innovation process to begin. That is to say, this is the information that entrepreneurs require in order to reduce uncertainty to tolerable levels.

The economic problem of innovation arrives when we realize that answering these questions involves eliciting cooperation in order to combine distributed knowledge, the value of which is ex ante unknown and only revealed ex post, once combined with other information. So this type of innovation problem is a *collective action* problem—which is a type of coordination problem, and specifically a *knowledge coordination problem*—that is resolved with *institutional governance*, that is, with mutually agreed-upon rules for coordination. This is an economic problem of efficiently incentivizing and processing distributed information. Moreover, it is not equivalent to the entrepreneur being bold or creative (in the Schumpeterian canon) or alert (in the Kirznerian story).

Allocation problems are essentially planning problems, and in many ways the modern innovation problem has been formulated as a variation on a classic industry-planning problem. But economic problems conceived as planning problems, as Hayek (1945) showed, are vulnerable to the "knowledge problem" critique.

The difference is the type of economic costs at the heart of the innovation problem. In the standard model, these are *production costs* that require investment to produce new technologies—as, for example, levels of R & D investment by innovating firms, sectors, or the whole economy, and modeled, in prime instance, with a production function for new knowledge (e.g., Romer 1990). But in our new approach these are *transaction costs* of innovation (Coase 1937), and they are a function of rules and institutions needed to coordinate knowledge in order to discover new opportunities. These are the costs that entrepreneurs face, not costs that research scientists incur. This defines the innovation problem as a strategic problem of *cooperation*, or *collective action*, in the first instance, and with solutions in the space of governance and contract (Williamson 2005) that will only under certain conditions be efficiently handled in competitive markets.

This is a different conception from the economic perspective of what the innovation problem is, and by whom and where it is experienced—namely in discovering new opportunities in the early phases of a new technology, rather than in producing new technologies. The economic problem of innovation here is that of a group of people seeking to discover value in dispersed knowledge by developing institutions to coordinate their actions. In this view, the innovation problem "is a problem of the utilization of knowledge not given to anyone in its totality" (Hayek 1945, 520).

This difference in analytic perspective also reflects a different focal point of the innovation problem along the innovation trajectory. In the modern neoclassical and Schumpeterian approach, the focal point of the innovation problem corresponds to the biggest and most conspicuous part of the innovation trajectory, namely the adoption and diffusion phase. This is the phase Schumpeter (1942) referred to when he wrote of creative destruction. It's the part Everett Rogers (1962) referred to when he wrote of the early-middle and late adopters. It's the part Zvi Griliches (1957) referred to when he wrote of technology diffusion (David 2015). It's the part Ed Mansfield (1961) wrote about when examining technological change and the rate of imitation. It's the part you can see.

But the innovation problem actually starts further back, in the parts you can't so easily see, where entrepreneurs, firms, and markets do not yet necessarily exist. What does exist is a prospect associated with a new technology or idea and distributed information carried by the enthusiasts of that new technology or idea. Yet this prospect, shrouded in uncertainty and still an uncoordinated mess of distributed knowledge, is fundamentally constitutive of an economic problem of innovation.

2.3 The Origin of the Innovation Trajectory

The Schumpeter-Nelson-Arrow conception of the innovation problem, and therefore innovation theory and policy, has little to say about the origin of innovation, about what happens at the very beginning, and specifically before there are innovating firms, entrepreneurs, and industrial dynamics. In the standard approach, which is constitutive of both neoclassical and evolutionary analysis, there is nothing before the entrepreneur and the venture-financed founding firm, which begins the creative destruction process. Anything prior is bundled under a broad heading of creativity, imagination, or serendipity, that is, not a consequence of systematic economic forces.

But there is actually an important phase that comes before "first entrepreneur, first firm, first market"—which is the conventional origin of innovation trajectory—and, moreover, it is governed by an explicable economic logic, which is to say that there is an economic problem of innovation associated with it. Call this *phase 0*, if you will, as the germinal phase in which a community forms, and figures out some rules for self-governance. Why does this happen, and why is this interesting and indeed crucial? The answer is that when that self-governance is effective, it enables something critical to happen, namely pooling and sharing of not just innovation resources, as might be gathered within a firm, but also information.

Phase 0 of an innovation trajectory—which I argue is the true origin of the entrepreneurial and innovation origins of the nature and causes of the wealth of nations—is the pooling of information to figure out the nature of the entrepreneurial opportunity associated with a new technology, or more generally a new idea. An economy is made of ideas, of human knowledge, and the growth of knowledge is the elementary process that describes the growth of all economies (Loasby 1999). This introduction of a zeroth phase updates Schumpeter through the lens of Hayek (1945) and Elinor Ostrom (1990).

This zeroth phase is the *innovation commons*, represented in relation to the standard three-phase trajectory in figure 2.1.

The innovation commons is institutionally different from subsequent phases in the innovation trajectory, largely made of entrepreneurs, firms, markets, and governments. Yet there are no entrepreneurs, firms, markets, or governments in the innovation commons; what there is, rather, is a commons—in Ostrom's (1990) sense of a rule-governed economic institution to oversee a common-pool resource among a community of users.[12]

The key question: What is that common-pool resource?

It's not what you think. It's not the new technology or proto-innovation per se. It's not the output of a laboratory, or the sort of thing that might be patented. Rather, in the innovation commons, the common-pool resource is the

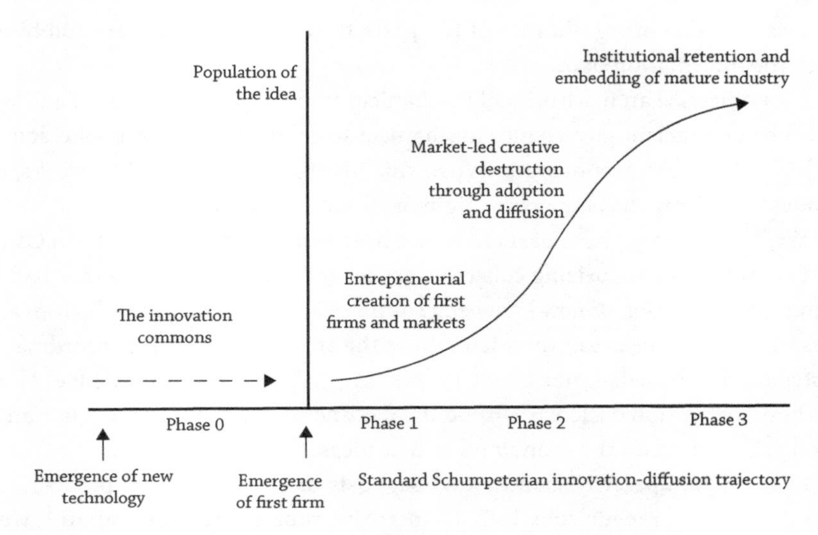

Figure 2.1 The innovation commons as the zeroth phase of an innovation trajectory

information about the innovation, and the role of the institutions of the commons is to govern access to that resource, and to coordinate the production of that resource.

The value of this information is that it enables people to overcome the uncertainty about the nature of the market opportunity, and thus to become entrepreneurs, to start a firm, to seek venture finance, and to move to the firms and markets phase of the innovation trajectory. The origin of innovation, in this new story, is not the first entrepreneurial firm (phase 1 in figure 2.1); rather, the innovation process starts further back, under a different institutional regime (i.e., a commons), which is an institutionally efficient mechanism to solve a different version of the innovation problem as an economic problem.

The standard definition of the innovation problem is an incentive problem facing individual economic actors: they allocate too few resources to R & D investment, compared to the social-welfare-maximizing ideal. That's a market failure problem, solved with government intervention. The economic problem that the innovation commons solves—and more efficiently than firms, markets, networks, or governments—is a different problem that occurs earlier in the innovation trajectory, prior to phase 1 in figure 2.1. It is the problem of pooling *distributed information*, and it is not a market failure problem, because markets have not yet formed, but rather is fundamentally a *collective action problem*.[13] This is because the information necessary to reveal the entrepreneurial opportunity is distributed and has little value until that information is pooled—that is, several people, perhaps many, each hold part of the total information, but no one knows the value or significance of the parts they hold until they are combined with the information of others.

A commons is an institutional mechanism to pool that information and will often be an efficient governance mechanism to create a common-pool resource of high value to entrepreneurs. When this institutional mechanism works, an innovation commons is the true origin of an innovation trajectory.

Yet, surprisingly, these parts have not been put together before. Both Olson and Ostrom were theorizing collective action and public goods. Neither had in mind the production of new knowledge or innovation (although see Ostrom and Hess 2006b). Hayek was theorizing how the market mechanism coordinated distributed knowledge, not about its role in producing new knowledge. None of these institutional theorists of political economy—Hayek, Olson, Ostrom—explicitly focused on the economics of new ideas.

In the Schumpeter-Nelson-Arrow diagnosis of the innovation problem, an *individual* entrepreneur runs into an incentive problem (market failure), with a government solution (innovation policy). In figure 2.1, that problem and its solution mostly unfold over phases 1 and 2 of the innovation trajectory. Yet a different conception of the innovation problem is the Hayek-Olson-Ostrom diagnosis, in which a group of people endeavor to solve a collective action problem to pool distributed information. They do this to create a common-pool resource to enable the discovery of entrepreneurial opportunities, and so to develop a new idea into an innovation.

This form of the innovation problem—and its solution in the innovation commons—exists because of fundamental uncertainty. This problem is solved with effective institutional governance rules of the innovation commons that facilitate the pooling of information, which dissipates the uncertainty, revealing entrepreneurial opportunities.

So this is a problem faced by a *group* (not an individual, the heroic entrepreneur in Schumpeter-Nelson-Arrow), it is a *collective action problem* (not a market failure problem, as in Schumpeter-Nelson-Arrow), and it is solved with community-level *governance* (not by government, as in Schumpeter-Nelson-Arrow).

The people in an innovation commons are therefore not yet entrepreneurs. They may be potential entrepreneurs or just technology enthusiasts. A number of different terms circulate: hobbyists, hackers, makers, amateurs, and so on. They may be contributing cognitive or some other resource surplus (Skirky 2012), or they may value the social or cooperative communitarian aspects (Benkler 2008). The simplifying working assumption we make is that they are behind a veil of entrepreneurial ignorance, and simply lack sufficient information to be effective entrepreneurs (which is to say that uncertainty is too high), but that there are enough compensating incentives in the commons to induce cooperation.

The innovation commons is the institutional solution to an *entrepreneurial discovery problem*. This discovery process takes place in the commons: indeed, it is the common-pool resource that is being produced. When that happens, the commons engenders a fundamental transformation: technology enthusiasts can become entrepreneurs, and the processes associate with the first and second phase of the innovation trajectory will get started. The commons is likely to collapse.[14]

The solution to this origin of innovation problem is governance, not government. It arrives bottom-up from civil society, not top-down from government. It is an emergent private *polycentric*[15] ordering of the sort studied by Ostrom (1990) and, as we will later see, is closely related to the models of idiosyncratic investment and hazards of opportunism developed by Williamson (1985a). The economics of this new approach to the innovation problem is not centered around policy recommendations to subsidize the *production costs* of innovation, but governance of collective action create an effective innovation commons, and how *transaction costs* affect that.

In both cases, the innovation problem is similarly constituted, namely on the economics of investment in research and development (i.e., new ideas). Yet a critical distinction, in both theory and policy, depends upon whether this is understood primarily as an allocation problem or as a coordination problem, which is to say whether it is viewed as a social welfare problem of *market failure* (in the Pigovian sense) or an institutional problem of *collective action* (i.e., a *social dilemma* [Dawes 1980; Ostrom 1990]). The first definition—allocation problem, *market failure*—dominates modern innovation economics, in both theory and policy. But the second definition—coordination problem, *social dilemma*—is an equally plausible and consistent model that fills many of the gaps left by the allocation-problem/market-failure model, particularly in relation to the economics of the origin and discovery of new opportunities, the formation of groups and the structure that may eventually become firms and industries, and the process of user-driven adaptation.

2.4 The Economic Problem of Innovation

What is the economic problem that society seeks to solve? How does the innovation problem relate to that?

If you're a microeconomist, the classic textbook formulation of the economic problem is unlimited wants and limited means—scarcity, in other words, requiring choice. The marginal revolution taught us how to resolve the economic problem as an allocative efficiency problem: namely allocate resources so marginal values are equal across all uses (in equilibrium, MR = P = MU). For this mechanism to work in a decentralized way, you need competitive markets. Where it doesn't work, you need governments to reallocate resources according to this principle by making transfers to equate marginal social benefit with marginal social cost. The innovation problem here is market failure (Arrow 1962b). But it is one of many market failure problems in an economy, and probably not the worst. The innovation problem is also a public goods problem—with new knowledge being the public good—and also one rarely high on the list of public good priorities.

If you're a macroeconomist, the economic problem is economic fluctuations or growth, depending upon your time horizon. In the first you're concerned with the causes of changes in income, employment, interest, inflation, and exchange rates; and in the second you're interested in growth and development through changes in savings, investment, institutions, and technology. The economic problem is to identify the stocks and flows of resources and economic activity, and the institutions that coordinate them, in order to target aggregate outcome, such as price stability, employment, or income growth. The innovation problem here is really a special case of the investment problem (in an aggregate production function for knowledge [Romer 1990]), which is ultimately a savings problem. Again, the innovation problem does not loom large in this story, hidden in the shadows of the problem of economic growth, and already set up as an institutional design problem, an industrial planning problem, or public spending problem.

But if you're an Austrian economist, that micro definition of the economic problem as "the best use of the available means" is not quite right because it neglects what Mises and Hayek called the "knowledge problem." What they meant is that the "how best to use society's scarce resources" definition of the economic problem is actually a planning problem, and, moreover, one that is trivial in logic if all the basic data about technology, resources, and consumer preferences are given. The knowledge to coordinate economic activity is never concentrated in one place and able to be operationalized by a planner, but as Hayek explains (1945, 519) consists of "the dispersed bits of incomplete and frequently contradictory knowledge which all the separate individuals possess." This is the knowledge problem, and it is solved by the information contained in market prices and relative price movements. So the innovation problem looks different from the Austrian perspective. It's not a market failure problem—that is, insufficient incentive to invest in new knowledge discovery, but a problem of opportunity discovery using the information contained in market prices.

And if you're an evolutionary economist, that macro definition of the economic problem is also not quite right. What it gets wrong, as Schumpeter explained (1911, 1935, 1942), is what it leaves out, namely the significance of endogenous transformation of the economy by entrepreneurship and innovation. Economies don't grow; they evolve. The measured growth in statistical aggregates of production or spending should not be confused with a real dynamical process of variation, selection, and differential replication of the habits, routines, and technological capabilities that constitute an economy, a formulation first articulated by Nelson and Winter (1982).

If the innovation problem is defined as an investment problem in competitive markets, and a diagnosis of waste or market failure is reached, then the solution will be to design market-correcting institutions such as new property rights, subsidies, competitive constraints, or public goods. This is, more or less, the gamut of modern innovation economics and innovation policy (Dosi and Nelson 2010).

But if innovation is seen as a problem of collective action, which is to say of coordinating distributed knowledge under conditions of uncertainty, then it presents as a choice problem over institutions, rather than one of modifying an extant institutional form. This is simply to recognize that, as technological historians have repeatedly pointed out, through the long and diverse history of capitalism, alternative modes for organizing the process of innovation have existed (Allen 1983; Scranton 1997; Meyer 2003; Nuvolari 2004; Moser 2012). The basic insight of the new institutional approach to innovation is that the most efficient institutions will be those that minimize transaction costs to the problems of innovation as a group activity. I summarize this in table 2.1.

2.5 The Innovation Problem Is a Collective Action Problem

Collective action problems (or "social dilemmas") are widespread in economics, social science, and evolutionary biology. They address the differing strategic incentives of individuals versus the group when facing the same problem. At its heart is the problem of *free riders*, that is those who seek to gain a benefit associated with a group but without paying the cost. Collective action problems are problems of strategic cooperation, where cooperation refers to an individual contributing to a group outcome, and in which the group seeks to design rules to constrain free riding.

Innovation is a problem of *strategic cooperation*. It is not just a problem of market failure. Many of the current diagnoses of market failure can be traced to earlier failures in strategic cooperation—that is, failures of governance that manifest later as opportunities for government intervention. We need to better understand how governance problems arise, and how they are solved, in order to mitigate the need for more costly and distortionary government solutions. A public choice perspective that sets the costs of government failure against the costs of market failure will never be far below the surface.

This new approach to innovation economics builds on both new institutional economics and on new public choice economics. It is also built upon information

Table 2.1 **The innovation problem as market failure versus collective action**

Innovation problem	*Market failure*	*Collective action*
Focus	Investment in R & D	Discovery of market information necessary for entrepreneurship
Economists	Nelson (1959), Arrow (1962b), Romer (1990), Freeman (1995)	Knight (1921), Hayek (1945), Ostrom (1990), McCloskey (2016)
Caused by	Fixed costs, copying, weak incentives to investment	Uncertainty, distributed knowledge
Specific form	Too little private investment in new technology development	Too much entrepreneurial uncertainty
Scarce valuable resource	New technologies	Information about opportunities
Concerns who?	Engineers	Entrepreneurs
Type of economic problem	Allocation	Coordination
Type of economic solution	Innovation policy, spending	Institutions, governance
Solving agent	State, organizations	Networks, civil society, organizations

economics and the economics of entrepreneurship. Which is to say the market failure view of the innovation problem is also offset by the market process view of the innovation problem. This is also reframed as a collective action problem.

Innovation is a problem of strategic cooperation because the introduction and development of any new idea in an economic system always runs into the fundamental problem of *entrepreneurial uncertainty*. In the entrepreneurial literature this problem is variously called "opportunity discovery" or "opportunity creation" (Alvarez and Barney 2007). However, in essence the concept recognizes that a technological possibility is not yet equivalent to an economic opportunity. The difference is that in discovering or creating a new economic opportunity a great deal of information needs to be revealed or assembled. This is information about costs and constraints, market demand and competitors, complementary resources and risks, and so on. These factors need to be experimentally discovered or assembled from distributed, possibly inchoate information. This is the sense in which innovation, as entrepreneurial discovery, is a collective action problem.

Joseph Schumpeter long ago characterized the entrepreneur as a heroic Nietzschean figure casting against the tides of conventional economic activity. Schumpeter's romantic portrait emphasized individual genius and force of will, and in so doing pushed into the shadows the extent to which entrepreneurial discovery is actually a group or distributed activity. Entrepreneurial action is an individual undertaking, but the entrepreneurial process as that of opportunity creation and discovery is a coordinated collective action over distributed information in order to resolve uncertainty.

This is where Hayek enters our story. For Hayek, the price mechanism was a marvel of distributed computation, with continually changing relative price signals leading to continual adaptation of the plans of economic agents to events throughout the economic system, and of which they may have only the dimmest awareness, but can quickly figure out a near optimal response simply by adjusting their actions based on input from changes in a few price signals. The genius of Hayek's insight was that the distributed price mechanism worked far more effectively and efficiently than any centralized planning mechanism.

Hayek's insight applies to all economic agents operating in markets and therefore whose actions are coordinated by the price mechanism. One limit is that much economic activity is coordinated by command mechanisms within organized hierarchies such as firms and other organizations (Coase 1937; Williamson 1975). This is also the domain of the innovating firm (Penrose 1959). However, Hayek's model is incomplete because there is still entrepreneurially relevant information not contained in prices (i.e., from markets). This is because early in the innovation process, markets don't yet exist. Actually, neither do firms. Schumpeter pointed up the innovation problem in terms of innovating firms, and Hayek pointed up the coordination problem in terms of markets. But both were implicitly operating in a world institutionally configured such that the relevant firms and markets already existed. Yet another class of coordinating institution that arises from civil society is the commons. The key insight here is that the innovation problem can be solved in the commons.

How do we complete Hayek's model of distributed information in markets, in Schumpeter's universe of disruptive entrepreneurs in firms? We add Elinor Ostrom's model of cooperation in the commons. Once we move the innovation problem away from seen entirely as market failure (in which firms invest too little in innovation from a social welfare perspective), and recast the innovation problem as a collective action problem (in which the innovation problem is that of pooling resources and information for opportunity discovery), then we can examine how effective governance mechanisms in the commons can solve such problems.

When in dealing with resource allocation problems, Ostrom explained that there is a third way between government solutions (which use mechanisms of command and coercion) and market solutions (which use the price mechanism). These are the governance institutions of the commons, which use the mechanism of rules. Ostrom mostly studied natural resource problems—in which the commons referred to fisheries, watersheds, forests, grazing pastures, and the like (and the common-pool resources they contain: e.g., fish, water, trees, and grass). The commons thereby refers to institutions that govern the shared use of those resources by a community. But the logic of her insight extends easily to knowledge resources, as her last body of works pointed to (Ostrom and Hess 2007), in which the shared resource does not preexist and must be created.

An innovation commons is a hybrid resource commons and knowledge commons because of the nature of an entrepreneurial opportunity as an economic good. It is produced with pooled information, making it seem cooperative and nonrivalrous. But this is true only up to the point of revealing the opportunity, whence upon, once revealed, the common-pool resource becomes rivalrous as an exploitable rent. The complex nature of an innovation commons as production and consumption is why its institutions of governance are so important.

By focusing on governance, we are developing a solution to the innovation problem that does not require a reallocation of resources, but instead requires particular configuration of institutions. Governance means people coming together to find rules to enable effective cooperation to explore and develop new technologies and the opportunities they contain. These rules are the *institutions of innovation*, and the basic idea running through this book is that such institutions are the first steps in solving the innovation problem. These innovation commons institutions set up the development of the subsequent processes of an innovation trajectory.

By adding Ostrom and Hayek to the Schumpeterian model of innovation economics, we reintroduce not only information and institutions into the innovation problem, but also the role of self-organizing communities of cooperating agents. Innovation is something we do together: it takes an economy to raise a technology.

The theory of the innovation commons builds from the insight that new ideas and technologies begin with a self-organizing community. These are often labeled enthusiasts or hobbyists, for example, and they are presumed to live in places like clubs, or hackerspaces, or perhaps somewhere on the internet, which might suggest a lack of seriousness or professional organization. But that would be a mistake. These club-like and commons-like forms are appropriate institutions for what is being produced, which is in essence, cooperation to pool resources, ideas, and information as efficiently and effectively as possible (Lakhani and Wolf 2005).

What these communities share is information: distributed, contemporary, idiosyncratic, often experimental information. It's gossip and tips and access to resources. The thing about these communities is that no one really knows yet how to be an entrepreneur, which is to say how exactly to exploit the economic opportunity latent in the new technology or idea. That's what everyone is trying to figure out. And to figure that out requires pooling and combining the relevant experimental information as it gathers in real time. So it's important to be in the community, for access to that information. But these same communities face a classic collective action problem, in respect of free-riders. You want the benefit, but the cost is contributing information, which you don't know the value of. Everyone is in the same situation.

The innovation commons is the institutional space that exists before the Schumpeterian world of firms and markets, because it creates the cooperative conditions to enable pooling of information to gather the distributed parts that assemble into a clear sense of the entrepreneurial opportunity. From this point, the firms and markets story of innovation begins. Institutionally speaking, an innovation commons collapses at the point that the entrepreneurial market institutions begin.

However, this is not just an early transitory process, as a kind of larval stage of the innovation butterfly. For the quality of the innovation commons carries through to the institutional structure of the resultant innovation trajectory. A major purpose of this book is to elucidate how that happens, for example, affecting the institutional development of an industry, including giving rise to industry associations and patterns of regulation. There are a great many operational institutions that have naturally emerged at the level of self-governed communities to solve this problem—that is, these are the innovation commons—and they are the institutional dark matter of the innovation problem.

By seeking to better understand how these cooperative community-forming institutions work, we might develop more effective innovation policy. This might mean less focus on the allocation of public investment, and more attention to the manner of supporting self-organizing institutions to pool information and resources to discover the entrepreneurial opportunities latent within new ideas. Innovation policy will be more about facilitation, less about allocation. It will be more focused on information discovery, less on resource planning. It will come from the bottom up, not from the top down.

2.6 Innovation Happens in Groups

The innovation problem is a knowledge problem of recombining distributed specialized knowledge in order to discover new opportunities and sources of value, including discovery of which bits of knowledge need to be combined. Knowledge is distributed because of specialization, with the value and meaning of the individual pieces not always apparent to those holding them (Lachmann 1994; Lavoie 2004). Because new knowledge is made of recombinations of existing knowledge, and that knowledge is invariably distributed and "not given to anyone in its totality," innovation is a coordination problem involving collective action. An appropriate maxim for the new transaction-cost-centered view of the origin of innovation is perhaps that *innovation is always and everywhere a group phenomenon*.[16]

A group, in this sense, is a group of people, such as a community, a club, or a network or an organization, such as a firm, whose mutual coordination is governed by a shared set of rules (i.e., an institution). Each person carries specialized knowledge (Dopfer and Potts 2008), and so a coordinated group is also a structure of knowledge. A different group is a different structure of knowledge. New knowledge is made, therefore, by making new groups (Hartley and Potts 2014).[17]

Because new knowledge is made of distributed heterogeneous knowledge, an outcome of specialization, this is a problem to be solved by a group, which requires institutions for coordination. The relevant economic problem, then, is the most efficient economic organization of those groups, where the innovation problem is both the discovery of these groups (i.e., who has what knowledge that needs to be combined) and the minimizing of the costs of effectively coordinating these groups. In both dimensions of the problem, the relevant innovation costs are transaction costs.

In the standard approach to the innovation problem—the market failure, allocation problem version—there are no groups. It is an autarkic model, in which the entrepreneur has already solved the knowledge coordination problem by assembling the relevant innovation resources within a single firm in order to exploit the known opportunity. The Coasian boundary problem between the firm and the market is not a foundational consideration, but a refinement of a closed innovation model to now include open innovation (Dahlander and Gann 2010). The locus of innovation—this brilliant entrepreneur, that enterprising firm, those clever patents—is manifest in singular identifiable measure-zero points (or their black-box equivalents) that are mutually coordinated by the price mechanism and, where markets fail, by government.

To see the innovation problem as a knowledge problem is to recognize that firms, markets, and governments are institutional mechanisms to coordinate the economic activity of discovering and putting to use new knowledge, but that there are also other institutional mechanisms involved as well. These other institutional mechanisms, beyond firms and markets, are not entirely alternative mechanisms, but also part of the same process of innovation and the growth of knowledge. But these mechanisms have a different institutional logic based on the creation of conditions for *cooperation* to pool and share information and knowledge in order to discover opportunities.

This is the institutional logic of innovation in groups, the fundamental premise of which is a starting position where the specific shape of the valuable opportunity is not yet known. This is true even when the underlying technology already exists, as for example in the early days of electricity, computers, lasers, internet, 3D printing, and, at the time of writing, blockchains. A technology, as an abstract mechanism (Arthur 2009), has no economic value until it is translated into a structure of capital and business models and market positions that can realize consumer value through adoption and use. Only then does it become an innovation in the economic sense.

This new conception of the innovation problem is centered on this discovery problem. It is a problem of the economic organization of groups of people to combine different pieces of knowledge. The economic problem of innovation, in this view, is to find the most efficient institutions to pool distributed information and knowledge. It concerns the economic organization of cooperation to create institutions for knowledge pooling, sharing, and contracting in conditions of high uncertainty. The modern institutional organization of firms and markets (and governments) do not always meet that condition in a transaction cost-minimizing way. Yet other institutions sometimes do have these properties—these tend to be commons, clubs, and other emergent cooperative institutions—and our new approach to the economics of the innovation problem is to integrate them into a more general theory of the innovation process.

Leonard Read once explained the efficacy of the market process with the story "I, Pencil." The point, channeling Adam Smith, was that because of the division of labor, no one actually knows how to make a pencil, but that market mechanisms coordinate distributed knowledge to produce something, even as simple as a pencil, that no one person can actually do. The corollary is that no one "innovated" a pencil either. The innovation process that gave us the pencil was similarly distributed. The problem for innovation economics is that the way our extant models work is that particular inventors, patents, entrepreneurs, and firms did innovate the pencil. Clearly, this happened. But missing from the story is how the knowledge was combined and the opportunities realized and then acted upon by the relevant market agents. Yet this is the economic problem we seek to understand. The logic of which technologies we have in our market economy and why is as much a phenomenon of the relative economic efficiency of particular institutions of cooperation that enabled this group and not that group to coordinate their knowledge in such a way that subsequently revealed profitable market opportunities as it is of any objective sense of ideally planned technologies.

Discovery Failure

Let us introduce the concept of *discovery failure* (as a corollary of market failure). Discovery failure occurs when the institutions of collective action in innovation fail, and the information necessary for entrepreneurs to see the pathway by which a new technology might benefit consumers fails to come together. In consequence the technology goes dormant. This probably happens more than we realize, because it leaves no trail. Like market failure, it is constructed only by comparing it to a hypothetical perfect outcome. So what then is *perfect discovery* (as the innovation analogue of a perfectly competitive market outcome)?[18] This occurs when all distributed knowledge is simultaneously available to an entrepreneur, who is then alert to the relevant prospects. When all relevant information is contained in price data, this is symmetric with perfect competition.

Discovery failure begins when the relevant information does not find its way into the entrepreneurial process. Lavoie (1994) and Lavoie and Prychitko (1995), following Lachmann's (1956, 1976) Austrian conception of heterogeneous capital, argues that entrepreneurs are keyed into a broader concept of the discovery of meaning than is contained in price signals. This generalizes the Misean/Hayekian notion of markets as communication mechanisms to a more general understanding of the communication platforms that guide an economy. Discovery failure is a concern with the institutions of communication and coordination that piece together the information about opportunities for the discovery of particular entrepreneurial actions to advance a new idea or technology. Discovery failure is a prime instance of the failure to efficiently resolve a collective action problem.

The innovation problem is a "knowledge problem," in the Hayekian sense, to the extent it is a discovery problem of finding combinations of different pieces of knowledge that reveal valuable opportunities on which entrepreneurs might act. The economic problem is to choose effective institutions to efficiently coordinate this knowledge discovery process. This is the new innovation problem.

Discovery Costs

Innovation discovery requires governance because innovation discovery requires coordinating distributed information, knowledge, and resources to reveal an entrepreneurial opportunity prior to the endeavor to realize it as an innovation. There are several institutional and organizational forms this governance can take. In the Schumpeterian canon these center on hierarchical organizations, such as the innovating firm (Nelson and Winter 1982) or a public science institute or a research university (Nelson 1959); a network of organizations (e.g., open innovation [von Hippel 2003]); or a market (e.g., the market for ideas [Gans and Stern 2010]). But discovery governance can also take the form of private orderings such as a club (Kealey and Ricketts 2014), or a commons (Ostrom and Hess 2007). Discovery failure is not the failure to discover an opportunity; that is a common occurrence in any search process under uncertainty. Rather, discovery failure is failure to realize and adopt an effective governance mechanism to coordinate the distributed information, knowledge, and resources toward opportunity discovery. The likelihood of opportunity discovery will be a function of the effect of institutional governance mechanisms on discovery costs.

Discovery costs are the dynamic entrepreneurial analogue of transaction costs. Transaction costs are the costs incurred in making an exchange, which includes the cost of exchanging property rights, of making and enforcing contracts, and of capturing the gains from specialization and the division of labor, including "the value of the labor, land, capital, and entrepreneurial skill used in making exchanges" (Wallis and North 1986, 97). These are often decomposed into search and information costs, bargaining costs, coordinating and enacting costs, and monitoring and enforcement costs (Dahlman 1979).

In this view, the world of economic costs divides between *transformation costs*—the costs of making and producing things, which are represented in the neoclassical theory of the firm—and *transaction costs*, the costs of using the market to coordinate those activities, which are broadly the domain of new institutional economics. Introducing discovery costs into this model seeks to recognize a domain of economic activity, and thereby of costs, associated with the creation and discovery of economic opportunities, which must then be produced and exchanged (transformation costs and transaction costs). This is the domain of Schumpeterian, evolutionary, Austrian, and entrepreneurial economics, although often shoehorned within the transformation or transaction costs frameworks (see table 2.2).

Discovery costs are incurred in developing an entrepreneurial opportunity, from the initial discovery and development of a novel idea, through the discovery and development of the entrepreneurial opportunity (Hausmann and Rodrik 2003). Discovery costs are the costs associated with the technical development of a new idea (R & D costs) as well as the costs of establishing the nature of the entrepreneurial opportunity, such as experiments, discovery of costs and business models, and costs incurred through incubator and venture capital stages of development. Discovery costs also include the broader costs associated with uncovering potential uses of the technology and potential benefits, and to whom, and the costs that the new idea might impose on others.

The process of accounting for discovery costs extends the approach used to account for transaction costs. Transformation cost accounting is focused on the value of the inputs required to produce a set of outputs in a firm. Transformation costs beyond the firm are usually expressed as public infrastructure, or simply public goods. Transaction costs extend beyond the firm as the institutions that

Table 2.2 **Transformation costs, transaction costs, and discovery costs**

Standard model of economic costs		*New model also includes . . .*
Transformation costs	*Transaction costs*	*Discovery costs*
Neoclassical theory of the firm	*New institutional economics*	*Evolutionary economics*
• Production function of inputs: capital, labor, technology	• Search and information costs • Bargaining costs • Monitoring and enforcement costs	• Technological discovery, R & D • Entrepreneurial discovery, experiments
Inputs to outputs	Facilitates exchange	Creates novelty, reduces uncertainty

contribute to the facilitation of exchange, such as the publicly funded legal and judicial system, or the civil society institutions of trust. This also involves a shift in the conception of the firm as an organization from the (Marshallian) transformation cost model in which a firm is a production function, to the (Coasian) transaction cost model in which the firm is a bundle of contracts. The accounting logic of transaction costs is based on identifying the total costs of creating and exchanging property rights over resources. The accounting logic of discovery costs, in turn, is based on identifying the total costs of creating and developing novel ideas that might become resources that will be subject to transformation and transaction.

Firms incur discovery costs (e.g., R & D expenditure of the innovating firm). But discovery costs are also incurred by economic agents outside a firm, such as consumers, users, hobbyists and hackers, and other enthusiasts engaged in the search of applications and value (see von Hippel 1986; Franke and Shah 2003; von Hippel and von Krogh 2003; Flowers 2008; Baldwin and von Hippel 2011). Furthermore, those agents who seek to constrain the development of the novel idea (such as protestors or agents engaged in rent seeking) will also help reveal those costs by revealing something about their distribution and magnitude. Discovery costs are the total costs involved both in the technological development of the idea and in figuring out the nature of the entrepreneurial opportunity. In this sense, they are the total costs in reducing uncertainty to the point that an entrepreneur can act, usually by starting a firm.

These total discovery costs are incurred by an economy in the same way that transaction costs are, such that some institutional configurations of a society will have lower transaction costs than others (e.g., because of trust). Similarly, some institutional configurations of a society will have lower discovery costs than others—because of information pooling and sharing, for example. These aspects are often associated with properties of technology and innovation clusters in an industrial context in reference to the information externalities they generate.

What might a national accounting of discovery costs look like? Wallis and North (1986) estimated that about 50 percent of the US economy over the first three-quarters of the twentieth century was *transaction services*, which is an income estimate of transaction costs. That figure is probably higher in a more developed economy than in a less developed economy. The corresponding figures for discovery costs (estimated with discovery services) can only be speculated upon, but will certainly be higher than the 3 or so percent that is accounted for in private and public R & D spending in most developed economies.

Discovery costs include those of technological discovery, not only science and R & D but also the capital and time costs of user and consumer experimentation. They will also include the full suite of entrepreneurial discovery costs ranging across venture funding and capital, entrepreneurial incubator costs, technology transfer costs, discovery of competitive and complementary investment, business models, and market barriers and opportunities. Discovery costs include finding and establishing property rights (Coase 1960; Demsetz 1967)—including ways to reduce transaction costs (Foss and Foss 2005) or revealing opportunities for value creation within a bargaining context (Lippman and Rumelt 2003). See table 2.3.

Many discovery costs are currently bundled in with transformation costs (production of innovation) and transaction costs (information search). By separately identifying these as discovery costs, a more robust dynamic accounting can be constructed.

2.7 Conclusion

Modern economics struggles with the innovation problem, underestimating the extent to which it is simultaneously a knowledge problem, a coordination problem, and a collective action problem. The innovation problem is also a metaproblem; you solve the innovation problem and you solve a whole lot of other economic problems too. That's why it matters.

Innovation is a process with a beginning, middle, and end. Most thinking about innovation problem focuses on the middle and end, because that's where all the action is (and the data too). This is innovation as competitive rivalry between firms. It's innovation as industrial dynamics. It's innovation as venture capital and market disruption and new business models and the creation of

Table 2.3 **Taxonomy of discovery costs**

Technological discovery
Basic science
Research and development
Prototyping, Beta-testing
Technology transfer
User experimentation
Entrepreneurial discovery
Uses and applications
Property rights
Complementary assets
Teams and partners, and locations
Venture finance
Start-up and incubator
Competitive and complementary investment
Costs (materials, inputs, regulations—transformation costs and transaction costs)
Business models and organization
Market discovery (intermediate and final demand, supply sources, distribution, price points, and segmentation)

new industries. It's innovation as adoption and diffusion of new technologies. Schumpeter's creative destruction is all middle and end. Innovation policy tends to be all middle (the evolutionary dynamics of firms, markets, and industries) and end (dealing with the economic, social, cultural, and political consequences). But the hard part of the innovation problem is the beginning. And the really hard part is the very beginning.

Notes

1. Among others, see Hodgson 1993. See Nelson and Winter 1982 for the modern classic analytic framework of economic evolution in terms of populations of firms (made of habits and routines) subject to entrepreneurial variation and market selection. See Metcalfe 1998 on evolutionary economic selection. See Dopfer and Potts 2008 for an account of the *General Theory of Economic Evolution* in terms of micro-, meso-, and macroanalytic domains.
2. Or the *generic rules* of the economy, as Dopfer and Potts (2008) propose. The idea that knowledge is a resource too wouldn't become clear in the mainstream until Romer (1990), but was foundational in the work of Joseph Schumpeter (1912) who introduced the concept of the entrepreneur as an agent of economic evolution, bringing variety to the knowledge base of an economy upon which market selection might operate (Alchian 1950). The economics

of knowledge as a resource concerns how it is allocated (the standard concern in the economics of resources), but also how it grows. The economics of the growth of knowledge has two solutions: an allocation solution, which has been widely studied, and a coordination solution, which has been barely recognized.

3. And the core of what Boettke (2012) calls "mainline economics" (cf. mainstream economics).
4. Demsetz (1969) cautioned against a policy approach that starts from the assumptions of perfect competition, calling it the "nirvana fallacy."
5. There is a more or less equivalent way of telling this story directly in terms of "externalities," and without requiring the concept of a public good, but we'll come to that later.
6. If you're wondering what the social optima is: it's artificially constructed by summing all individual preferences to produce a "social welfare function." The social welfare function is a model of society allocating scarce resources and receiving benefits as if it were a single agent.
7. And yes, Eisenhower did initially include "academic" in that infamous lineup, although it was deleted from the final draft. See Giroux 2007.
8. Arrow (1962b, 619) wrote: "We expect a free enterprise economy to underinvest in invention and research because it is risky, because the product can be appropriated only to a limited extent, and because of increasing returns. This underinvestment will be greater for more basic research. To the extent that a firm succeeds in engrossing the economic value of its inventive activity, there will be an underutilization of that information compared to the ideal allocation."
9. Richard Nelson went on with colleagues (including Sidney Winter, David Mowery, Giovanni Dosi, Nate Rosenberg, among others) to found modern evolutionary economics, which is both methodologically and theoretically distinct from the neoclassical approach to innovation economics and policy that grows from Arrow's work.
10. Ken Arrow pretty much defines modern neoclassical microeconomics, just as Dick Nelson defines modern Schumpeterian or evolutionary economics. The models and policy frameworks based on their work have gone in different directions (e.g., patent races versus innovation systems), but both ultimately present the innovation problem through the lens of an allocation problem, a social welfare function, and market-failure diagnostics.
11. This point is repeatedly made in the Schumpeterian literature (e.g., Metcalfe 1994, 1998). The canonical statement in the mainstream literature is Romer 1990.
12. In 1990, Elinor Ostrom, also a political economist, published *Governing the Commons*, which explained why these small groups could nevertheless sometimes produce local public goods through the effective governance of a common-pool resource (explicitly arguing against Hardin's [1968] "tragedy of the commons" thesis). What Ostrom showed was that, under certain conditions, civil society could create institutions to manage and produce a common-pool resource without the necessary involvement of government. Rather, such coordinating institutions emerged from the bottom-up actions of civil society.
13. In 1965, the political economist Mancur Olson published *The Logic of Collective Action*, which, as subtitled, was about the "public goods and the theory of groups." Free-rider problems meant that small, organized groups could defeat large disorganized groups, explaining why collective action to produce public goods often failed, producing rents instead (Krueger 1974). This is why "government failure" (cf. market failure) is central to public choice economics.
14. We will see in chapter 7 that an innovation commons can transform into a different institutional form, namely an industry association.
15. It should be noted that the idea of an innovation commons is consistent with both singular and multiple communities of governance forming to pool information and other innovation resources. An innovation commons can in this sense be polycentric. Examples are the various chapters of hackerspaces or meetups that form around makerspaces, or in blockchain or crypto-communities.
16. Cf. Milton Friedman's quip that "inflation is always and everywhere a monetary phenomenon."

17. In the Hartley and Potts (2014) framework of "cultural science," the evolutionary function of culture is to make groups (distinguishing "we" from "they"), and the evolutionary function of groups is to make knowledge by creating a common pool of elements. In this evolutionary model of culture and knowledge, changes in the boundary of groups causes changes in knowledge.
18. Cf. the concept of "perfect innovation" in Potts 2017 in the context of behavioral innovation economics.

3

Innovation Is a Knowledge Problem

In standard innovation economics, the core models are essentially stories about problems that arise in the context of innovation in markets. In a stylized way, this can be represented in the work of Ken Arrow (welfare economics, information economics, as the market failure model), and Joseph Schumpeter and Richard Nelson (evolutionary economics, the innovating firm, and the creative destruction model of an innovation trajectory).[1] This is the Schumpeter-Nelson-Arrow framing of the innovation problem.

Our new approach to the innovation problem builds on a different set of key theorists and reference models, of which I suggest there are four:

1. *Deirdre McCloskey* in the *Bourgeois* trilogy, on the moral and cultural foundations under which innovation can occur as an evolutionary social process
2. *Friedrich Hayek*, both in his famous "use of knowledge in society" paper and in his later work on cultural evolution, on the ideas of both distributed knowledge and group selection
3. *Oliver Williamson*, on the coordination problem of idiosyncratic investment under uncertainty, and the hazards that contains
4. *Elinor Ostrom*, whose work provides a resolution to the Hayek and Williamson knowledge conditions with a general solution to the collective action problem of knowledge discovery by pooling knowledge through institutional evolution

So on one side we have a Schumpeter-Nelson-Arrow model of the innovation problem centered about a *choice-theoretic* analysis of individuals (including firms) endeavoring to innovate in competitive markets, the things that go wrong, and the sorts of solutions that follow. This approach, based on a market failure and market externalities definition of the innovation problem, has been enormously useful for understanding market capitalist dynamics and for designing innovation policy.[2] On the other side, in this chapter, will be a McCloskey-Hayek-Williamson-Ostrom model of the innovation problem centered about a *contract-theoretic* analysis of a collective action problem of discovery of entrepreneurially valuable knowledge.

3.1 Innovation Problem I: Social Contract Problem (McCloskey Version)

The ways in which the innovation problem is fundamentally a collective action problem begins with the second innovation problem, the problem of disruption and the uneven costs innovation brings by devaluing some existing positions, and the implications that has for *social justice* (Wilkinson 2016). The first economic problem that needs to be solved is *permission to innovate*.

The problem of weak incentives to innovate—the classic modern formulation, à la Arrow (1962b)—is a foundational innovation problem only in a perfectly competitive market economy. Such an economy has a utilitarian model of distributional justice, in the welfare-theoretic sense (Pigou 1932; Samuelson 1954). There is no individual ethical dimension here, just incentives, or "prudence only" as Deirdre McCloskey (2010) says. Yet the origins of the modern market economy that produced "the great enrichment"—the spectacular rise in global wealth beginning in northwestern Europe in 1800 (Mokyr 2011)—are the same origins from which the modern innovation economy emerges. McCloskey (2006, 2010, 2016) argues that the cause of this epoch-making shift was not discovering new resources or markets (coal, colonial empires), nor, contra Douglass North et al., was it imposing "good institutions," but rather it was an ethical shift in the moral rhetoric (the conversations in society) about liberty and dignity, in which respect for betterment and its practitioners, the bourgeois, gradually took hold, even and indeed especially among the commoners. McCloskey (2016) explains:

> What mattered were two levels of ideas—the ideas in the heads of entrepreneurs for the betterments themselves (the electric motor, the airplane, the stockmarket); and the ideas in the society at large *about* the businesspeople and their betterments (in a word, liberalism).

The permissioning of innovation comes from this second level of ideas, and McCloskey's point is this was, and remains, a fundamentally egalitarian revolution in virtue ethics. The origin of the innovation economy was a change in the moral position of those introducing new ideas into society through the market channel of trade-tested betterment. The rise in the status of merchants and traders—the good bourgeois—was a simultaneous rise in the status of entrepreneurs and innovators, what Mokyr and Voth (2009) call the "knowledge elite" (Mokyr 2016).[3]

Yet what McCloskey calls "bourgeois deal" was a profoundly inclusive one. By permitting not just freedom but also according respect to all who sought to explore the possibilities of the liberal market order, the bourgeois deal was based on a collective understanding that the benefits would be shared and that no one would be left behind, that is, a social contract of distributive fairness (Tomasi 2012). The moral underpinning of the bourgeois deal, and therefore of the innovation economy, is the principle of social justice. Social justice is bourgeois virtue: it is a society-wide agreement, manifest in what Adam Smith called "moral sentiments" and only subsequently and sometimes expressed in laws and "policies," about how to share the gains from cooperation. It is a social contract based in moral sympathy that extends equal rights and dignity to all members of a society. Without this ethical foundation, there is no innovation economy because there is no basis for the sorts of cooperation such an economy requires.

Think of this ethical revolution as a massive shift in the *social technology for cooperation*. A social contract that grants permission to innovate,[4] in return for an understanding that the gains from innovation will be shared in some way, and that the costs of innovation upon whom those fall will in some sense be compensated, can be modeled as a technology that fundamentally lowers the transaction costs of innovation, or of the pursuit of trade-tested betterment. The welfare state and other rights-based social insurance and universal public provision of higher education are both plain instances of this Rawlsian contract that strengthen social cooperation. It is *special* treatment of particular incumbent positions (e.g., industry protection, occupational licensing, and other monopolies) based on political power that violates the contract because it weakens cooperation by entrenching inequality.

The innovation economy is sometimes characterized as an "experimentally organized economy" (Eliasson 1991), a "venturesome economy" (Bhide 2010) and a "free market innovation machine" (Baumol 2001) of "restless capitalism" (Metcalfe 1998) powered by Schumpeterian animal spirits. The policy implication is that to drive "mass flourishing" (Phelps 2013) we need more entrepreneurship, which can be purchased with stronger incentives through better institutions.

McCloskey's argument is that this is actually bad economics. An ex ante commitment to social justice is costly for a society because it weakens the high-powered incentives to enterprise. But the other side of the deal—the permissioned social contract—has a substantial payoff by lowering the (transaction) costs of cooperation in the face of *uncertainty* of outcome. Innovation is a Rawlsian veil of ignorance: it is difficult to know ex ante where you will find yourself on the other side, and how the new idea will impact on your own consumption, wealth, and status. Individually rational loss avoidance and risk minimization withdraws cooperation, withholding resources and raising costs of the discovery of value. But the bourgeois deal is always to play "cooperate" on the first move and allow exploration to see where this goes, on the secure understanding that fairness will prevail and no one will be left behind.

The economics of the innovation problem is not in the first instance that of incentivizing individual entrepreneurs to create an innovative society. The foundational economic problem of innovation is the collective action problem to generate ex ante cooperation prior to individuals knowing how it will affect them, or whether they themselves will be entrepreneurs. An ex ante commitment to liberal social justice, as an a priori agreement about how to share the gains from cooperation when these are not yet known (and so too with how to apportion the costs), achieves this social contract through a moral revision of status. The bourgeois deal is that commerce is ethically valued, and with it the quest for improvements in commerce (i.e., innovation) is ex ante permissioned, in return for a strong commitment to inclusiveness and fairness. The result is lowered costs of cooperation and a wider sphere of cooperation in the discovery of new ideas.

Social permissioning of innovation is the first collective action problem that needs to be solved in the economics of innovation. Social justice is the other side of this bourgeois deal, and its effect is to lower the transaction costs of cooperation in the discovery of value by implicitly contracting a post hoc redistribution of the surplus generated. This is secured through fundamental moral principles of inclusive liberty as social justice. We now consider how the opportunities for knowledge discovery are limited by the extent of low cost cooperation.

3.2 Innovation Problem II: Distributed Knowledge Problem (Hayek Version)

The innovation problem continues as a collective action problem in consequence of two distinct aspects of the ideas of Friedrich Hayek: first, in his work on distributed knowledge and the price mechanism (Hayek 1945); and second, in his work on cultural group selection (Hayek 1973, 1988).

Hayek (1945) argued that the socialists who sought to centrally plan an economy using shadow prices had fundamentally misunderstood what the price mechanism does. Prices, he argued, were highly efficient information signals to communicate distributed information and knowledge about the state of local conditions, allowing a great many people, none of whom need know each other or their particular situations, to nevertheless coordinate their separate actions so as to arrive at an orderly meshing of individual plans.[5] For Hayek (1945, 519), "The economic problem of society is mainly one of rapid adaptation to the particular circumstances of time and place." The price mechanism is an economy of knowledge that enables this dynamic mutual coordination of decentralized actions.

The adaptations Hayek had in mind were exogenous shocks to supply or demand conditions over goods, and for which there already exist markets and therefore prices.[6] So what, then, is the role of the price mechanism in innovation? In one sense, the price mechanism fails completely here because it cannot coordinate over new goods that do not yet exist, that is, have prices. But it does provide information about the need for new substitutes (rising prices), or the benefit of new complements (falling prices), each of which involves entrepreneurial alertness and judgment to changes in these prevailing prices. It also provides information about prospective costs of inputs into the innovation process (R & D costs), opportunity costs (alternative returns on factors), and the rents available (extant profits). So there is a penumbra of price information in markets for innovation (Akcigit and Lui 2016).

However, the identification of efficient price-equivalent mechanisms in a sense misrepresents Hayek's fundamental insight, which is that knowledge is distributed and that the value of markets is that they are an *efficient* institutional mechanism to coordinate that knowledge. Hayek's insight was pre-Coasian, so he did not have a transaction cost concept of markets firmly in mind. But when we add transaction costs, markets for new and partial information of the sort needed to furnish information to input into entrepreneurial decision-making quickly fail (Arora et al. 2001; Gans and Stern 2003, 2010). But the relevant question is not whether markets can always do this job, but whether there is any institutional mechanism that can efficiently perform this function.

The standard answer to this question is the innovating firm: the contractual organization of resources by an entrepreneur in order to undertake a particular new venture (Teece 1992), which is then multiplied by many innovating firms exploring different parts of that space in parallel, the efficiency condition resolved ex post with a market selection mechanism (Nelson and Winter 1982). This is the model of the innovating firm in an evolutionary process of industrial dynamics. Note that there is no price mechanism in this account, just selection on profitability (Alchian 1950). Entrepreneurs could be acting randomly, or under strong conditions of uncertainty.

An alternative mechanism is ex ante cooperation, that is, from behind the veil of ignorance about where one will be with respect to the outcome of the innovation. This manner of cooperation is the *innovation commons* (Allen and Potts 2016). We will refine and develop this idea in section 3.4, when we turn to Elinor Ostrom's work on knowledge commons. But the key idea is that a potentially efficient institutional solution to the Hayekian problem of coordinating distributed information and knowledge about innovation possibilities in order to reveal entrepreneurial prospects is to identify low-transaction-costs solutions, the minimum of which is invariably to pool the information into a commons, that is, to create a common-pool resource. A social contract that sets up ex ante cooperation is precisely the low-transaction-cost condition that facilitates a potentially commons-based, rather than market- or firm-based institutional solution.

To recap: the Hayekian knowledge problem also applies to innovation in the context of the identification and coordination of distributed knowledge necessary for the entrepreneurial discovery of opportunities. But the problem is that this information is not entirely, or even generally, communicated through the price mechanism. Much of the information requires the extraction of meaning from nonprice information (Lavoie 1994). The innovation problem *for an individual* is how to position himself with respect to the loci of such information so as to maximize his chance of gathering the right information while minimizing the costs of doing so. This is a planning problem. But the innovation problem *for a society* is different: it is how to create institutions that efficiently gather and pool that information so as to minimize the effort needed in individual planning (or to maximize the prospective reward).

This brings us to the second line that Hayek opened up, the emphasis in his later work on the role of cultural group selection. This has been critiqued in economics (Vanberg 1986; Beck 2018) and noted in fields outside economics (Sober and Wilson 1998) for Hayek's seeming abandonment of methodological individualism for a rejected model of evolutionary theory, namely group selection.

But what is now called "multilevel selection theory" has had a significant revival in evolutionary theory (Gintis et al. 2003; Wilson and Wilson 2007; Nowak et al. 2010), rehabilitating Hayek's original position (Zywicki 2000). Multilevel selection theory can be summarized as "cooperation *for* competition," and groups that can successfully cooperate, and thus realize the gains from cooperation, can outcompete groups that cannot (Turchin 2015; Bowles and Gintis 2013). Hayek's arguments against "scientism" were the basis of his reasoning about cultural group selection, namely that a society could through differential evolutionary selection acquire habits and traits that were mutually beneficial, even when not rationally explicable, a point he worried about in the context of civilizational collapse (Dekker 2016).

A society that can lower the transaction costs of cooperation for innovation, that is, to effectively "permission" innovation, through an effective commitment to a social contract of principled egalitarianism whatever the outcome of that innovation, is a society acting as a group, and can potentially outcompete a rivalrous society with higher innovation transaction costs. It does so by having lower barriers to innovation entry, and therefore a higher expected innovation payoff. And to the extent that that makes that society economically stronger and more prosperous, able to marshal greater resources against an external threat or offer a higher standard of living to increase sustainable migration, that cooperative "cultural group" can outcompete rivals on a regional or even global stage.

3.3 Innovation Problem III: Idiosyncratic Risk (Williamson Version)

The third layer of the innovation problem as a collective action problem arrives with the integration of the contract-theoretic (rather than choice-theoretic, i.e., market failure) perspective on governance of the innovation problem through the lens of Oliver Williamson's (1985a) operationalization of transaction cost economics (Coase 1960) in terms of uncertainty, asset specificity, and opportunism. Oliver Williamson (1985a, 11) once explained that "any issue that can be formulated as a contracting problem can be investigated to advantage in transaction cost economizing terms." So how is the innovation problem a contracting problem?

In essence, it is a contracting problem caused by Hayekian distributed knowledge and heterogeneous capital (Foss et al. 2007), or the need to arrive at cooperative solutions that are mutually beneficial to all parties. The noncontracting version of the innovation problem is what can be called "innovation autarky," or the presumption that all relevant information is concentrated at one specific and functionally complete locus, namely the entrepreneur. Note that I explained previously that whether this is true or not does not matter from an evolutionary market selection perspective that ignores transaction costs (Alchian 1950). But from the Williamson perspective on innovation economics, the fundamental choice is between autarky (acting along, in markets) and contracting (seeking efficient governance institutions). I represent this in figure 3.1, to distinguish between the choice-theoretic market school of innovation economics (neoclassical and Schumpeterian) and the contract-theoretic governance approach developed

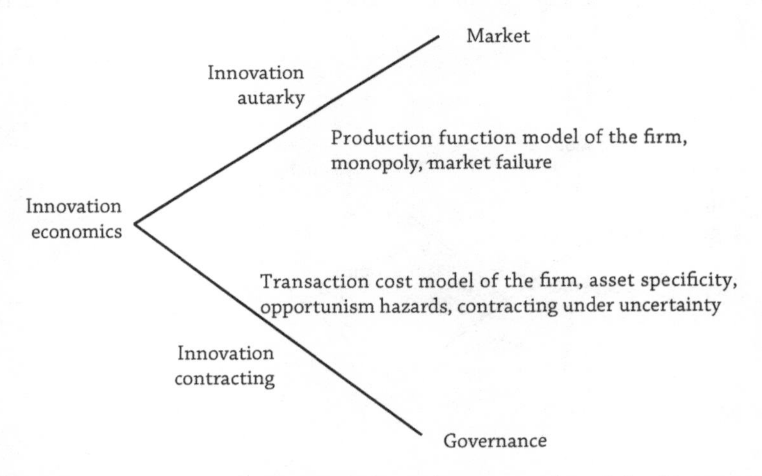

Figure 3.1 Market (choice) versus governance (contracting) models of innovation economics

here, which begins with a collective action problem of seeking to find others with whom to cooperate in an uncertain venture.

In the Williamson framework, agents economize on transaction costs by choosing an efficient governance structure to minimize hazards of opportunism and maximize quasi rents. Quasi rents are returns to mutual cooperation in consequence of specific investments that pay off only if the counterparty also makes specific investments (Klein et al. 1978). Such contracts expose each party to hazards of opportunism: the other party can defect and capture all rents once an irreversible investment is made.

This is a game-theoretic problem of trust in the narrow sense, but more generally it is a problem of optimal institutional or mechanism design. It is also a problem of uncertainty, which both exposes and magnifies trust problems. Where there is certainty of outcomes, complete knowledge, and low transaction costs, economic coordination is efficient in markets. But where the payoff to particular idiosyncratic investments depends on assured complementary investments, the hazards of holdup can lead to failure to make those idiosyncratic investments in the first place. Bringing these contracts within a firm using employment contracts (as in the hierarchy branch of figure 3.2) is a partial solution to this problem because dynamic capabilities also develop (Robertson and Langlois 1995).

However, under conditions of high uncertainty of the value of particular knowledge, and of what knowledge needs to be combined, such contracts are uncovered risk for an individual firm.[7] In consequence, we expect that differential governance institutions will emerge in proportion to the levels of uncertainty and the costs of contracting (figure 3.2).

The Williamson (1985a) problem—idiosyncratic investment in complementary assets, creating conditions of opportunism, resolved contractually

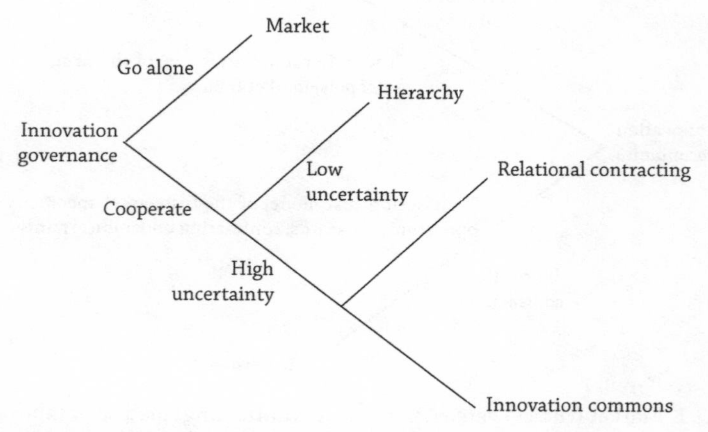

Figure 3.2 Comparative institutions of innovation contracting

to minimize transaction costs—translates into the space of innovation when those idiosyncratic investments are the distributed (Hayekian) components of knowledge that need to be combined in order to reveal and manifest entrepreneurial opportunities.[8] Transaction costs are part of the total costs of innovation that arise from the need for groups of people to make highly idiosyncratic investments to generate quasi rents only if others in the group make complementary investments. Those quasi rents correspond to the identification of opportunities for value creation, which can be observable to all involved, whether or not they've contributed through specific investment. It is reasonable to suppose that most revealing of information is costly, and that this information has limited alternative uses (i.e., is of most value when combined with other specific information about the technological and market opportunity). This exposes all parties to opportunism hazards, otherwise known as "asset specificity," which is the irreversibility of an investment.

The basic economic problem, in this view, is that innovation requires multilateral investment in transaction-specific assets with uncertain value. But with extreme uncertainty, coupled with asset specificity, the investment problem is one of contractual assurance that whatever happens, the investor has no bargaining power or recourse, but for reputation. Furthermore, realizing this value is contingent on coinvestment by others, the investor is widely exposed to the hazards of opportunism. In equilibrium, no rational agent would ever cooperate.[9]

How is this resolved? Cooperation within a social construct (i.e., from behind a veil of ignorance, but with an assurance of social justice) affords an implicit moral framing of the costs of defection and the benefits of cooperation, furnishing a low-transaction-cost, collective action mechanism for dealing with the innovation problem. There has been a great deal of interest in recent decades on the rise of innovation networks, and open innovation, and the new sharing economy, and platform economies (Chesborough 2005; Lerner and Tirole 2005; Sundarajan 2016; Evans and Schmalensee 2016), all trading on the idea that humans are more cooperative than they used to be (Bowles and Gintis 2013) and social networks are more effective (Lessig 2004b; Benkler 2006), a development attributed to the deep penetration of the internet and social media in lowering the cost of information and increasing the value of reputations (i.e., cooperation) and the cost of reputational damage (i.e., defection). But an alternative hypothesis is that the fall in the costs of cooperation, and therefore in the transaction costs of innovation, has only a proximate explanation in the new internet affordances, but an ultimate explanation in the efficacy of the social contract (McCloskey) and the outworking of cultural group selection (Hayek).

Williamson's arguments about the significance of transaction costs, and how they play out in the context of uncertainty and the private incentives to idiosyncratic investment in the shadow of the hazards of opportunism, suggests a reconsideration of the basic economic analysis of the situational logic of cooperation in the pooling of resources for innovation. Williamson (1975, 1985, 2002) emphasizes the role of private ordering, rather than government ordering, in resolving coordination problems through efficient institutions for contracting, for both Coasian and Hayekian reasons: that is, the interaction of local knowledge and transaction costs.

A parallel idea is that this same logic might apply in the context of innovation. The investment problem in the Williamson view concerns idiosyncratic investment that is of value, yielding quasi rents only when combined with other such investment, thus subject to opportunism. But the Williamson critique applied to innovation suggests that government intervention in public funding of R & D, for instance, might actually displace or distort deeper forms of private ordering (i.e., rules for governance) in resolving the investment problem in the distributed information and resources needed for innovation.

3.4 Innovation Problem IV: Rules for Cooperation (Ostrom Version)

In the final chapter of our four-part story of the collective action problem in innovation we turn to the work of the institutional economist Elinor Ostrom, both her studies of effective institutional rules for governance in dealing with common-pool resources in natural common-pool resources (Ostrom 1990, 2010), and her subsequent work on knowledge commons (Ostrom and Hess 2006a; Hess 2008; Frischmann et al. 2014). Ostrom helps us understand how the innovation problem is finally solved as a collective action problem with effective rules for cooperation.

Innovation is socially disruptive and so requires social cooperation (section 3.1, the McCloskey innovation problem); that cooperation is needed because knowledge for innovation is local and distributed and so requires coordination (section 3.2, the Hayek innovation problem); but that specialized knowledge is also idiosyncratic, and so investment is at risk of opportunism and requires governance (section 3.3, the Williamson innovation problem); the governance problem is resolved with locally adapted rules to overcome the collective action problem in a particular context (the Ostrom innovation problem).

This last step in the collective action resolution of the innovation problem involves the development and evolution of particular local institutions, or rules-in-use (Ostrom 2005, 2010), to resolve particular local coordination problems in a way that works for the local group of potential entrepreneurs, each with partial information, each at the margin of trusting the others in the group as they explore and share information, ideas, and other innovation resources about a potential new technology or idea. This governance model is unfolding today in hackerspaces throughout the world, as new technologies are being incubated and accelerated in these entrepreneurial commons (Williams and Hall 2015; Allen 2016).

However, my hypothesis is that this governance structure made of local rules for common-pool innovation is not new at all, but has existed since the beginning of market capitalism in the seventeenth century and accords with the origins and modern institutions of open science (Mokyr 2016). The innovation commons has long existed and has been powerfully effective in delivering wave after wave of new technology as consumer product and viable industry.

The innovation commons is hard to see, even as it happens, leaving little historical trace. This is because commons governance emerges from enthusiastic amateurs who find each other and thus form a collective (a group). This group, however, soon enough collapses at the point of entrepreneurial insight, when the exact shape of the opportunity becomes clear to all, including what the key assets are and what business model will work. From that point, the commons collapses with a rush to entrepreneurship.

This collapse of the commons is the origin of entrepreneurship and the origin of the innovating firm. It is the Schumpeterian alpha moment in which the creative and confident entrepreneur emerges. But that entrepreneur, like all who came before him, emerged from the commons. The commons is the origin of entrepreneurship in all complex modern economies, and the origin of all firms in their ideational component. In a sense this is like the dynamic enclosure movement, but run hundreds of times a day globally. The emergence of all new technologies into industries, powered by innovating firms, is, analytically considered, a collapse of a commons.

This is the new theory I propose: innovating firms and successful entrepreneurship emerge from the collapse of an innovation commons. Therefore, the origin of entrepreneurship and innovating firms is modeled in terms of the theory of an innovation commons.

An innovation commons has the same logic as commons elsewhere in the society and the economy. The only difference is that an innovation commons is usually temporary (Allen and Potts 2016). The basic logic, as a species of knowledge commons (Frischmann et al. 2014; Potts 2018), is that it is the creation of a local public good. It is the product of cooperation, under institutions of governance, where these institutions seek to deal with "social dilemma" problems of free riding. The local public good is information about the entrepreneurial opportunity. That information is distributed and specialized and requires investment. It is Hayekian in its context and Williamsonian in its aspect. From a prudence-only perspective, it does not and cannot exist, because why would it? Only a fool would contribute such costly and valuable information to a common pool that would seem to resolve into a "tragedy of the commons" (Hardin 1968). This, in essence, is the case made by the market failure model of innovation: namely, because of this seeming collective action problem, the only solution is government intervention, whether as public provision or as intellectual property, that is, a market or state solution.

But Ostrom (1990) showed that in situations where local knowledge mattered to the efficacy of an outcome and where incentive mechanisms, including punishments, needed to be locally constructed and enforced, commons-based solutions were often superior to externally imposed regulatory, legislative, or government-imposed property rights solutions. The reason is transaction costs. Effective commons governance made much better use of local knowledge and conditions.

However, Ostrom also showed that commons-based solutions often failed due to ineffective rules. Ostrom's study of the actual working rules of thousands of common-pool institutions revealed eight design principles of success (Wilson et al. 2013). These eight rules also seem to apply to innovation commons (Allen and Potts 2016) as set out in Chapter 1, section 1.2 above.

The innovation problem is a collective action problem in the primary instance at the level of a society, in permissioning innovation. It is about social cooperation, where the social group is everyone in society. But as we move closer to the frontiers of a new technology or the exploration of the implications of a new idea, the innovation problem moves closer to a collective action problem of a smaller group of people, people who don't know each other but who need to form a new community. This is not yet a firm, and it is not yet a market. It is certainly not yet an industry. What it is, at this gestational stage, is an *emerging community*, and the entire prospect of any subsequent industry and any creation of entrepreneurial value depends crucially on the instrumental success of this early-stage process of community formation (Feldman and Tavassoli 2015) and the ability to pool information to identify, accurately, entrepreneurial value propositions upon which the participants can confidently act, with swift and risk-managed entrepreneurial decisions.

Who are these participants? They are the members of the club, those with access to this commons. But now, when it has such information, this is an incredibly valuable club, membership being of obvious value. But that is post hoc reasoning. The relevant analytical way to think about this is ex ante, which is behind the veil of uncertainty when all that is real is a novel technology or new idea and the prospect of contribution to a common-pool resource to unpack and explore its value. Ex ante, the innovation commons is pooling nonrivalrous information for discovery; ex post, it has produced a rivalrous opportunity for entrepreneurial exploitation.

That local social contract is governed by particular rules that on the surface mostly encourage free cooperation and contribution, but where they succeed tend to have rules made by the community itself, based on specific context, and with explicit layers of access and punishment for violation, along with effective community monitoring. These constitutional rules in large part determine the success or otherwise of the attempted cooperation. And the success of the attempted cooperation under the governance rules of the innovation commons will likely affect the shape of the technology development toward value discovery.

This suggests a testable hypothesis: new technologies that develop under effective innovation commons will tend to give rise to viable new industries, and not otherwise.

The alternative hypothesis is that new technologies that emerge without the governance support of an innovation commons will tend to fail (unless under exceptional circumstances) because they will be extremely unlikely to experience the full relevant input of distributed information necessary to discover the relevant lines for commercial market success. This is because they will have been, as it were, bred in a lab, subject only to the limited information available therein. This will be an instance of *discovery failure*, and an expression of the knowledge problem. Where such failure occurs, it will not be observed, because nothing actually happened.

Of course, in practice, we do get to run history over and again, as many firms have many attempts with each new technology and learn from each other's failures, and such are the rewards of venture finance, all of which is a great virtue of the market economy as an evolutionary mechanism. It does eventually get there, where enough resources are marshaled. But it will be noted here that that is also a supremely wasteful economy. And the origin of waste can be identified in the moment of the shift between the undertaking of innovation discovery in cooperation in a commons and innovation as competition in a market.

The logic of competition is most efficiently conducted in market institutions *once it is clear where the entrepreneurial opportunity lies*. This is because production cost economies and the efficient allocation of resources to that end become, once this information is elucidated, in effect just a planning problem. Innovation policy tends to line up behind such reasoning.

However, this argument does not hold in the early stages of innovation, when there is a new or potentially new technology or idea, but the exact shape of the entrepreneurial opportunity remains undiscovered. In that situation, the game is not competition, but selective cooperation. And the relevant parameters are the costs of cooperation (social justice, McCloskey); whom to cooperate with (distributed knowledge, Hayek); the incentive problem (Williamson); and how to cooperate with others (rules of governance, Ostrom).

3.5 Conclusion

The economic problem of innovation is not how to incentivize innovation investment under hypothetical perfect competition. Nor is the problem how to incentivize innovation by aligning entrepreneurial investments to optimally designed forms of government systems. The real innovation problem is a knowledge problem, the one that has been true since the origin of the modern economy, and indeed the solution to which created the modern economy (McCloskey 2016). The real innovation problem the *catallaxy* (cf. the *economy*) must continually solve in order to grow, develop, and evolve is to discover new ideas and how they create value. An *economy* is the particular structure of actions and orderings of resources to achieve this end, and economics is the science that studies the most productively efficient way to do that.

This pushes the innovation problem outside of economics. It involves psychological behavior in a sociocultural, political, and historical context, conceived as an exogenous change. Modern neoclassical and Schumpeterian economics of innovation endeavors to reclaim this as a variation on a market failure approach and to endogenize the change by focusing on the problem of inputs to innovation investment.

But the new approach I have proposed here—a collective action view of the innovation problem—returns the innovation problem to economics. The problem is that it was focusing on the wrong sort of costs. The innovation problem as a resource allocation problem (a *market failure* problem) focuses on production costs, but a knowledge coordination problem view (a *discovery failure* problem) focuses on transaction costs. Transaction costs matter because they are the economics of cooperation. And cooperation matters because it is the lowest-cost individual solution to the problem of how to coordinate the distributed knowledge needed for innovation. Societies that can generate low-cost cooperation among a knowledge-sharing group can innovate, and societies that can successfully innovate can outcompete other societies and gain in wealth and status (Hartley and Potts 2014; Turchin 2015). An economy is a solution concept in this space.

Institutions of cooperation differentiate economies. This is the real innovation problem, because innovation depends on cooperation at different levels. So what causes innovation? Economies that develop entrepreneurial firms and new markets and innovative industries—that is, the sort of economy that most governments want and most citizens desire—are those with the institutions that solve the collective action problem of the innovation commons.

In what sort of society will this economy thrive? Such societies have existed for many hundreds of years, some of which have become nation-states. But most are actually not. They are self-organized communities, catallaxies, many with formal anchors in the nation-state, such as firms and other official organizations. But many are private, and many are temporary. New such organizations form whenever the costs of organization fall below the benefits of cooperation (MacDonald 2015).

The innovation process is also a society. It is a group of people, each carrying some knowledge, forming to explore the prospects of a new idea by cooperating to pool that knowledge, creating a common-pool resource. An economy occurs when that common-pool resource yields insight into the nature of the value proposition, the execution of which we call entrepreneurship in the first instance and innovation in the second instance and thereafter.

Entrepreneurship is not the origin of innovation. Entrepreneurship is the market expression of ideas about what creates value. The origin of innovation is the creation of those ideas. As an economic problem, any solution must work through four layers: first, it must solve the collective action problem of social cooperation; and then solve the collective action problems of, second, distributed knowledge, and third, specialized knowledge; and then fourth, solve the problem of local cooperation. This is a discovery process of innovation. It results in market economic action, and so in entrepreneurship and innovation, but it is not caused by entrepreneurship. It is caused by the effective creation of an innovation commons.

The new economics of innovation is the study of the institutional logic of an innovation commons.

Notes

1. There are of course other representatives we might have considered, for example, Nelson (1959), Usher (1964), and Stiglitz (1999) on the information economics problems of investment in R & D. On the evolutionary path, Penrose (1959), Rosenberg (1982), Nelson and Winter (1982), and Dosi (1982) are alternative paradigmatic representatives. Note further that our new approach is not a critique of these approaches per se, but rather an attempt to recognize that what they abstract from and analytically ignore—in essence, transaction costs and collective action problems—is sufficient to reconstruct a whole new approach to innovation economics. This new approach should be considered a mostly complementary framework for analysis.
2. "The strong evidence of under-investment in technological advance justifies public action to support private innovation" (Martin and Scott 2000, 446).
3. A similar idea is expressed by Robert Lucas (2009, 1): "It is widely agreed that the productivity growth of the industrialized economies is mainly an ongoing intellectual achievement, a sustained flow of new ideas. . . . What is central, I believe, is the fact that the industrial revolution involved the emergence (or rapid expansion) of a *class* of educated people—thousands, now many millions—of people who spend entire careers exchanging ideas, solving work-related problems, generating new knowledge."
4. What has recently come to be called "permissionless innovation" (Thierer 2016) is perhaps better understood as an appeal to a return to the original contract of "implicitly-permissioned innovation."

5. This orderly meshing of plans through such a spontaneous ordering mechanism Hayek, following Mises, calls a "catallaxy" rather than an "economy." An economy, in contrast, is the product of order through design.
6. This same logic carries through in the Austrian model of price discovery and entrepreneurial alertness to opportunity through the price mechanism (Kirzner 1973).
7. Research-leading firms in an industry tend toward monopoly, so as to capture all talent within a single organization (e.g., Bell laboratories). Or concentrated, cluster-based labor markets with low exit costs and high transparency of marginal product will need to emerge (e.g., Silicon Valley).
8. The economics of the governance of innovation is a well-explored field. See, for example, Klein et al. 1978; Holmstrom 1989; Aghion and Tirole 1994; Pisano 1991; Langlois and Foss 1999.
9. It is perhaps worth pointing out that this is not equivalent to stealing an idea, that is, copying a design or downloading a file, which intellectual property laws are designed to protect. That legal process references an idea whose value is known and manifest. The specific issue here is investment in components of ideas of uncertain value, and which gain in value only by complementary coinvestment, which then needs to be coordinated.

4

Four Theories of the Innovation Commons

The innovation problem can be diagnosed through four different levels of knowledge problem. These were associated in chapter 3 with Deirdre McCloskey (social contract problem), Friedrich Hayek (distributed knowledge problem), Oliver Williamson (opportunism problem), and Elinor Ostrom (collective action problem). In this chapter, I want to look for solutions in the space of efficient institutions to solve the innovation problem as a knowledge problem.

My argument should by now be clear: the foundational innovation problem is not market failure but rather opportunity discovery, and the shape of this problem is largely about pooling and coordinating distributed information, knowledge, and other resources, all from behind a veil of uncertainty. Several institutional and organizational forms can be used for this, including small or large firms, relational contracts, networks, markets, clubs, commons, or government. There is diversity both among and within these different institutional forms (Hall and Soskice 2000; Williamson 2000; Ostrom 2005; Hodgson 2015). For any particular economic problem, a variety of institutional forms can solve it. The most efficient—in the sense of minimizing transaction costs—institutional form for solving the innovation problem is, generally, in the commons, namely, the "innovation commons," referring to the rules to enable an emergent community to create and govern a common-pool innovation resource.

This particular institutional form—the innovation commons—while it has definite costs and problems associated with it, in particular that it emerges from civil society and relies mostly on informal norms and rules, will nevertheless under certain circumstances be distinctly superior to alternatives, including firms, markets, and governments, and especially so at the very beginning of the innovation process.

This is not a recent development. It has been true since the origin of market capitalism (McCloskey 2016; Mokyr 2016). Yet it has been overlooked in the innovation literature, with its strong propensity to see innovation originating exclusively from firms, and where that fails, from government policy. Yet that issue is for later chapters. Our immediate goal is to unpack the reasons why, and the conditions under which, the commons can be an effective and efficient mechanism to solve the innovation problem. To that end, I've assembled four distinct theories.

The first is the "two commons" theory. The reason the commons is effective and efficient is because it works as an efficacious screening mechanism by having the truly valuable commons of entrepreneurial information accessed only through the commons of technological knowledge and material innovation resources.

The second is the "evolution of cooperation" theory. Drawing on modern evolutionary theory (specifically multilevel selection theory, evolutionary game theory, evolutionary psychology, and sociobiology), I argue that cooperative or sharing behavior is actually far more likely than the selfish rational actor model supposes. In this theory, the commons is simply an easy, low-cost solution.

The third is the "defense against enclosure" theory. In this account, the commons is a preferred institution for first movers because it raises the cost of alternative institutions and therefore minimizes the risk of loss of control of the technology to private agents or to government control. The value of this defense is that when it works well, the technology is protected from enclosure and remains open for development along all possible frontiers.

The fourth is the "institutional uncertainty and real options" theory. Early in the life cycle of a new technology there will be uncertainty about what the best institutional form to develop a technology will take, and the particular way in which property rights will develop. The innovation commons is a good way to keep options open while learning about possible uses and the property rights that will work best in those domains of application. This builds on Dixit and Pindyck's (1990) real options approach to investment under uncertainty, and Luppi and Pasari's (2011) asymmetric Coase theorem. A further aspect relates to reducing uncertainty of the new property rights associated with new technology.

Consider these distinct but overlapping theories of the mechanisms and evolutionary logic behind how and why an innovation commons works.

4.1 Two Commons

The first key to understanding the nature of an innovation commons is that it is not one commons, but two. And the first commons, the commons of material and technological innovation inputs and resources, is a screening mechanism for the second and more valuable commons, the commons of entrepreneurial information. The price of entrance to the second, valuable commons is cooperation in the first, material commons.

If this theory is true, it predicts that on the surface an innovation commons will appear to be that of pooled physical and technical resources, including kit and knowledge of the sort that engineers value. A hackerspace is a prime example, in which a defined group of people pool their physical equipment (3D printers, say) or resource equivalents (club fees) along with their embodied skills and expertise for sharing within a well-defined community. Think of the technically useful resources embodied in physical and human capital as one class of resources in the commons, and with an obvious correlate with the grazing pastures, trees, water, or fish in a natural resource commons.

Economists who study innovation tend to focus on these resources. They include basic science and the translation through engineering into prototypes of technologies. These innovation resources include everything under the heading of research and most things under the heading of development. However, my claim is that these are not the most valuable resources in an innovation commons. Rather, there is another resource that also accumulates in the commons, namely Hayek's "knowledge of time and place" about, for instance,

- how the technology works in particular circumstances
- how particular consumers use the new technology in specific instances
- price points that matter, and those that don't
- ways to discriminate in the market
- complementary and competitive investments being made
- sources of technical expertise and talent
- qualities of different (global) locations for production and distribution from a regulatory, political, and cultural perspective
- sourcing of critical resources, and the risks and costs involved
- the prospect of potential competitive or complementary investment, and by whom
- problems that arise when attempting to scale up, and the value of particular incubators or accelerators
- specific sources of expertise in particular aspects of production and development
- regulatory and legislative risks and barriers
- possible markets that might exist and how
- the fit of different business models (and platforms) and the consequences of each
- sources of venture finance, and who might be a possible investor, and why
- how property rights work over the new technology, and so on

None of this information can be patented or protected, and all of it is context specific. Every bit of it is acquired by experience, and much of it has been accumulated without intention. Its value decays fast if not used, and information is usually only of value when combined with other related data. Yet this is the information that entrepreneurs need.

An innovation commons is of value to an engineer, as someone seeking to put together or to access technical information about how to do something. This is usually assumed to be the prime value from the perspective of peer production of new technology (Williams and Hall 2015). But an innovation commons also has value to an entrepreneur, as someone seeking to organize resources to coordinate economic activity. What the entrepreneur needs is broader than what the engineer needs. An innovation commons is thus two commons. It is a pool of resources and information that engineers need, or those who are building the technical prototypes, but which can also be effectively assembled in alternative institutional forms. Yet this will often function as a gateway for the real reason that people are in this commons, namely to gain access to the information that entrepreneurs need, which is all of the bits of information about the costs and prospects of the idea or technology that when taken together provide sufficient information for the entrepreneur to act upon.

An innovation commons consists of two commons—one of technical resources, and one of market information. In the two-commons model the most valuable resource is the latter, but the cost of access to it is contribution to the former. An innovation commons is thus a kind of club, where the price of admission into the community is to contribute technical resources, which is in effect a screening mechanism: if you cooperate in the first you get access to the second. But once in this club, entrepreneurially relevant information circulates. That is the reason that people are there, in the innovation commons, namely to gain access to entrepreneurially relevant information.

4.2 Evolution of Cooperation

The basic argument for the efficacy of institutional solutions built with markets, hierarchies, and governments is that they economize on the need for cooperation. A market system works when each person pursues her individual self-interest and does not rely on her behaving altruistically. The mutual benefit to others, as Bernard Mandeville explained in 1714, is an emergent order—a *catallaxy*, as Hayek (1960) subsequently called it. Firms and governments also do not rely on altruistic cooperation, but respectively on the coercive power of the threat of contract breach, or as Thomas Hobbes put it, on the "monopoly on violence." Obviously, things go more smoothly when agents cooperate under the shadow of these implicit threats, resulting in the "as if" cooperation better known as the social contract.

The problem is that cooperation and trust is expensive and vulnerable.[1] It is not usually an evolutionarily stable strategy (Maynard Smith 1972; Axelrod

1984). It is a well-established finding in evolutionary game theory that when an altruistic cooperator is matched with an agent who plays defect, the cooperator will lose. Evolution is in this sense "selfish," as Dawkins (1976) famously explained. However, modern evolutionary theory has arrived at a new understanding of the evolution of cooperation in the framework of multilevel selection theory in which competition and differential selection operate not only between individuals, but also between groups (Nowak 2011). Lower-order selection operates within groups and predicts that selfish individuals will outcompete altruists. Higher-order selection operates between groups and predicts that groups of altruists (or agents who have found a way to mutually cooperate) will outcompete groups of selfish agents. We will elaborate this theory more fully in chapter 6. As technology improves, social coordination also becomes easier, and we can proceed more directly to efficient cooperative institutions. As the costs of cooperation (and coordination) fall, we can embed more of our institutions into cooperative frames. By this mechanism, innovation commons emerge and strengthen as we cooperate socially to discover individual opportunities.

4.3 Defense against Enclosure

A third explanation for the existence of the innovation commons emphasizes the role of endeavors, whether self-interested or public spirited, to ensure that a new idea of technology is not controlled or monopolized by any one group. This pursuit is driven to prevent monopoly control, regardless of the source of that control, whether from the private sector side, such as a firm controlling a technology by copyright and refusing license it or extracting significant rents from that monopoly position (e.g., pharmaceuticals), or from the public side in rendering a technology illegal or controlling it for limited purposes that meet the government's interests with regulation or enforcement (e.g., cryptography, maps, or weapons).

The demand for the commons comes from the demand to constrain the ability of private or public actors working through private or public institutions to control a technology and its course of development. Placing an idea in the commons is a highly effective defensive gambit. The institution of creative commons licensing, for example, has been developed to achieve this.[2] The innovation commons is a highly effective mechanism to ensure that an idea cannot be exclusively controlled by other private agents.[3] Even the threat of the prospect of placing an idea in the commons, that is, simply the existence of the commons, can condition strategic behavior in mutual games of development of an idea toward socially beneficial equilibria.

A mutual public benefit of development in the commons is the more likely discovery of unintended consequences. The longer an idea is in the commons, the better it gets "shaken out" and all of its potential problems and applications discovered. This has a parallel in code, and in part explains the success of open-source projects, which was expressed by Torvalds as the hope that "with enough eyeballs, all bugs are shallow." The innovation commons can under many often-met conditions be an efficient debugging institution because it can concentrate diverse perspectives on an idea.

4.4 Institutional Uncertainty

A fourth theory to explain the existence of the innovation commons turns on the problem of institutional uncertainty with respect to the best fit between a new idea and an institution within which to develop that idea, coupled to the notion that once placed in a particular institution (e.g., private or public domain), this tends to be an irreversible investment decision (à la Dixit and Pindyck 1994). There can be substantial benefits (i.e., consumer and producer surplus) to the development of a technology or industry to a good match between idea and institution, and substantial costs (i.e., opportunity costs) to a poor match. The key insight here is that the innovation commons is a kind of "real option" for institutional choice, a way of deferring institutional choice while more information is gathered, so as to minimize the likelihood of a poor irreversible choice.

The basic model here is that there is an allocation problem of matching each new idea to a particular institution. Assume that each new idea or technology has inherent qualities that give it an institutional "true type," which is the institutional context or environment in which the idea or technology will best flourish. However, this true type is unobservable in the beginning and only revealed through experience.

New ideas can develop the idea in public institutions, or in private institutions. Assume that different types of ideas (say, up-type and down-type) perform better under different institutional settings (private and public), and that ideas exhibit path dependency in institutions such that there is institutional stickiness and that institutional switching is costly, and in the limit impossible. With fundamental uncertainty about idea type (up or down), and therefore about optimal allocation over institutions (public or private), the innovation commons is a gateway institution. Ideas of uncertain type are first placed in the commons to induce information pooling that reduces uncertainty, eventually revealing an idea's true type (up or down). This facilitates efficient matching of new ideas to institutions.

Innovation commons are effective institutional mechanisms for pooling information to reduce uncertainty about an idea's true type. Innovation commons will be likely therefore to be temporary institutions. Their usefulness will eventually fade by the logic of their success in reducing entrepreneurial uncertainty.

We should expect to observe innovation commons at the nascent stages of any new idea, technology, or industry as an essential but transient component of an innovation system. An innovation commons is an *emergent, temporary institution* that forms in the early phases of a new idea when uncertainty is highest with respect to the institutional form that the innovation trajectory will best develop along. An innovation commons is thus a mobile institution in a national innovation system, forming at the frontiers of new technologies with high entrepreneurial and institutional uncertainty and decomposing when that uncertainty resolves. It will collapse into a public, private, or mixed institutional form once it has done its job in reducing the fundamental uncertainty about the nature of the idea and the economic opportunity it represents.

The specific form of this private uncertainty could emerge in several dimensions. It could be that the potential size of a private market for the idea is completely unknown and ex ante unknowable (e.g., genetic cloning), or development costs are unknown and ex ante unknowable (e.g., commercial space tourism), or it could be that the externalities are unknown, including whether they are positive or negative (e.g., nuclear fusion technologies). The uncertainty may be due to problems of unknown competitive or complementary investment (Richardson 1972), including knowledge of what types and scale of complementary investments might be required, and of who might undertake them, and when. The upshot is that in such circumstances, which are presumed to be common, it can be exceedingly difficult to know where to place an idea for development.

There are substantial risks and costs associated with misallocating a high-type idea in public institutions. The most obvious cost is the forgone private income that could have been associated with either ownership of the intellectual property or from owning a private company that successfully exploited the idea. The Google search engine was developed at a private university (Stanford) and quickly moved into a private company (Google, and subsequently Alphabet), currently valued at over US$400 billion. On the other hand, Tim Berners-Lee developed HTML at a public research institute (CERN) that released it as a public good in the form of the World Wide Web. Berners-Lee has received many awards and much acclaim, including a cash prize $1.3 million for inventing the web, but he is not rich (Wright 2001) compared to the economic value the web created (Goolsbee and Klenow 2006). Jonas Salk's research and development of the polio vaccine was publicly funded; meaning that while he did receive fame, he could never have achieved the great wealth such a patented vaccine could have accrued.

And there are substantial risks and costs associated with wrongly placing a low-type idea in private institutions. One is the potential waste and duplication that comes from multiple replicated private investments where firms are not able to signal to others that the particular line of investigation is a dead end

(Akcigit and Lui 2016). Another is the social cost due to ransom and holdup problems. Bessen et al. (2011) estimate these costs on the order of hundreds of billions in relation to "patent trolls."

More generally the risk is that the idea remains underdeveloped due to insufficient investment, inability to access complementary resources and capabilities, weakness in lobbying for regulatory exemptions or special treatment, or overly narrow application, perhaps due to exclusive licensing. For the agent developing the idea, these costs manifest in low private earnings or losses, but also in the opportunity costs of failing to access the reputational and associated benefits from developing the idea in public institutions. Examples can be seen in experimental alternative energy technologies that are flourishing under public innovation institutions (in the sense of providing income for proponents of the idea), but widely failing under private innovation institutions (examples are wave energy and wind energy and fusion reactors). In contrast, technologies for hydraulic fracturing of shale gas formations technologies were successfully developed under private innovation institutions (by Halliburton, a private US oil services company) and would likely have failed under public institutions. Recently, Lockheed-Martin (a private US defense contractor) has announced a design breakthrough for a portable nuclear fusion reactor.

An implication of this framework is that innovation institutions are sticky, or at least partially irreversible (or equivalently, that the development of an idea exhibits institutional path dependency, or that there is a hysteresis effect), such that an idea that starts under public innovation institutions can never completely transfer to private innovation institutions, or vice versa, without loss. The strong form of this claim is that ideas that begin in private institutions stay in private institutions, and those that begin in public institutions also stay in public institutions. This stickiness may be an artifact of bounded rationality and organizational problem solving (von Hippel 1994). Strong-form stickiness is likely to be observed when dominant patents are privately held. (Patent buyouts can mitigate this [Kremer 1998].) It is also likely to be observed where a group of firms collectively holds information essential for subsequent development. (Patent pools can mitigate this for these insiders [Lerner and Tirole 2004]). Stickiness in public institutions will often be due to constraints in developing new business models that do not depend upon control of intellectual property, or due to direct crowding out. Stickiness may further be due to development of specialized (research) capital such as laboratories or complementary skills (Williamson 1975; Teece 1986a) that are costly to transfer between institutional regimes.

The resolution of institutional uncertainty in the commons is a partial consequence of the Hayek-Williamson innovation problem discussed in the previous chapter. To the extent that capital has a structure, and that some capital investments are complementary (Hayek [1941] 2007; Lachmann 1956;

Richardson 1972),[4] there will also be a corresponding innovation structure, so there will also arise a need for a *coordinated institutional choice* of each of the distributed investments in an innovation. This is a *focal point* coordination problem (Sugden 1995), in that the payoff is maximized when all parties choose the same institution. But it is also likely to be a *path-dependent* process for that same reason. Initially developing an idea in the innovation commons provides an institutional space to facilitate coordination on subsequent institutional choice.

Another way of thinking about institutional choice derives from the Coase theorem, which says that the initial allocation of property rights doesn't matter so long as there are no transaction costs to inhibit bargaining. Luppi and Parisi (2011) point out that there is an asymmetry here, in that the transaction costs are higher for bundling and rebundling than for unbundling or fragmentation. This leads to an entropy prediction, namely that property tends to fragment. If we think of a firm as a particular or bundled structure of ideas and capital, then the asymmetric Coase theorem suggests that the emergence of an innovating firm is an unlikely event because of the transaction costs to be overcome in making the bundle.[5] But the utility of an innovation commons is that it is an institutional solution (an allocation of fuzzy property rights) that minimizes transaction costs to maximize the probability of an innovating firm emerging from the commons.[6]

In this model, the source of the negentropy (or increased order) is from the clarification of the institutional rule through the elucidation of property rights over the idea. An idea becoming an innovation is monotonic with elucidation of institutional rules. A commons, then, is the institutional space in which the rule is still fuzzy, and so opportunities and property rights are uncertain. The logic of the innovation commons is that it is a low-transaction-cost environment to elucidate institutional rules, thus clarifying property rights, and in so doing thereby sharpening the information set necessary to reveal entrepreneurial opportunities.

4.5 Conclusion

Why do we expect the innovation commons to emerge at the origin of any new idea or technology? The key insight is that any fundamentally new idea or technology emerges without labeling, and therefore with uncertainty about the particular opportunities and value that it harbors. They must be discovered. And the commons can be an efficient institutional space for this discovery process to unfold by furnishing an efficient governance mechanism for pooling distributed information. The innovation commons is the missing quadrant in the theory of innovation institutions beyond private, public, and club-like institutions.

An innovation commons is a site of peer production to reduce uncertainty to generate entrepreneurially relevant information that will yield both private and social benefit. The innovation commons exists for several distinct reasons: (1) because of uncertainty about the nature of new ideas and the entrepreneurial opportunity they represent, which requires solving a collective action problem to pool distributed information; (2) because cooperation expresses itself efficiently in a commons, such that successful groups can form that are highly technologically progressive; (3) because the commons is an efficient mechanism to distribute power in the development and adoption of an idea, making it difficult to control the path of development of a technology once it is in the commons, thus ensuring that power never attaches itself to a technology; and (4) because of uncertainty about the most effective innovation institution to develop the idea. The innovation commons can be temporary and mobile institutions that form at the origin of a new technology, and then collapse when the entrepreneurial opportunity is fully revealed, but that are nevertheless of permanent value because they shape the development of an idea and the pathways along which it develops.

Notes

1. Novak et al. (2018) estimate that the "cost of trust" is around 35 percent of GDP.
2. Creative Commons licensing was founded by James Boyle, Laurence Lessig, and Hal Abelson in 2001.
3. Madison et al. (2010, 692) offer the following examples (italics added): "A commons is constructed *as a defense against potential privatization* of commonly useful resources. Examples of such arrangements might include constructed commons for basic biological building blocks such as the Single Nucleotide Polymorphism (SNP) consortium or the publicly available databases of genomic sequences that are part of the Human Genome Project. . . . Formal licenses and related agreements assure that participants in the commons become part of what amounts to a *mutual nonaggression pact* that is necessary precisely because of the possibility that intellectual resources may be propertized. So long as the resource is in the commons, it can be shared among commons members, and neither commons members nor outsiders are able to appropriate that resource, patent it, and then assert a patent claim against a commons member."
4. In contrast to Keynesian and neoclassical models in which all capital goods are substitutes.
5. Thanks to Trent MacDonald for suggesting this model.
6. As negentropy (Raine et al. 2006).

5

Origin of the Innovation Trajectory

From where does innovation originate? What is its true source? And how do we know when we find it? The problem with our current generation of innovation theory, as Geroski (2000, 620) explains, is that "diffusion stories which are designed to explain the S-curve [i.e., the logistic adoption path of an innovation] usually take the appearance of '*the*' new technology for granted, and focus on the question of why it takes so long to diffuse."

Modern innovation economics broadly adopts the cartographical imperative, from which any mighty river of technological change ought to trace back to a single wellspring. This notion could equally be called the epidemiological imperative, where any observed pattern of technological adoption and diffusion (the analogue of infection) must originate from an index case, a patient zero. It was Schumpeter who taught us that the entrepreneur was always that source, or at least to stop looking when we located the entrepreneurial fountainhead. But this is also, to use Georgescu-Roegen's (1971) analytic diagnostic formulation, an *arithmomorphic*[1] imperative that maps a dynamic process along a count of natural numbers, starting at the zero-to-one threshold. And so there is "the" origin of the technology, as Geroski (2000) mentions, implying that if you just keep searching, you will eventually find the creative, imaginative, insightful, alert, or perhaps just lucky mind that is the singular and true source of the innovation.

In the standard Schumpeterian analytic model, it is from this distinctly individualistic and broadly entrepreneurial conception of origination, which is to say from purposeful and identifiable human action, that the innovation trajectory begins. The line of this book, however, is that this perspective is often wrong. Along the innovation trajectory, the number that comes before one isn't zero but "some" or "many." This has been little noted because modern innovation studies are not much concerned with what happens before one (zero, obviously!), and so tend to put that into a separate basket of affairs—creativity studies, for instance, or the history of invention—and to focus instead on the subsequent phases and processes of the growth trajectory. Innovation studies of the dynamics of technologies, markets, industries, and economies is then broadly, although not always, associated with the three phases of a logistic or

S-shaped diffusion curve that align with the distinct inflection points in the adoption or growth process.

In "The Creative Response in Economic History" Joseph Schumpeter (1947) pointedly distinguished between invention and innovation, noting that his analysis was entirely concerned with innovation.

> In short, any "doing things differently" in the realm of economic life—all these are instances of what we shall refer to by the term Innovation. It should be noticed at once that that concept not synonymous with "invention." Whatever the latter term may mean, it has but a distant relation to ours.

Schumpeter's point is simply that innovation refers to an economic impact, and that technical invention, however creative, important, or subsequently valuable, is not by this fact alone an economic action. Someone has to make it so, and that person is the entrepreneur, and thus the origin of innovation. It is a simple, clear, and profound point. It is not under dispute here.

What is under dispute is whether there is in fact a prior *economic* phase that comes before the entrepreneurial phase of origination. I argue that there is indeed such a phase, and that which comes before the so-called first phase of the standard innovation trajectory I call the *zeroth* phase. The innovation commons is the zeroth phase of the Schumpeterian innovation trajectory, the true germinal phase that is antecedent to the standard innovation trajectory. It is a distinct phase because it is behaviorally, epistemically, strategically, and institutionally distinct from what comes after. Entrepreneurs, firms, and markets are not yet part of this germinal zeroth phase. The reason is simply that uncertainty is still too high for these institutional forms to emerge.

The transition between the zeroth and first phase is an institutional transition from the commons to the institutions of firms and markets. Extending a term first used by Williamson (1975), let us call this the "fundamental transformation."

To develop this idea let us also introduce the concept of the *proto-entrepreneur* and the *dual-discovery problem* in which the proto-entrepreneur has to first solve the discovery problem of finding who else has the relevant nonprice information to input into solving the entrepreneurial discovery problem. This higher-order discovery problem is solved in the innovation commons. Entrepreneurship therefore has an institutional origin, emerging from the innovation commons when collective action works to pool distributed information in order to reduce uncertainty and so reveal opportunities, rendering entrepreneurial action possible.

The surprising argument of this chapter and the next chapter is that societies with effective innovation commons can, under some circumstances, outcompete societies with effective innovation policies, or even those with effective entrepreneurs, because what matters is *the rate of entrepreneurial discovery*: the efficacy of the innovation commons is a principal although underappreciated determinant of this. However, societies with effective entrepreneurs, effective innovation policies, *and* effective innovation commons are unbeatable.

5.1 The Zeroth Phase of the Innovation Trajectory

An innovation commons, as in figure 2.1 in chapter 2, is the true, although opaque, first phase of an innovation trajectory. While there are many different definitions and theories of the temporal and spatial process-structure of innovation (variously as waves, trajectories or processes, viz., long or short waves, innovation or technological trajectories, industrial dynamics, adoption-diffusion process), they all have a first phase that represents germination or the origination of the novel idea or technology. So either the nominal "first phase" is really a true second phase or there is a phase prior to the already identified "first phase." Taking inspiration from the "zeroth law of thermodynamics" inserted before the first law of thermodynamics, we can adapt to these extant models not by redefining their own internal phase structure, but by referring to the innovation commons as the *zeroth phase*.

An innovation trajectory is an analytic conceptual representation of the widely observed and robust empirical patterns relating to the time-path of a new technology or idea into an economy. Models of how new ideas and technologies enter an economy invariably reach for some analogy with a process elsewhere in nature or society. However, the standard economic model of Walrasian market dynamics is singularly unhelpful here (Mirowski 1989) because innovation dynamics are poorly modeled as if analogous to a shock or disturbance in a physical field (i.e., an electromagnetic or gravitational field), that is, jumping from one equilibrium to another. Instead, technological historians chose the metaphor of a *waveform* (derived from a theory of cycles) when representing the observed pattern of technology diffusion, noting the frequency and amplitude (length and significance) of the wave (Schumpeter 1939; Soete and Freeman 1995; Louca 1997; Louca and Freeman 2001; Perez 2002).[2]

However, innovation scholars modeling technology adoption in markets as a process (rather than seeking to understand the new equilibrium) soon refined the metaphor in the organic direction, fixing on the epidemic model of diffusion derived from ecology or population-dynamics (Griliches 1957; Mansfield 1961, 1963; Rogers 1962; Bass 1969). In an epidemic model, the metaphorical transfer is this: consumer adoption of a new technology is "like" a viral infection process, in which the probability of an event for each agent (a Markov state-transition function, i.e., infected/not; cf. did / did not adopt the new idea) is proportional to the state of immediate neighbors on a lattice, or the frequency of the trait in the population. The epidemic model is a special case of a population dynamic, both modeled with replicator equations. This was a key conceptual insight for the historians and scholars of technological change who explicitly adopted an evolutionary model (e.g., Basalla 1988; Mokyr 1990; Arthur 2009) in which technological dynamics is modeled as a form of selection process (i.e., differential replication) corresponding to the relative frequency of a particular technology in a population of other technologies.

The characteristic functional form of these models is a partial differential equation, known as the logistic-diffusion curve (Geroski 2000). This S-shaped curve has three distinct phases corresponding to its inflection points between an origination phase of early adopters (phase 1), followed by the takeoff phase (phase 2, the steep part of the curve) due to feedback effects, and then the saturation or maturation plateau (phase 3), when most of the potential adopters have adopted and the curve flattens out again.[3]

The entrepreneur-driven innovation trajectory (i.e., the meso trajectory [Dopfer et al. 2004]) is the unit of evolutionary dynamics that describes how growth and development occurs in a market capitalist economic system. Schumpeter's three great books elucidated the logic of the innovation trajectory. In *Theory of Economic Development*, Schumpeter ([1912] 1934) introduced the role of the entrepreneur as the origin of the new ideas that disrupted the long-run equilibrium, or the circular flow, and began the growth and development process. In *Business Cycles*, Schumpeter (1939) built on detailed historical records to construct a model of real economic fluctuations arising from short and long waves of industrial innovations. And in *Capitalism, Socialism and Democracy*, Schumpeter (1942) located this evolutionary conception of economic dynamics within the broader institutional feedback of political economy. The evolutionary approach to economic growth and development is built on a model of industrial dynamics driven by perpetual waves of innovation trajectories. Each innovation trajectory has entrepreneurship at its origin and a new institutional order at its conclusion, with the process of creative destruction playing out in market dynamics as firms enter and exit and differentially grow (Alchian 1950; Nelson and Winter 1982).

While the notion of an innovation trajectory as a historical process implies a beginning (origination), middle (adoption-diffusion), and end (retention), it is always viewed from the endpoint backward. It was the economic historians, and particularly those focusing on technologies and industries, such as the eponymous Kondratiev, whose long waves Schumpeter reported, who documented and marshaled the evidence that suggested such an understanding of industrial dynamics and economic change. In all cases, they were looking at a trajectory from the perspective of having already seen it unfold, and observing patterns across many different such trajectories. Schumpeter, in particular, analytically framed this as a departure from a circular flow, or what the classical economists called a stationary state.

The evolutionary process of change begins with a disruption or disturbance of the initial economic order. For Schumpeter, and all evolutionary economists to follow, that disturbance was the entrepreneur, or the innovating firm. But viewed from the endpoint of a trajectory, it doesn't really matter what that actually is, or whether it's the same thing each time, because something must have caused it. There must have been a seed. From that point on—from the first entrepreneurial actions through the emergence of the new products, new markets, and new firms that mark the origin of a new industry—we are in the domain of industrial dynamics that unfold until a new economic order is established. It is entirely reasonable for the economic theory of industrial dynamics (and of growth and development) to view the range of such a trajectory as complete, and to map this to historical and statistical data defined in terms of an industrial population (i.e., number of firms, total sales, and so forth).

Yet the three-phase innovation trajectory is an artifact of a historical selection bias in the economic data. This is because we only see the trajectories that get started and move through all three phases, not the ones that failed at the start, or otherwise collapsed. We only see a trajectory clearly once all uncertainty is removed, which by definition is only from the perspective of the third phase, once embedded as part of the new economic order. From that backward-looking perspective, with uncertainty removed, there is a tendency (the *post hoc fallacy*) to refract the manifest certainty of the final outcome to suppose a similar absence of uncertainty in earlier phases in the trajectory. But this is invariably false and misleading. Uncertainty was indeed real for contemporaries in earlier phases; and the earlier the phase, the higher the uncertainty.

By this account, the origin of a trajectory is the point at which someone elucidates the entrepreneurial opportunity and so develops the first product, starts the first firm, or establishes the new market, founding the new industry. This looks like the origin because in microcosm, all the things that will be there through the trajectory—the innovating firm, the new product or process, the new markets, the new industry—are initially in place, as can be seen from a post hoc perspective. By this reasoning, the origin of the innovation trajectory is the point at which someone figured out how to proceed and got things started, even if many others turned out to be mistaken. For Schumpeter (1912), this was the successful entrepreneur, the bold, heroic, and visionary entrepreneur who sees through the uncertainty and acts decisively (Mises 1949), and to whom the innovation trajectory, along with the broader dynamics of market capitalism, is subsequently owed. The entrepreneur is the *primum movens*, the first cause. There is nothing in this model that comes before the entrepreneur.

In our model, however, there is a phase in the innovation trajectory before the entrepreneur, the zeroth phase *from which the entrepreneur subsequently emerges* and more or less as the Schumpeterian model above describes. The zeroth phase is thus usefully thought of as the "origin of the entrepreneur" phase, which is, as discussed in chapters 3 and 4, the phase where uncertainty is significantly reduced to a level that allows entrepreneurial action to be feasible at all. The key point of chapters 2–4 was that uncertainty is processed in order to reveal entrepreneurial opportunities, and that this is achieved by pooling distributed information, none of which has much value by itself, or at least has ambiguous value, but yet is costly in its parts, and so presents a collective action problem. This high uncertainty and ambiguous value of distributed information is the state of nature. Without intervention to process this uncertainty and organize this information, innovation will indeed be reliant on the happy accident of a heroic, visionary, and perhaps lucky individual coupled with the similarly low-probability event of all relevant information also forming a nexus at the locus of that same individual. Now sometimes this does happen, just as some rare genetic mutations have high value to the host carrier. But the conjecture that there exists a zeroth phase to the innovation process is the claim that there exists a mechanism—in the form of an emergent institution, the innovation commons—that can significantly improve the likelihood of entrepreneurial emergence, or opportunity discovery, beyond the autarkic reliance on heroic accident.

What evidence exists for this alleged zeroth phase? Why hasn't it been apparent to scholars of the innovation trajectory?

First, the evidence is perhaps hard to see because an innovation commons is an institution of private governance and so will often not leave an official trail or record. It is not a registered company or a government program. It does not show up in official records, data, or statistics. Yet the signatures of an innovation commons in the norms of governance have been widely observed by economic sociologists, business ethnographers, innovation strategists, and scholars and researchers examining contiguous domains, such as the emergent norms used to coordinate open-source communities.[4]

Innovation scholars were also not actually looking for an earlier pre-entrepreneurial discovery phase because the origination phase was already defined expansively to include search and discovery, or effectuation and creation of opportunities (Sarasvathy 2008). Innovation scholars have never really sought to explain the deep origin of the creative impulse (Galenson 2007), or the "invention" as it is referred in the engineering context, which for the most part was already relegated to studies of creative genius (Simonton 1999). These origins lie inside the (individual) human mind, in the neurocognitive domains of psychology, not the institutional-governance domains of economics. And where they lay outside the mind, they could be modeled as search, in which the economic input is the cost of search and the output is read off a production function for information (Stigler 1961). However, the innovation trajectory focuses on economic agents, which means entrepreneurial actions, innovating firms, and the dynamics of markets. The origin of creativity and inventiveness, while manifestly a form of human behavior, falls outside the legitimate domain of economic inquiry and can be treated as exogenous, allowing analysis to concentrate on the observable growth phases that are centered around an adoption-diffusion process that occurs in and between firms and other organizations.

However, the zeroth phase of the innovation trajectory—the innovation commons phase—is fundamentally distinct from the origination phase in which entrepreneurial actions unfold to establish the new firms and markets (and which leads into the second phase of Schumpeterian competition, and the third phase of a new economic order). The distinctions between phase 0 and subsequent phases 1–3 are that (1) the institutions are different; (2) the agents, with respect to identity, behavior, expectations, and strategy, are different; and (3) the states of uncertainty and knowledge are different.

The institutions are different in that firms and markets do not yet exist in phase zero, where coordination is achieved through the institutions of the commons. And because the agents are in a different institution, they behave differently because of the different incentives. They will have a different identity and specifically will not yet see themselves as entrepreneurs, employees in a hierarchy, or market participants, and so will not adopt the norms of behavior, the strategies of interaction, or the expectations of outcomes associated with those institutions. And the reason that the behaviors and institutions are different is because knowledge is in a different state. As legendary Hollywood producer Sam Goldwyn said of his own industry, "No one knows anything." In an innovation commons, no *one* knows everything, but most people know something—it is a Hayekian (viz. Hayek 1945) context of distributed information that must be assembled into meaning (Shackle 1972; Lachmann 1976). It is that pooling and assembly process which takes place in the innovation commons that is the mechanism by which uncertainty is processed in order to reveal entrepreneurial opportunities to those who are in the commons.

This suggests a conjecture, the strong form of which is this:

> An innovation commons always exists at the start of an innovation trajectory.

The weaker form is this:

> An innovation commons usually exists at the start of an innovation trajectory, with exceptions.

The strong form of the conjecture claims that while an innovation commons may not be obvious, nor necessarily record a significant and lasting trace owing to its status as a private order, it was always there. This suggests a research heuristic that if you look hard enough you will find it. The logic of this existence conjecture is an argument from probability and efficiency: it is unlikely that all necessary information to elicit an entrepreneurial opportunity from a new technology appears neatly in one mind; and when that information is distributed across several people, it is unlikely that they have already organized into an alternative institutional form that has lower transaction costs than an innovation commons.

The weak form of the conjecture is typified by a context when a firm or research organization, which already existed for some other purpose, is able to develop a new technology and bring it to market to create a new industry. Examples from legendary and remarkable organizations such as Bell Laboratories, Du Pont, and Xerox Park, and more recently Google and Apple, fit this definition. In this case, something like an innovation commons forms inside an existing firm. Another class of exceptions occurs when an innovation commons is prohibited from forming because the technology is already enclosed such that its exploration is illegal or rendered artificially costly, as for example with weapons, military, or security technologies. An interesting counterexample is the development of cryptography and encryption (e.g., PGP) in an innovation commons by a community that called themselves cypherpunks (Popper 2015; Vigna and Carey 2015) and who subsequently developed cryptocurrencies.

To summarize, the innovation commons is a distinct and originating phase of the Schumpeterian innovation trajectory, but it occurs prior to the phase of entrepreneurial discovery. However, it is still subsequent to the particular invention or creative insight that furnishes the generic seed idea about which it forms. But the innovation commons is an economic process because it is a process of coordination and production. What is being coordinated is distributed information, and what is being processed is uncertainty in order to create the fundamental scarce and valuable resources the innovation commons produce. These are the conditions for the discovery of the entrepreneurial opportunity.

5.2 The Fundamental Transformation

What then is the nature of this transition from phase 0 to phase 1 of the innovation trajectory? Oliver Williamson's notion of the "fundamental transformation" furnishes a way to think about this. In Williamson's (1975, 1985a) new institutional reinterpretation of Coasian transaction costs, within a model of boundedly rational agents and sunk cost investments, the individual firm's ex ante idiosyncratic investments create quasi rents because the value now depends upon a web of other investments and contracts, which creates ex post hazards of opportunism. The very act of mutual investments that are not costlessly reversible thus transforms the ex ante competitive market that exists prior to contracting and investment into an ex post bilateral monopoly, fundamentally changing the bargaining relationship, for example, by creating hazards of opportunism through holdup. This is the fundamental transformation, and it is inherent in any situation of mutual or joint investment, or what Williamson termed asset specificity. In a world of boundedly rational agents and positive transaction costs, and therefore of incomplete contracts, Williamson explained, the market fails because of this "fundamental transformation." In consequence, an efficient solution is to endogenize these contracts and investments within the boundaries of a vertically integrated firm. From this perspective of anticipated ex post inefficiencies in market contracting (i.e., hazards of opportunism), agents needing to make idiosyncratic investments will instead arrive at private governance solutions to this coordination problem, using hierarchies rather than markets.

Like Coase (1937), Williamson (1979, 2002) focused on the boundary between firms and markets. Subsequent innovation economists who developed Williamson's new institutional framework (e.g., Monteverde and Teece 1982; Teece 1986a; Teece et al. 1997) have similarly examined this same boundary problem, using the logic of bounded rationality and transaction costs to explain why innovation takes place in firms rather than markets (although, importantly, this analysis extends to integrate the theory of *dynamic capabilities* [Langlois and Foss 1999]).

But a firm is not the only institutional private governance solution to a joint-production problem. Indeed, a similar problem arises in the innovation commons, and in this case the efficient transaction-cost-minimizing solution is also to integrate into a firm. But now we have an explanation of the origin of the firm emerging not from the market (à la Williamson) but at the boundary between the commons and the firm. We propose also identifying this as an instance of the fundamental transformation, but rather than explaining the onset of vertical integration, it explains the phase transition between the zeroth phase of the innovation commons and the first phase of the Schumpeterian innovation trajectory.

There are two distinct transaction cost explanations of the origin of the firm: one emerging from the market, the other emerging from the commons. The market-firm boundary is largely a story of idiosyncratic capital investment and the problems of the unrelieved hazards of contractual enforcement in joint production. The commons-firm boundary, however, while also a problem of the hazards of joint production, is due to a different problem, namely one that is largely a consequence of mutual uncertainty (and therefore the hazards of opportunism) about the respective value of the idiosyncratic investments for the purpose of opportunity discovery.

An innovation commons is an institutional mechanism to pool distributed information and knowledge in order to jointly produce the discovery of an entrepreneurial opportunity from a new *generic idea* (Dopfer and Potts 2008) or new technology (Arthur 2009). The individual bits of pooled information and knowledge will therefore have a property similar to Williamsonian asset specificity, in that each bit is an idiosyncratic investment, the value of which depends on other such idiosyncratic investments also being made, that is, contributed to the pool. The quasi rent, however, exists only when a sufficient and ex ante unknown number of other such investments are also made. This is the coordination and commitment problem (to which we will return soon, to show how a dual commons of technological resource pooling combined with market information pooling can resolve this by creating a screening mechanism). The opportunism hazard for each individual agent is that another agent will gain access to the commons and harvest or exploit the entrepreneurial opportunity, while minimally contributing or even guilefully furnishing misleading contributions to the pool.

On the face of it, this straightforward tragedy of the commons predicts a Nash equilibrium of mutual defection. Actually, this is less a prediction that the commons never forms in the first place than that the origin of entrepreneurial discovery will be constrained to situations where either (1) all relevant inputs into opportunity discovery are already public (e.g., as market prices, in the case of Kirznerian alertness to arbitrage opportunities [Kirzner 1973]) or (2) a contractual governance mechanism to pool distributed information and innovation inputs already exists, that is, inside the innovating firm. That is, the origin of innovation is entrepreneurial discovery from within firms or markets.

Therefore, the conditions for an innovation commons to emerge at the origin of a new generic idea or technology require a context in which not all entrepreneurially relevant information for opportunity discovery is (1) public, that is, in observable prices, or (2) contained within a known contractible set of other agents or capital, that is, an existing or potential firm or able to be contractually acquired by a firm. Yet these approximate conditions are far from special and widely pertain at the early stages of any new idea or nascent technology, and have done so throughout history. So we predict that to the extent that new ideas exist, manifest conditions for the emergence of innovation commons should be widely prevalent.

So why are they so hard to see? How will we recognize them when we do see them? We need to further elucidate the specific economic problems being resolved in the innovation commons, how they relate to the transaction costs of discovery, the critical resources involved, and the problems of opportunism that subsequently arise.

5.3 The Proto-entrepreneur, the Dual-Discovery Problem, and the Two-Commons Solution

Let us be clear about who are entrepreneurs in this story, and when they are. The essential point is, by definition, *no one is an entrepreneur in the innovation commons*.

Entrepreneurs arrive at the onset of phase 1 of the innovation trajectory, just as Schumpeter said. Rather, those in the innovation commons are what we will, for the sake of continuity of the theory, call "proto-entrepreneurs." The difference is that you're not an entrepreneur until you can see the opportunity upon which to act, that is, engage in purposeful entrepreneurial action. Whether you succeed is not the issue: it's that you're acting based on a plan that is organized about a perception of an opportunity. So we're hewing to an operational definition: an entrepreneur is someone engaged in entrepreneurial action. And for that perception to be realized into coherent action, a quantity of information and knowledge of sufficient quality must be effectively pooled that the fog of uncertainty lifts enough to catch a glimpse of the opportunity.

Yet "proto-entrepreneur" is also potentially misleading as a concept, implying that all those in the commons have definite designs to become an entrepreneur. Strictly speaking, this orientation to entrepreneurship is only realized at the fundamental transformation, at the onset of phase 1 of the innovation trajectory. Furthermore, explicit intention to become an entrepreneur in the innovation commons may not even be an optimal public strategy, as it effectively announces an intention to defect from the cooperative game at first opportunity. A better, or at least more descriptive, name for those in the innovation commons is *amateur*, in the sense of an amateur enthusiast, hobbyist, or, the increasingly preferred term, hacker. *Amateur* is French, from the Latin *amator*, meaning "lover of."[5] A proto-entrepreneur is a lover of a new idea, someone who seeks to explore the new idea or technology for its own beauty and interest. An innovation commons is the institutional forum for seeking others to join in that pursuit, such that they might share their passion. But the implication is still manifestly that they are searching or seeking something deep in the idea, which we can assume is potential value. The discovery of entrepreneurial opportunities may thus present not as profit opportunities in an avaricious Marxian sense, but rather as potential profit opportunities in the Misean sense of guiding action toward creating sources of much deeper value when others too can come to share that passion and realize that value (e.g., as consumer surplus).

Proto-entrepreneurs, or amateur enthusiasts, thereby face several distinct but interrelated problems.

First, because the object of their enthusiasm is not common knowledge but something new, there is presumed to be little information in prices alone, nor in other sources of easily observable public information. Markets, which as Hayek (1945) explained, do effectively process local distributed knowledge into a public signal from which to coordinate action, are in this case not enough. The proto-entrepreneur requires nonprice information as well.

Second, it is not ex ante obvious who will have that nonprice information. So, before one can seek to discover the entrepreneurial opportunity, there is a prior problem to solve, namely, to discover who has that information. This is the *dual-discovery problem*. It should be noted that this is in fact a mutual coordination problem, as you can reason that others are trying to solve this same problem too, and you know that they know that you know that.

Third, even when you discover your group, there remains the underlying collective action problem of how to create effective governance institutions to make cooperation in this space stable and efficient. One solution is a kind of screening mechanism in which the innovation commons separates into *two sequential commons* of distinct innovation resources: a primary resource commons of technology and things; and a second commons, accessed only through that commons, of the ultimately more valuable and scarce resource, the entrepreneurially relevant market information. The first commons screens for the second commons, and it is only in the second commons that the innovation commons problem is solved.

Consider the context of the proto-entrepreneur. Entrepreneurial discovery uses information to infer opportunities to create value. Price information from competitive markets is an efficient concentration of distributed local information, yet will likely be incomplete in proportion to the degree of novelty or newness of the underlying idea or technology because products, firms, and markets may not yet exist, so information cannot yet accumulate in prices. Nonprice information exists in other people, and a proto-entrepreneur seeks this information, but doesn't necessarily know who or which other people have that information. If he did know, he could more efficiently contract with them through the market to buy that information (exchange), or form a partnership or an organization (hierarchy) or an ongoing interaction (relational contracting). The particular institutional configuration would of course be determined by transaction costs. Even when the relevant information set includes nonprice information, the entrepreneur can still solve this problem and discover the opportunity if she knows who has the relevant nonprice information, or where it can be found. There is no proto-entrepreneurship then, as opportunity discovery can be resolved in firms and markets by actual entrepreneurs.

The Proto-entrepreneur Seeks Nonprice Information

In Kirzner's (1973) model of opportunity discovery the entrepreneur is alert to new information in relative prices and price movements and uses this information to develop plans for entrepreneurial action.[6] However, as Don Lavoie (2004, 23) explains, "Markets are an extension of language," and the language of markets is not limited to just price signals, and so entrepreneurial action depends upon extracting rich meaning from a context. "The 'seeing' of an entrepreneurial opportunity is best understood not as perception, but as a kind of reading of a meaningful situation in a language-constituted world." In Lavoie's postmodern extension of the Kirznerian entrepreneur into a richer context of complex capital structures and embedded meaning (Lachmann 1954, 1994), the entrepreneur is perceptively reading a text and subtext of the market, looking for messages and meaning from which he might discover or reveal opportunity.

There is much to like in Lavoie's model of opportunity discovery in markets through entrepreneurial alertness that is achieved with a richer understanding of, as it were, entrepreneurial language capabilities (or deep textual reading, as postmodern scholars would say). The entrepreneur in this model specializes in reading the market, including its hidden messages and subtext, not just those obviously legible through prices. But the point is that the locus of this model is still an individual "reader." There is no community here, and thereby no underlying coordination problem, and so no comparative institutional opportunities.

When an entrepreneurial opportunity can be read directly in prices (for example, an arbitrage opportunity, à la Kirzner 1973), or even Lavoie's (2004) broader text of prices and meaning (Lavoie and Prychitko 1995), then the market mechanism, as an institution, is an efficient discovery mechanism (Hayek 1937; Kirzner 1997; Ikeda 1990; Holcombe 2003; Salerno 2008; Bostaph 2013). But when discovery of an opportunity requires *assembling* and not just reading nonmarket, nonprice information as well, then we have a different sort of problem.

A simplifying assumption is to treat this as a higher-dimensional information space: we assume the entrepreneur is searching through price space and also nonprice space, which is in a sense what Lavoie (2004) does. Yet that misrepresents the nature of the problem, because it will usually be far from clear who or what is actually in that nonprice space. Indeed, if you knew that already, even probabilistically, then you could still arrive at a contracting solution, or offer to buy that information on a market for ideas (Gans and Stern 2003, 2010). Some entrepreneurial researchers have argued that judgment fills this gap (Knight 1921; Foss and Klein 2012). An alternative approach is to suggest that the information exists, but not subjectively from within the entrepreneurial imagination (Eckhardt and Shane 2003), but that other information, or more valuably its meaningful interpretations, will be in other people. So finding those other people (to communicate with) is a substitute for a deep reading of hidden context in price information, and a complement with your own nonprice information.

For the proto-entrepreneur, the entrepreneurial discovery problem is actually a dual-discovery problem: to discover the entrepreneurial opportunity, one must find the set of information, much of which is nonprice information, and much of that will be located in other people. An efficient solution to entrepreneurial discovery will therefore need to trade off the costs of processing the publicly readable or market tradable information yourself versus seeking to discover who those other people are, and where they can be met, all the while knowing that they too will be trying to solve the same problem. The proto-entrepreneurial discovery problem in this way implies a dual-discovery problem.

The Proto-entrepreneur Faces a Dual-Discovery Problem

When the information necessary for entrepreneurial discovery is distributed and involves nonprice information, *proto-entrepreneurial uncertainty* relating to the discovery of the opportunity will exist at two distinct levels. First, there is uncertainty about the group of people or the distribution of information necessary to solve the entrepreneurial opportunity discovery problem. Second, there is uncertainty about the entrepreneurial opportunity itself. The innovation commons thus solves a dual-discovery problem: who or where, and then what. Note this first aspect of the opportunity discovery problem—who or where?—is not present in the firms-and-markets conception of the discovery problem, because the answer is trivial, namely in the firm or in the market.

Entrepreneurs search in markets for information without needing to contractually cooperate with others. They are nonstrategic in their institutional aspect. The proto-entrepreneur, however, searches in other people for information, and furthermore does so cooperatively, allowing others to search him too. The dual-discovery problem is therefore not just a problem of finding other people, but of strategically acting in such a way as to facilitate others finding oneself. The innovation commons is in this sense potentially viewed as a multisided market problem, or a platform (Rochet and Tirole 2003; Evans and Schmalensee 2016).

Yet the epistemic problem is worse than dealing with multisidedness, because that would imply a matching problem, albeit with asymmetric information. But that ignores a basic epistemic problem that attends the early stages of any new idea or technology, which is that when initial information and insight is distributed, not only do you *not know what you don't know* (i.e., the value of the information held by other people, which is an information asymmetry problem), but you also *don't know what you know* (i.e., the value of your information, because of its complementarity to others' information, but which you do not know ex ante). This problem exists because information is distributed, and you know it is distributed, but you don't know *how* it is distributed (although you know you don't know, and moreover you know that others do not either).[7] This is the essential problem the proto-entrepreneur faces, namely that of *mutually* discovering the information set necessary to discover the entrepreneurial opportunity, and knowing that others are trying to solve the same problem.

This first discovery problem—finding others when you don't know who they are or what they know, but worse, you don't necessarily know what you know—is simultaneously a collective action, a coordination problem, and an uncertainty problem. This is why is it a hard problem not readily solved in firms or markets, which even when they can adapt to the collective action and coordination aspects still fail at the uncertainty level of this problem. Quite simply, how do you contract or establish property rights when you don't know what you don't know? Prima facie, it seems hopeless.

But the innovation commons can work as an efficient solution to this first discovery problem, because of how it works as a solution to the *coordination problem* by functioning as a focal point, or Schelling point (Schelling 1960; Potts and Waters-Lynch 2017). Proto-entrepreneurs, without necessarily knowing other proto-entrepreneurs or what they know, can nevertheless coordinate on meeting in the innovation commons in the expectation of mutual sharing of information. The innovation commons is a solution to the *collective action problem* by entraining mutual expectation that the behavioral norms of a commons will govern interaction, thereby facilitating cooperation, because each agent can reasonably know that the other agents also suffer this same problem.

This is a subtle point. The innovation commons solves an economic problem that few economic institutions face, namely *mutual comprehension through collective revelation*. This is an economic problem because it reveals the economic value of the information and knowledge that individuals hold, information that is otherwise ambiguous and uncertain. But it does so by finding other partners for cooperative exchange, or mutual pooling. The revelation does not occur until the mutual exchange happens, and the efficiency of the revelation is proportional to the size of the exchange, or the collective pool.

In one sense, this is akin to price discovery (Kirzner 1997), in that the more participants in the market, and therefore the more Hayekian information is compacted, the more efficient is the price discovery mechanism—except there are no prices, or prices are only a part of the meaning to be apprehended (cf. Lavoie and Prychitko 1995). This is opportunity discovery, but at one layer removed from a production function model, because what is being discovered is also what each individual agent herself knows. And that matters, because opportunity discovery proceeds along the line of each proto-entrepreneur, each amateur enthusiast, seeking to refine and understand what she knows in order to arrive at a coherent perception of an opportunity. The intention is to establish a competitive position, yet the entire process proceeds cooperatively, else it breaks down.

Pursuit of an entrepreneurial opportunity associated with a new technology or idea—with mutual uncertainty about who has what information, when information cannot be valued without placing it in the context of complementary information, and when one's own information is uncertain—is a special sort of economic problem. It is not an entrepreneurial bargaining or allocation problem, but a proto-entrepreneurial coordination and collective action problem.

It is a game in which each proto-entrepreneur will reason that because information is distributed, his information is unlikely to be the complete set and will be of value to others, and that others are in a similar situation.[8] Furthermore, they will reason that others are likely to be holding different information, which is of value to them as a complementary good. Moreover, each actor will reason that others will arrive at a similar conclusion. This situation is characterized by high uncertainty that prohibits individual action to cross the entrepreneurial threshold. Although there is strategic value in faking that information to trick others, say, into dropping out of the game or declaring an entrepreneurial position too soon, each agent is presumed to be aware of that possibility, as a kind of inverse trembling-hand equilibrium (cf. Selton 1975). Each agent knows she doesn't have enough information to act entrepreneurially, that others are in the same situation, and that they all know that they know. The institutional formation of an innovation commons, as a set of rules to govern this collective action in order to coordinate a mutual revealing of information, solves this problem.

The relevant question is whether it can do so efficiently: that is, at lower transaction costs than alternative institutional solutions, including firms, markets, or government action (i.e., innovation policy). The economic logic of the innovation commons is the prospect of mutual expected gain if a group of agents can find each other and coordinate on a cooperative solution to pool their information in order to reveal the entrepreneurial opportunity. The prospective payoff to the proto-entrepreneur in the commons is the prospect of transformation into someone able now to act and engage *individually* in entrepreneurial actions. But he also knows that that same prospect is motivating other proto-entrepreneurs. It is mutual cooperation under the shadow of expected competition.

An innovation commons is a crucible for making entrepreneurs. At this point the innovation commons would collapse, as its raison d'être was realized. Yet the underlying problem is still a social dilemma of incentivizing free-revealing of oneself in the commons without being exploited by those who have little to reveal.

The Two-Commons Solution

The resolution of this problem is *screening* (Spence 1973; Stiglitz 1975). An effective innovation commons will efficiently screen entrants into the commons. In this sense, an innovation commons is like a club (Buchanan 1965), but with the additional problem that membership needs to be emergently rule-governed, rather than controlled. Now, in practice many innovation commons I studied did conform to the club model, in which a particular member occupied a position as the gatekeeper for the commons, making the innovation commons in effect a club. In reality, this operational criterion was widely observed. But it is not generally true of an innovations commons, nor is it essentially true. The reason is that the innovation commons has widely evolved the structure of two commons—an institutional structure that seems to get rediscovered anew in the process of innovation, that is, to evolve multiple times and in parallel. The first commons screens the second, but it is largely the second that is of value in entrepreneurial discovery.

An effective innovation commons will often have two commons: a *primary commons* of psychical innovation resources and technology, of things of interest to engineers and makers of stuff, and a *secondary commons* of market and quasi-market information, including nonprice information, that is of interest to proto-entrepreneurs. This first commons is largely composed of things that cost money or are difficult to make, have obvious value, and are targets of R & D and instruments of innovation policy. The second commons is different, primarily being entirely made of information, usually evanescent information, none of which can be patented, traded, or indeed meaningfully written down as facts for posterity, yet all of which must be consumed immediately, under high competitive pressure. That secondary innovation commons, however, contains the most economically valuable information because that is the information that unlocks the entrepreneurial opportunity. The entire existence of the primary innovation commons (the pooling of innovation inputs as things), which would otherwise be inexplicable, and is the identified market failure that innovation policy seeks to solve (and, might we note en passant, at enormous cost) is to function as a screening mechanism for the secondary commons. It is the secondary commons that is the valuable commons to proto-entrepreneurs: it's the reason they're there in the first place.

The innovation commons is not a public pool of information and knowledge about a new technology, undertaken for public-spirited and globally altruistic reasons. To the extent that wonderful and generous behavior happens—and it does, to be sure, by those keenly spirited tinkerers, experimentalists, and brilliant and far-sighted citizens among us, even those who accidentally or unintentionally reveal such information, deep humanists and heroes all, and I unreservedly salute them and their contribution to the public good—its heroes are not whom I mean to include in the innovation commons. They may put that information, those ideas, and these technologies into a commons, whether into a local commons for their people or into a global knowledge commons (Stiglitz 1999). However, the group I refer to are those who carry such information, irrespective of stated pretext, but with the private prospect of gaining access to the second order of the innovation commons, in which subsequent information about market opportunities is pooled and shared.

Action in the innovation commons is assumed to be economically rational. Entering the commons is a first-best action and strategic response. The reason the agent does not contract—whether by forming a firm or seeking to trade in a market—is because fundamental uncertainty rationally forecloses that prospect of entrepreneurial action. The agent is in a *proto-entrepreneurial* state; she does not have enough information to act at all. And, as in the *dual-decision problem*, she does not know what she knows, only that she needs to find others to pool information in order to reveal what is known (and she knows others face a symmetric problem). But realizing that problem, they all, individually, now face a collective action problem, which is resolved with the *two-commons solution*. The rational enthusiast of a new idea or technology faces a problem that can be resolved with open cooperation under a certain configuration of rules, in which others are similarly incentivized. That emergent private governance ordering is the innovation commons.

5.4 Modeling the Innovation Commons

How might we model this process? I have emphasized that the logic of an innovation commons fits within a rational actor model. Agents do the best they can in given circumstances with the resources and information available. This formulation also fits within a strategic model with rational expectations. Each agent acts as a best response to how he expects other agents to act, knowing that other agents are making similar strategic calculations with similar information. The key constraint for agents, however, is that the "given circumstances" are known to have incomplete, distributed knowledge. Not only does each agent know that, but each agent knows that each other agent knows that, and each further knows that other agents know that they know there is missing and distributed information. Each agent does know that he doesn't know everything, and that other agents know different things. Yet, paradoxically, it is this *mutual assured knowledge of incomplete and distributed information* that provides the impetus for the emergence of an innovation commons. There are several analytical frameworks that, while not developed here, might be used to model the emergence of an innovation commons.

An innovation commons is a constructed social form of organization, and so sociological models might usefully apply. But we are not concerned with actors buffeted, as it were, by "social forces" (in the Durkheim/Parsons sense), but rather seek to explain the emergence of "the social," as per Bruno Latour's (2007) constructivist framework of actor-network theory (ANT), which is used to study how relational ties between actors (including people and objects) within a semiotic network generate emergent meaning.[9] An innovation commons is a prime example of a social form that is forged or formed for a purpose (discovery), under uncertainty, and that can be understood in terms of the microprocesses of group formation and maintenance. The case study approach developed by Latour and colleagues might therefore usefully be applied to the sociological analysis and modeling of the emergence of innovation commons.

An innovation commons is a complex system (a lattice of edges and vertices, a network of nodes and connections) and so its topology and structural dynamics can be modeled using complex systems theory. Specifically, an innovation commons can be analytically treated as an open network or *dissipative system* (Raine et al. 2006); as a *nonintegral network* poised at the edge of chaos (Potts 2000), affording it dynamic efficiency properties; as a *small-world network* (Watts and Strogatz 1998) with both clustering and fast communication; and, owing to the fact that it is a network of knowledge and expectations, as what Foster (2005) calls a *fourth-order complex system*.

A computational model of an innovation commons as a complex system can be further developed by modeling each vertex as a computational agent specified in terms of rule-governed interactions on a local network with other rule-governed agents (Epstein and Axtell 1996). The agent-based modeling approach is highly suited to the study of emergent social phenomena—what Epstein (2006) calls *generative social science*. A benefit of this approach is that it can be further developed, as Epstein (2014) does, to focus analysis on richly specified neurological and behavioral models that seek to explain emergent or generative social phenomena.

Both sociological approaches (from actor-network theory) and computational network approaches (from complexity and agent-based modeling) are likely to be useful frameworks for a broader social science analysis of innovation commons because they abstract key aspects that we have observed in the examples discussed so far, including their emergent properties, generative social nature, interacting mutual expectations, and their dynamic efficiency (compared to alternative institutional or governance forms of organization). Many of the known properties of complex networks—scale-free or power-law behavior, clustering, dynamic efficiency, emergent properties—are observable in innovation commons. Moreover, innovation commons are both autopoietic (self-making) systems and semiotically complex, suggesting that a complex systems or computational modeling approach will need to be combined with cultural and sociological analysis of evolving knowledge systems.

5.5 The Innovation Commons in Institutional Space

The innovation commons solves a type of innovation problem—namely the coordination of distributed information and other innovation resources necessary to reveal the entrepreneurial opportunity. This is the first innovation problem, and while there are many different potential institutional solutions, an innovation commons can be an efficient solution because it minimizes transaction and discovery costs. (The focus on firms, markets, and governments, as the presumed default solution to this problem, was a consequence of ignoring transaction costs and the organization of the entrepreneurial discovery aspects of innovation). We can therefore locate this *innovation problem*, and the innovation commons as a possible solution, in an *institutional space*—in the context of firms, markets, governments, networks, clubs, and other forms of commons.[10] Moreover, it also locates the innovation commons in relation to an *innovation trajectory* (see figure 2.1)—as the zeroth phase in the standard three-phase Schumpeterian trajectory. We observe that an innovation commons is *institutionally different* from that which comes after it, which is to say that the collapse of the innovation commons is the "fundamental transformation" associated with the entrepreneurial origin of an innovation trajectory. We also emphasized that the innovation commons is a private ordering, emerging from civil society and thus requiring governance institutions, rather than a product of innovation policy enacted by government.

Putting this together affords us a strong case for claims about the existence of the innovation commons (because of entrepreneurial and market uncertainty); its relative position in institutional space; and its location in time, particularly in relation to the innovation process and industrial dynamics. Indeed, this suggests a conjecture:

> Conjecture: *All (Schumpeterian) innovation trajectories originate in the innovation commons*
>
> *Corollary 1: Entrepreneurs are prior members of the innovation commons.*
>
> *Corollary 2: Innovating firms emerge from the innovation commons.*
>
> *Corollary 3: The fundamental transformation (collapse of the innovation commons and arrival of the entrepreneur and innovating firm) occurs when common-pool resources in the innovation commons elucidate the entrepreneurial opportunity.*

Missing from this account is a theory of the size and spatial organization of the innovation commons. We know it is larger than $n = 1$ (autarky), but smaller than N = all (the population of the nation-state). Our initial observations of innovation commons suggest that they tend to be "club-sized" (a paradigmatic example of an innovation commons was the Homebrew Computer Club at Stanford University, between 1975 and 1985, which had about 300 members [Meyer 2003]). Other examples of innovation commons are hackerspaces and makerspaces (Allen 2016; Williams and Hall 2015), and coworking spaces (Potts and Waters-Lynch 2017), which tend to scale between dozens to at most a few hundred members. Innovation commons are therefore about as big as an intermediate-sized firm. But to develop a theory of the size of innovation commons we need more than a sample distribution. We also need an account of the forces that cause an innovation commons to grow and to stop growing or to shrink.

Suppose an entrepreneurial opportunity is revealed only when k bits of information are combined into a single set, where k is an unknown random variable. Let the probability that a person, drawn from a random distribution, has one of those k bits be p ($0 < p < 1$). The minimum size, n, for a commons to reveal an opportunity is k only when there is certainty that each person has one of the necessary parts of the information (i.e., as $p \to 1$, $n \to k$). But where each member of a commons has valuable information with probability p, then minimum expected size is $n = k / p$. Furthermore, as $n \to \infty$, the probability of discovering the opportunity goes to 1. The basic logic that causes an innovation commons to grow, and for a larger commons to have a higher expected value to joining than a smaller commons, other things equal, is the increased probability that a commons contains the necessary information to discover an entrepreneurial opportunity. This can be decomposed into two aspects: (1) the larger number of knowledge carriers in the commons (n); and (2) the higher the probability that each carrier is carrying high-quality information (p). This model predicts that an innovation commons will exhibit increasing returns, growing toward infinity from any arbitrary starting point, stopping when it crosses the *k-threshold*.

To contain that explosion, we add two sorts of costs.

First, let there be a cost to being in a commons, as a kind of periodic fee, or contribution cost, C_i. This is a fixed cost, paid by each n, every time she enters the commons, and can be thought of as the individual cost to contributing information. With zero communication and coordination costs, $C_i = C^*$, which is the value of that information once in the pool. (The information is assumed to have zero value by itself.) The total value of the common-pool resource is therefore $\mathbf{C} = \Sigma C_i^n$, for all n. For communication costs c, $\mathbf{C} = \Sigma C_i^n - \Sigma c$.

The second cost is proportional to the number of people already in the commons (the analogue of a congestion cost in a club good [Buchanan 1965]). The value of an innovation commons to a "commoner" is access to k. But the value of that is proportional to the number of others who also have access to exploit it. So the exploitable value of k is $E(k) = k / n$. The more people are in the commons, the higher the probability that it contains k, but also the lower is the expected value of k after the fundamental transformation. Therefore $E(k) = p$.

Note that n drops out of that equation. The upshot is that with the assumptions above, there is no optimal size of the innovation commons. That is a consequence of the interaction of individual and group incentives. For a group, bigger is always better, yet each individual's best contribution is zero, and the smaller the group, the greater their probability of being the entrepreneur on the other side of the fundamental transformation. So in theory, an innovation commons can be any size at all. Which is to say that we need to look for other factors to determine optimum size.

Communications and coordination cost is a possible factor. If a particular group can improve its technology of communication and coordination, then, other things equal, it can lower aggregate transaction costs, Σc, for k-discovery. This increases the value of the rent in the commons **C**, and so increases the optimal size of the commons. An example is when members in an innovation commons share physical or social technologies that lower communication and coordination costs. However, in the other direction, because a commons is peer governed, the larger the size of the group, the more costly is individual monitoring and so the likelihood of free riding (Olson 1965).

Tacitness of information will affect the scale of the innovation commons. If information is highly tacit (or sticky [von Hippel 1998]), then the costs of transmission of information beyond the source (or the fidelity of that transmission) will tightly constrain the size of the innovation commons.

Screening is another factor. The higher is p, the more valuable is a commons to each new entrant. Therefore an innovation commons that can effectively screen (imposing an entry cost that only high-quality contributors can afford, causing low-quality types not to enter the commons) will be smaller in n for the same expected k, but with a larger ex post probability of entrepreneurial payoff after the fundamental transformation. An example is when an innovation commons has club-like exclusivity or costly membership, for example, the Homebrew Computer Club.

Density/subsidy/surplus is yet another factor. An innovation commons may opportunistically form to exploit surplus resources whereby the costs C_i are being contributed by some other mechanism (Shirky 2010). It is as if there are more n in the commons than there actually are, and so the ex post exploitable payoff from k-discovery $E(k)$ has higher apparent value. This may also be a product of critical density of some function in a population (e.g., technical literacy, wealth, access to a technology), where below some threshold λ, an innovation commons does not form, but above that threshold it is increasingly likely to form due to some feedback effect. An example is when an innovation commons forms about a public university.

Culture might determine the size of an innovation commons. The theory of culture-made groups (or *demes* [Hartley and Potts 2014; Potts et al. 2016]) is an evolutionary theory of the group formation for the purpose of pooling knowledge. The size of a deme and the size of an innovation commons will be correlated. An example is when a cultural group (e.g., a religious community) has high trust (low transaction costs), permitting an innovation commons to form about a technological prospect (e.g., the documented entrepreneurial success of Israeli Army veterans in technology, or the origin of the wine industry in Australia from Protestant German immigrants [McIntyre et al. 2013]).

Historical and institutional specificity may also explain the size of particular innovation commons. Allen (2011) argues that a revolution in technological measurement of performance in the late eighteenth century facilitated a shift toward modern institutions. A similar argument may apply to the institutional technologies of innovation where the ability to track and measure contribution and to monitor reputations can increase the viable scale of the innovation commons, in the first instance as an escape from autarky, but more recently with the arrival of information and communication technologies and social media (Benkler 2006; Shirky 2008).

The innovation economy is the original sharing economy. If you trace back to the beginning of almost any innovation process, you will observe the same economic coordination problem being solved in the same way: namely, a group of people with a shared enthusiasm for a new technology pooling and sharing "innovation resources"—data, information, know-how, equipment, material, access, connections, and so on—under a commons-like institutional governance structure. Observe that this sharing economy is not a free-for-all—it is not a public good. There are rules about what you give and what you take, and there are consequences for breaking those rules, the most significant being exclusion from the shared innovation resources, that is, banishment from the innovation commons, and therefore from access to the resources it contains. But these rules are ad hoc, adapted to the local circumstances, and both made by and enforced by the community itself. And these rules are, because of that process, legitimate. The core of the innovation sharing economy resides in the effectiveness of these governing rules.

5.6 The Innovation Commons as Higher-Order Discovery

Where the institutions of the innovation commons form and succeed, new ideas are, through a process of information pooling, transformed into entrepreneurial opportunities that can then be exploited. A corollary of this logic is that societies or economies that can successfully engender innovation commons will have more effective levels of opportunity discovery, and therefore entrepreneurial origination, as the onset of phase 1 of an innovation trajectory, than economies that rely on random genius.

An economy that relies on its supply of creative individuals—or what the modern analytic economic history literature now calls *upper-tail human capital* (UTHC) (Mokyr and Voth 2009; Squiccrini and Voightländer 2014; Gennaioli et al. 2013; Mokyr 2016)—will be limited by that very supply. It can seek to engender more supply, including by institutional means, but this is a hard constraint on economic development. Indeed, the endogenous growth models that underpin this line of work (Lucas 1978; Glaeser et al. 2004) indicate that this is ultimately the fundamental constraint on economic growth and development. But the theory of the innovation commons suggests that this is actually a societal variable, conditional upon emergent cooperation. Societies that can form effective innovation commons can potentially outcompete societies that have less ability to do so, to the extent that innovation commons productivity exceeds some certain fraction of individual genius or UTHC density.

So a prediction: societies with low UTHC and low levels of innovation commons will be weak; societies with high UTHC but low innovation commons will compete with societies with high innovation commons but low UTHC, and a society with high UTHC and high innovation commons will dominate. The reason why is simple: low UTHC and low innovation commons means low entrepreneurial discovery, which means the economy is forever behind the frontier. A high UTHC and low innovation commons, and vice versa, is a trade-off, as these different institutional strategies are potentially equivalent in terms of arrivals at phase 1 of the innovation trajectory. It's possible the underlying different institutions may have different subsequent effects, an issue we explore in chapter 7. High UTHC combined with high innovation commons is an unbeatable combination. It is the maximum flow of starting points into phase 1 of an innovation trajectory.

Such an outcome will appear as an innovation cluster, or some other measure often attributed to increasing returns in the geography of innovation, and may well therefore be confused with the consequences of innovation policy. Note that a successful innovation commons may cause a result (a high flow of entrepreneurial discovery) that may otherwise be interpreted as the consequence of innovation policy, which indeed aims at the same output and devotes resources to that effect. I raise this policy issue, however, because innovation policy affects group behavior, particularly at the level of a nation-state and a region. An innovation commons is an emergent, spontaneous group. It does not necessarily form at the level of a nation-state or a region and can form at levels both above and below that.

5.7 Conclusion

The innovation trajectory, I have argued, begins in the innovation commons. Societies with effective innovation trajectories evolve. A society that can successfully develop an innovation commons can, under certain circumstances, outcompete a society that can do everything but that. Innovation trajectories drive economic evolution, and economies that have such trajectories are at the forefront of global wealth. So the cause of an innovation trajectory is a critical factor in understanding the prospects of economic evolution and the causes of wealth, whether regional or national.

The origin of innovation is explicable. But, perhaps surprisingly, it is not the quantity of entrepreneurs in an economy. It is not even the quality of entrepreneurs in an economy. It is not the public support to entrepreneurs, nor the support to R & D, nor the level of public spending on innovation, nor the number of patents, nor the index of top universities. These things are measures of public effort, but they are not measures of what actually matters, which is the discovery of new entrepreneurial opportunities that successfully reach meso 1, and so begin the innovation trajectory. The theory of the origins of such meso 1 opportunities, as the origin of entrepreneurial discoveries, does not rely on the supply of entrepreneurial talent or endeavor, nor on resource supply, geography or cultural conditions, nor critically on government actions, but on the depth and effectiveness of the civil society institutions of the innovation commons. The technical origin of innovation is a new idea that makes logical sense and can be verified. The institutions for that have taken thousands of years to develop and reify into standards for philosophical truth and scientific veracity that are now mostly robust in the best of places, although they require eternal vigilance. The institutions for innovation are no less fragile and precious. They are the market economy, the subsequent application and development of a valuable new idea, and the innovation commons in its origination.

Innovation originates as the economic discovery of opportunity, and that requires pooling distributed information under high uncertainty. That's hard to do. It requires special cooperation and passionate commitment and enthusiasm to achieve opportunity discovery. Entrepreneurial discovery is a precious flower, not because entrepreneurs are precious—indeed they're among the hardiest human specimens we have. Entrepreneurial discovery is precious because the institutions it requires are precious and easily disrupted by social, cultural, and institutional disorders that endanger cooperation with strangers under uncertainty. This is why we need a better understanding of the institutional origins, that is, the rules, of innovation.

Notes

1. In *The Entropy Law and the Economic Process* Georgescu-Roegen (1971) distinguished between arithmomorphic and dialectic concepts. Arithmomorphic concepts are suitable for mathematical reasoning, while dialectic concepts (distinct but overlapping) are suitable for qualitative reasoning.
2. The technology diffusion model is the characteristic feature of the distinctly Schumpeter-inspired Science Policy Research Unit school of innovation economics at the University of Sussex, as founded by Chris Freeman. Key building blocks are Dosi's (1982) technological paradigms and trajectories model, and Pavitt's (1984) taxonomy of types of innovation trajectory.
3. Dopfer and Potts (2008) represent this as a generic "meso trajectory" composed of (meso 1) an origination phase, mapping to the entrepreneurial origination of the new idea; (meso 2) an adoption phase, mapping to the adoption of the generic idea into the population of carriers, which unfolds through a market process of creative destruction; and (meso 3) the retention or embedding phase, in which the idea is institutionalized into the economic system.
4. See, for instance, Lakhani and von Hippel (2003), Lee and Cole (2003), O'Mahony and Ferraro (2007), Fauchart and von Hippel (2008), Gächter et al. (2010), Bauer et al. (2016), Potts and Hartley (2015).
5. Recall *entrepreneur* is also Old French, meaning "undertaker of."
6. Note that the claim that the entrepreneurial opportunity can be discovered in an information set of market-determined prices is not the claim that prices are a complete information set, but rather that the market process that determines prices is a computation of emergent information that *embodies* the distributed information in an economy, including local knowledge of circumstances and how they have changed. Market prices summarize distributed information, which as Hayek (1945, 519) explained is "the knowledge of the circumstances of which we must make use never exists in concentrated or integrated form but solely as the dispersed bits of incomplete and frequently contradictory knowledge which all the separate individuals possess."
7. There is an analogue of a "no-trade theorem" (Milgrom and Stokey 1982) here, where if someone endeavors to start a firm, he is signaling that he does indeed know that he has the information sufficient to identify an opportunity. We might call this the "no-entrepreneurship theorem."
8. An overconfident entrepreneur might make a systematic mistake here, a behavioral bias well known to entrepreneurship and innovation researchers (Potts 2016).
9. See also Hartley and Potts (2014) for an evolutionary theory of socially constructed meaning making through group, or *deme*, formation.
10. For more on the concept of innovation and institutional space, see Davidson and Potts 2016b; they use the institutional possibility frontier (Djankov et al. 2003) to array the different institutional forms of innovation policy.

6

Rules of the Innovation Commons

An innovation commons emerges when a group of people can successfully work together—can act collectively—to share innovation resources. The product is not just a pool of resources, including knowledge, but the prospect of discovering opportunities in that pool that could not be seen in the individual bits and pieces of information prior to their being pooled. The pooled resources and knowledge have more value than the individual parts. On the face of it, there should be an incentive to create innovation pools. We should see them everywhere. But the reason we don't is that there is an economic problem in the midst of this that arises because the pool has the structure of a *social dilemma* (Dawes 1980; Kollock 1998): it is individually costly to contribute resources to the pool; the value of the pool depends upon the quality and extent of individual contributions; yet individual benefit can be had without making a contribution. An innovation commons therefore requires that a group of people be able to solve a collective action problem, and this requires *governance*, or *rules*.

Such collective action problems can present insurmountable barriers to cooperative outcomes. Yet as Ostrom (1990) showed, under certain circumstances, particular rules of governance can emerge that enable a group to cooperate in order to create a valuable common-pool resource. The key insight is that it while the quality of the people—their trustworthiness and cooperative intent—certainly matters in determining the prospect of cooperation, the quality of the rules that govern those people usually matters more. Furthermore, these rules are often invisible to innovation policy. As Ostrom (2005, 240) observes: "The groups who have actually organized themselves are invisible to those who cannot imagine organization without rules and regulations issued by central authority."

We will explore the innovation commons through the lens of these rules that enable a group to form and that make cooperation a safe and effective strategy within the group. Social scientists and evolutionary theorists alike have long known that cooperation is a puzzle to be explained (Axelrod 1984), and that an effective way to explain cooperation is to inquire into the rules and strategies that generate it. An innovation commons is made of resources, people, and rules. In this chapter, it is these rules that we seek to understand.

This chapter proceeds in two steps. First, I examine why cooperation is such an important part of this story, and how it fits into a broader evolutionary account of the economic agent in the context of innovation. A key insight is that the value of mutual cooperation is a direct consequence of high levels of uncertainty or ignorance. This is perhaps surprising, because high uncertainty or ignorance usually militates against action. When the input conditions for rational choice are absent, when crucial information is missing, a strategically dominant action is to make no choice at all. Yet what matters is not uncertainty per se, but knowledge of uncertainty and knowledge of others' knowledge of that uncertainty (Shackle 1972). It matters that people know that they are ignorant, or in a state of uncertainty, and therefore that the expected value of cooperation is the chance to reduce their own uncertainty. Of course, they cannot individually reduce their own uncertainty in a pooling context without reducing other people's uncertainty too. This interdependent aspect makes this situation institutionally interesting—only some types of rules are able to resolve this collective action problem and give rise to effective innovation commons. We seek to elucidate the nature of these rules and why they work.

Second, I locate this prima facie special claim within a more general context as a mapping of the behaviors and rules in the innovation commons according to Ostrom's (1990) *eight design principles* of the commons (listed in section 1.2 in chapter 1), showing that the innovation commons has microbehavior and microstructure similar to other commons. The rules of the innovation commons form a suite of constraints and incentives that increase the likelihood of successful group cooperation, suggesting a further evolutionary mechanism at work, namely *multilevel selection* (Wilson et al. 2013). The core argument is that group selection also applies to the evolution of innovation, or as Wilson and Wilson (2007, 345) explain: "Selfishness beats altruism within groups. Altruistic groups beat selfish groups. Everything else is commentary."

6.1 Cooperation behind the Veil of Ignorance

This book is about the institutional microstructure at the very beginning of the innovation process. The standard mythology is individual and heroic, typified by the Schumpeterian *Übermensch*, as the creative visionary entrepreneur, a leader of people and a disruptor of markets. Nevertheless, our story is fundamentally communitarian (McCloskey 2016; Howes 2016).

In the beginning: the germ of a new idea emerges—a technological prospect—along with a lot of ignorance and uncertainty about its value and the ways that value might be realized. In the beginning, the mix is one part excitement, nine parts uncertainty, and zero parts basis for entrepreneurial action. What happens at the origin of innovation is that people cooperate to create a pooled resource in order to deal with ignorance and uncertainty and to create some basis for action.

In the standard models of innovation, that basis for action is realized by investing in enlarging that one part of excitement into two or more parts research and development, seeking to raise the basis for entrepreneurial action accordingly. In the model here, the basis for entrepreneurial action comes from reducing the nine parts uncertainty to fewer parts. Not to zero, but to something more manageable for entrepreneurial action. This is achieved not individually, as in the investment model, but collectively by creating a rule-governed group whose purpose is to clear the fog, to figure out just where they actually are and what they might do. Only then, as it were, is world made safe for Schumpeterian heroes.

What type of person enters this group? And why does it work? An innovation commons is a *group* that forms to pool distributed knowledge, and it is a *cooperative* group because of ex ante fundamental uncertainty about the value of the information and bits of knowledge and other resources that are pooled. Yet the cooperative and social quality of these groups is largely independent of, and sometimes in spite of, the cooperative and social quality of the people who compose them. Cooperative groups are not necessarily made of cooperative people. The efficacy of the innovation commons does not assume a population of altruists (although that helps by lowering transaction costs). Rather, cooperative people are made by the institutional incentives to cooperate. It is shared cooperative rules that matter, that is, incentives, not cooperative people.

While it is undoubtedly true that, as with all collective instances of the human animal, some members of an innovation commons are generous and gregarious, with others taciturn and misanthropic in equal measure. Some members of that Invisible College of the Republic of Letters sought out their peers in writing, while working hard to maintain their preferred natural state of social isolation (Mokyr 2016). Many of the mathematical and engineering geniuses at the beginning of many a technological revolution are easily recognized as lying well outside the neurotypical spectrum, finding social interaction challenging and difficult. Yet still they seek out or create these social groups.

So the simple hypothesis—that these animal groups are formed by groupish animals—cannot possibly be the whole story. Among humans, cooperative social groups are made by social rules interacting with social animals, not by social animals alone (Bowles and Gintis 2011). They come together not because they are social, but because they need what sociability offers, and what sociability offers is a resolution to the problem of uncertainty. Innovation commons are cooperative groups that need to solve collective action problems in order to form and to function effectively, and do so by resolving individual uncertainty through social mechanisms. The social, in other words, is a means to an end. Social interaction pools resources to reduce uncertainty to facilitate individual action. Rational individuals cooperate under uncertainty to discover opportunities.

An innovation commons is actually a rather exotic species of Rawlsian "veil of ignorance"—from behind which you don't know what the shape of the economic order associated with the new idea or technology will look like, nor the a posteriori distribution of asset values or the strategic value of market positions. Now, if you could see through the veil of ignorance that shrouds entrepreneurial opportunities, even probabilistically (viz., Shackle 1972, building on Simon 1955 and Knight 1921), you could unilaterally act in expectation of profit, using price discovery mechanisms as feedback into exchange and contracting. In this pure situation, there is no need for cooperation or for society. Individual action is sufficient. Or more to the point, cooperative group action through resource pooling would be expected to have the structure of a "lemons market" (à la Akerlof 1970): if you have high-value resources (private information), why would you pool them? The only resources in the pool coming from others will be low value. Ergo, we would expect "commons failure" (*cf.* market failure).

But from behind the veil of sheer ignorance, a Bayesian strategy of cooperation and egalitarian distribution—à la John Rawls's (1972) notion of distributive justice; John Harsanyi's (1962, 1967) bargaining with incomplete information; and Robert Axelrod's (1984) experiments in the evolution of cooperation—will most likely be optimal. Sheer ignorance invites cooperative pooling.

However, this situation has the structure of a social dilemma (or collective action problem [Olson 1965]) from which mutual cooperation will emerge only with some institutional covenant to constrain free riding or ex post opportunism (Williamson 1979; Ostrom et al. 1992). The incentive structure of the commons, as Ostrom (1990) explained, depends on social coordination, social understanding, and social monitoring. So it is in the innovation commons.

The innovation commons is not a public good, but closer to a stag hunt game, as Sam Bowles (2004, 449) observed:

> Pursuing good ideas with practical applications is a costly and uncertain project, much like hunting large game. Success is rare, but its fruits are immensely valuable. . . . A new drug or a software application is not so different in this respect from an antelope. Thus it is not surprising that the system of prestige and norms in some parts of the modern information-intensive economy . . . in many ways parallel[s] the culture of the foraging band.

The innovations commons requires private institutional governance, or a local social contract of rules that specify the conditions of cooperation, the allocation of the rewards from cooperation, and the consequences of defection. Rational self-interested individuals, in the sheer face of fundamental uncertainty, can become hard-core communitarians with surprising alacrity when institutional conditions make that option safe.

6.2 An Emergent Social Order

The innovation commons is an economic institution but is rarely a designed institution. For the most part, it is a spontaneous institutional order that emerges from the bottom up to harness innate human propensities and social instincts (Hayek 1967; Bowles and Gintis 2011), expressing what Smith (2003) calls "an ecological rather than constructivist rationality." The human animal is adapted to group-making for collective action through language-based cultural processes of mutual and collective identity construction and meaning-making—it's our evolutionary niche (Dunbar 2003; Pagel 2012; Hartley and Potts 2014, 2015; Turchin 2015). The innovation commons harnesses this instinctive propensity to form cooperative, purposeful groups.

The mechanics of these groups works through a mix of evolved social instincts and incentives. A central mechanism is *social learning*, paying attention to the information others have and cooperating in order to access this information. Social learning is often more efficient and effective than individual (or experimental) learning and is the primary driver of cultural evolution (Herrmann et al. 2007; Mesoudi 2011; Mesoudi et al. 2016).

The other basic mechanism the innovation commons harnesses is *social signaling*, in which individuals acquire social status or prestige through conspicuous high-value cooperation and contribution, accruing a reputational currency that can be spent in various ways, including as a target for social learning (Gintis et al. 2001; Fehr and Fischbacher 2003).

The model we use to represent the economic agent in the innovation commons is not *Homo economicus*, and the reason is obvious: *Homo economicus* is not a model of an evolutionarily adapted, social-learning, group-forming agent. Indeed, these aspects are precisely what is abstracted from in order to define an agent—Deirdre McCloskey calls him "Max U"—who interacts through exchange and contract, and is a well-defined element in a social welfare function. Rather, our model of an economic agent in the commons is what Dopfer (2004) and Dopfer and Potts (2008) call *Homo sapiens economicus*—a rule-making and rule-using agent. This is a generalization of the work of Herbert Simon (1990, 2005), Cyert and March (1963), and Nelson and Winter (1982), who modeled a firm as made of habits and routines, or microinstitutional rules. A firm is a contractually organized cooperative group. A commons is a similar institutional structure, but much flatter organizationally and without the benefit (or costs) of formal contracts. Cooperation in a commons comes from implicit contracts. These are mutual understandings of rights of access in return for behavioral regularities.

They are usually enforceable at the intensive margin by limited sharing or shading (Hart and Moore 2008), and at the extensive margin by exclusion.

6.3 The Use of Society in Knowledge

In 1945 Hayek published "The Use of Knowledge in Society" in the *American Economic Review*. The paper is conceptually among the most important in modern economics. This was not a singularity, but built on key ideas developed by Ludwig von Mises and the Vienna school (Dekker 2016). Its significance was as the first clear expression of distributed information in relation to the nature of the market process. It was the beginning of economics as a science of complexity.

Hayek's paper explained the efficacy of price coordination by imagining the market process through the cybernetic computational metaphor of parallel processing of distributed knowledge with feedback from market prices to adaptive human actions.[1] A market is a socially organized mechanism that makes use of distributed knowledge: society uses knowledge through markets. The idea is pure *mainline economics* of spontaneous order, along the same line that connects Adam Smith to Vernon Smith (Boettke 2012). The price mechanism, in this account, is an efficient coordinating institution for processing distributed knowledge—that is, specialized and technical or local and tacit knowledge in the minds of a great many other people—without any agent needing to know what other agents know, or even who they are. Prices communicate distributed knowledge, facilitating adaptation to coordinate individual plans into an emergent order (a catallaxy).[2] In Hayek's mainline model, the price mechanism coordinates the use of knowledge in society.

An innovation commons is the reverse mechanism: that is, "the use of society in knowledge." It coordinates not on prices, but on rules that make an effective group, or microsociety, that pools distributed knowledge in order to make new knowledge. In such a group, with effective rules for private governance, it is individually safe to cooperate, and so to pool distributed knowledge for the prospect of revealing a hidden order (of mutual value). An innovation commons is a *social* form of production to create new knowledge—that is, discovery of an entrepreneurial opportunity—by coordinating distributed knowledge—for example, individual but partial insights, information, experiments, resources, and so on—through the governance of rules.

Institutional economics distinguishes between the *institutional environment*, which are the rules of the game and background constraints in law and social norms that guide individual behavior (Davis and North 1971; Hayek 1973; North 1990), and *institutional arrangements*, which are the governance structures designed by groups of agents to mediate particular economic relations

(Ostrom 1990; Williamson 1996). The rules of the innovation commons are institutional arrangements, in the sense of groups of people making rules within an institutional environment in order to provide governance to coordinate their interactions. However, note that while groups of people make institutions to solve coordination problems (Schotter 1981), institutions also make groups, in the sense that well-functioning, mutually adopted rules bind a group of people into patterns of cooperation. Groups make rules (Aoki 2007), but rules also make groups (Dopfer and Potts 2008; Hartley and Potts 2014).

The purpose of these institutional arrangements is to solve particular economic problems, mostly about coordination, that arise in the very early stages of the innovation process. Effective institutional arrangements enable a group of people to successfully cooperate to solve innovation problems. Once we identify these economic problems, we can search for adapted institutional solutions across different instances of innovation commons. This will enable us to infer the rules of the innovation commons.

In the Nelson-Arrow (Nelson 1959; Arrow 1962b) account of the economics of innovation, the economic problem is *fixed costs* in a production function for new knowledge under perfect competition, free appropriation (because innovation is an information good), and uncertainty. From an aggregate social welfare perspective, this is an allocation problem—that is, allocation of resources for investment in innovation. The economic problem is market failure: from a social-welfare-maximizing perspective, the incentive problem with perfect competition (price = marginal cost < average cost, because fixed costs > 0) is that too few resources are allocated to investment in innovation. In other words, innovation has public good-like properties.

However, the innovation problem represented here differs for two reasons: one, because it concerns the entrepreneurial discovery of *value* and not just scientific or technical novelty; and two, because we start with an additional assumption, namely that information inputs and innovation resources are *distributed*. The economic problem of innovation is how to coordinate distributed information in order to discover value in the shape of an entrepreneurial opportunity. These are problems of forming groups and creating incentives to pool distributed information under multilateral conditions of uncertainty.

For each individual, the economic problem of innovation is essentially whether to cooperate or not. To *cooperate* is to contribute to the common pool and to abide by its rules; to *defect* is to seek an alternative institutional arrangement, perhaps starting or joining an organization, or seeking to contract through a market, or choosing autarky. Yet an innovation commons emerges only with mutual cooperation or the expectation of mutual cooperation, because this is the necessary condition for the pool to have value. But recall that each agent is cooperating under conditions of uncertainty in respect of the value of the information and resources that she and others hold, and also of the *ex post* value of the pool. This fundamental mutual uncertainty is not incidental, but the sine qua non of an innovation commons. If agents did know the value of the information they and others held, then contractual or hierarchical institutional arrangements would invariably be a more efficient mechanism to combine knowledge and resources into an innovation output (e.g., Coase theorem). It is precisely the fact that you don't know the value of the information and resources that you and others hold, and that this is only revealed by combining them, that renders the commons a potentially efficient institutional solution.

In contrast, under conditions of such uncertainty, firms and markets are not efficient coordination solutions because property rights are costly for ad hoc bits of distributed information and because contracts are costly to write and enforce when it is unclear who has such information, what information they have, or its value. Firms and markets tend to be inefficient institutions for solving economic problems in the very early stage of the innovation process.

For an idea to become an innovation—that is, phase 1 of an innovation trajectory—the economic problems that need to be solved include coordination problems, collective action problems, agency problems, incentive problems, allocation problems, information problems, and knowledge problems. But really, these are different aspects of the metaproblem of organizing and incentivizing mutual cooperation under conditions of uncertainty in order to engage in a production process with several very peculiar characteristics. Specifically, you're seeking to produce something new (you don't quite know what), with a group of several others (you're not sure how many), using variable inputs (you're unsure of the value you or any others bring), on an open timeline (you're not sure how long). The only thing you do know, and you know that others know, is that you'll all know it when you see it.

Markets and firms don't work well under these conditions. They require greater specificity, less fuzziness. But what the innovation commons is producing is greater specificity and reduced fuzziness about the nature and shape of an entrepreneurial opportunity. What we called the "fundamental transformation" in chapter 5 occurs when the innovation commons creates sufficient clarity that markets and firms can work to develop the innovation. To do this, the innovation commons needs to first solve several distinct economic problems associated with the novel idea itself and with the economic organization of cooperation to discover its opportunities.

6.4 Problems the Innovation Commons Must Solve

Problem 1: Identity

The first problem the innovation commons must solve is its own identity in terms of "who and what"—that is, whom to cooperate with (and how much) and what to cooperate about. The "who and what" are interrelated as a joint problem of refinement of *subject* and *object*. What a commons focuses on depends on who is contributing to it, and who contributes and how much they contribute will shape its identity. This is the problem of identifying and refining the object of a commons and its subjects.

The focus of an innovation commons (the object) is the new idea or technology, but almost by definition this will emerge in an imprecise and fuzzy state. Yet the progenitors (the subjects) may well have a tacit sense of what the innovation commons is about, even when that is not necessarily obvious to outsiders. For instance, in the Republic of Letters discussed in chapter 1 (see Mokyr 2016) we can retrospectively see that the subject focus was what we now call "science." But the participants didn't call it that, themselves seeing what they were doing as a kind of cosmopolitan experimental philosophy. The refinement into that which we now call science was a product of the innovation commons. For the Homebrew Computer Club innovation commons, the object of focus was integrated circuit hardware and software (see Meyer 2003), but that didn't need to be spelled out to participants because of their mutual backgrounds in electrical engineering and computers. The "who and what" were codetermined.

The identity of an innovation commons works as a focal point (Schelling 1960, 1978), enabling potential entrants into the commons to coordinate on the same point, improving the chances of finding each other (Potts and Waters-Lynch 2017), and providing a seed for emergent identity to cohere about. The name of something—including the act of naming, the associations and meaning it implies, and the common knowledge of and agreement about the meaning of that name—will be a factor affecting the viability and success of the innovation commons.

Identity matters because of the substantial uncertainty about the meaning of the generic idea or technology in the innovation commons, and because of the importance of transfer of particular associations. The new sport of windsurfing emerged from an innovation commons (Shah 2005) and was by that name understood in the commons as wind*surfing*, that is, a new form of surfing, and understood to bring with it that culture, rather than, say, "stand-up yachting," which would imply different associations and paths of development. Similarly, the new sport of snow*boarding* was associated with other "board sports" (surfing, skateboarding) rather than say "side-standing skiing." It was the innovation commons of 3D *printing* rather than "additive manufacturing" (technically they refer to the same thing) that took off in the MakerBot community of Thingiverse,[3] with printing being something amateurs can do in their own home, whereas manufacturing was something done by corporations in factories. Names matter in the innovation commons because they not only define a domain, making a focal point, but create a web of associations to condition the subsequent development of the innovation paradigm and trajectory.

The refinement of "what" is closely connected to the problem of "how much" and "with whom." In a basic economic sense, this is an allocation of scarce attention and resources for the individual. The agent chooses to commit time and resources to the commons, balancing this allocation against next-best alternative uses. But rarely is the choice problem that straightforward. It is more likely to be a *search-and-match problem* for each individual. An innovation commons by definition is focused on something new and of uncertain provenance and quality. But it is also like a multisided market (or a platform [Rochet and Tirole 2003]) in that not only must you choose the innovation commons, but the innovation commons must also choose you. It is, in this sense, an instance of *nonprice coordination*. Moreover, for the innovation system as a whole, this is also a *coordination problem*. One agent may find another agent with complementary information or innovation resources, but for those agents to pool resources, the assessment that others have value to contribute, and that they are cooperating toward the same goal, needs to be approximately mutual, or have a common focal point (Sugden 1995).[4]

A related problem in respect of "who" is "Who else?"—that is, how big should the pool be? This is a *stopping problem* (when configured as a dynamic sequence) or an optimal-size problem as a one-shot pool. This is solved by a sequential check on whether the entrepreneurial opportunity has been discovered; else keep growing the pool. However, this process might not converge because it could have the wrong focal point, or the wrong elements might be in the pool. Yet that information is ex ante unknowable, so there remains fundamental uncertainty about whether an innovation commons has value, at least up until the point where value is revealed.

Yet uncertainty, and specifically mutual uncertainty or fuzziness, can actually facilitate pooling by creating a mutual expectation of similar value (i.e., mutual recognition of uncertainty, such that uncertainty itself is the focal point), or a fuzzy set that still covers somewhat different interpretations of what the innovation commons pool is seeking to discover. The origin of an innovation commons is always a new idea and the purpose of an innovation commons is to create a common-pool resource from which entrepreneurial opportunities for innovation can be created and accessed. But before specific economic problems associated with the design of effective incentives and internalizing externalities even arise, there is the fundamental problem of coordinating the existence of the innovation commons across people (who, who else?) and scope (what is this about?). These are economic problems because they involve choices and are resolved only through the coincidence of mutual choices (i.e., coordination).

Problem 2: Cooperation

An innovation commons needs to create rules or governance mechanisms that incentivize cooperation. It must establish an expectation of fairness and proportionality between effort or contribution and reward, and of protection from exploitation. It must make cooperation safe and render it a desirable, first-best option.

Market institutions create such incentives through well-defined and secure property rights and sanctity of contract, along with technologies to minimize transaction costs. Organizations create such incentives through effective management and operational control hierarchies. In firms and markets, competition and reputation constrain exploitative behavior, and standardized accounting conventions furnish precise consensus about who owns what, who did what, and who owes what at any point in time. In a commons, however, property rights are deliberately weak, contracts are general and multilateral, hierarchy is mostly nonexistent, and resources are by definition pooled.

So it seems that incentives for cooperative behavior are weak. Ostrom (1990) showed, however, that in many cases the assumption that common property resources will experience inevitable exploitation and collapse (what Hardin called the "tragedy of the commons") is profoundly misleading. Ostrom's point was not that the commons is never a tragedy, but that effective governance rules can be created to produce incentive mechanisms that are powerful enough to overcome the otherwise inherent tendency to exploitation and collapse. The same principle applies to the innovation commons.

An innovation commons does not have formal property rights that can be exchanged, nor price signals to guide action, or command hierarchies to direct people and resources toward a desired end. Prima facie, the incentive mechanisms in a commons seem weak, in effect limited to granting entry or access and disciplining opportunistic behavior with the threat of exclusion or exit. (A commons, in this sense, is like a club [Buchanan 1965].) But innovation commons can sometimes be highly effective when they harness powerful prosocial human instincts for cooperative behavior identified with an in-group (Bowles and Gintis 2011).

Homo sapiens evolved under powerful selection pressure on the human ability to play social games, that is, to engage in social learning, to read and monitor the social behavior of others (Dunbar 2003; Mesoudi et al. 2006; Boyd et al. 2011), all as a consequence of sexual selection and multilevel selection driving cultural evolution (Wilson and Kniffin 1999; Miller 2000; Richerson and Boyd 2006; Wilson and Wilson 2007). The economic agent in the innovation commons is not *Homo economicus*, the rational utility-maximizing individual, but rather *Homo sapiens economicus* (Dopfer 2005; Dopfer and Potts 2008) the rule-using and rule-making economic agent who is an intensely social animal and a product of cultural evolution. An innovation commons is a natural environment for *Homo sapiens economicus*. It is a cooperative space, but only with an in-group, which whom there are intense social interactions, monitoring, and boundary policing to ensure that the cooperation is mutual. The innovation, technology, and entrepreneurial discovery part of this is evolutionarily new, but social behavior and monitoring for cooperation in the commons are deeply atavistic (Congleton and Vanberg 2001). This is perhaps even more so than in a firm or market, which have in turn evolved specialized organizational and legal mechanisms, or at least a distinct formal and government shadow under which they occur, to monitor and enforce cooperation.

Like a market, an innovation commons is a competitive space. But where market action is guided and disciplined by price competition, individual action in a commons is guided and disciplined by *status competition* (i.e., competition for social position, a zero-sum game). The functional role of the prestige, reputation, or allocation of attention as a social currency or asset—giving rise to what some call a prestige economy, a reputational economy, or an attention economy (Henrich and Gil-White 2001; Lanham 2006; James and English 2009)—has long been understood as central to the cultural incentive mechanisms of knowledge production (Gaspart and Seki 2003). For example, the economic sociology of science or scholarship has long emphasized the central role of status competition and reputational economies in incentivizing cooperative behavior in the form of contributions (Merton 1973; Dasgupta and David 1994). This is a consequence of social learning in human evolution (Mesoudi et al. 2006; Boyd et al. 2011). New information, computation, and communication technologies not only improve the efficiency of search and coordination, which improve the technical efficiency of the commons, but they also, and possibly more importantly, improve the efficiency and effectiveness of in-group or "demic" signaling (Hartley and Potts 2014), which thus becomes an important mechanism in the coherence of an innovation commons.

Innovation commons also an opportunity to accumulate cultural and social payoffs that come not simply from being a shareholder in a cooperative social venture, but from *being seen to contribute* to that venture (Gintis 2000; Gintis et al. 2015). These payoffs come from the granting of reputation and prestige[5] from other agents who are in a position to observe altruistic cooperation and to communicate that information to other agents (Bowles and Gintis 2011). Such *conspicuously cooperative behavior*, when observed, elevates social status within a group, which in turn has the expected payoff of a greater access to the resources of that group, including power and mating opportunities (Turchin 2016).

Another prospect is that the value of status may accrue to residual control and bargaining in organizational forms *after* the fundamental transformation (e.g., in allied entrepreneurial ventures or industry associations) where such control depends upon the consent or preferences of others, and is thereby accumulated as status capital. In these situations, status is accumulated through multilateral cooperation as a rational investment to acquire a fungible asset that can be subsequently converted into utility. An innovation commons can incentivize cooperation by constructing an environment in which status can be produced and allocated. Furthermore, while this is, analytically considered, *selfish cooperation* entirely consistent with individual rational utility maximization, it does not work as investment in status capital if that pecuniary goal is perceived as such by others. Status is a good that one does not acquire but can only be given, that is, conferred by others based upon perceived altruism. We therefore expect to observe sincere cooperation.[6]

The potentially weak incentives within the commons may not matter that much if everything is in effect in the shadow of the real game that occurs after the fundamental transformation, once firms, markets, and other organizations form. In this respect, the extent of cooperation advanced in the innovation commons by the proto-entrepreneur will be directly proportional to the agent's expectation of the size of the entrepreneurial rent (and its distribution) that accrues from the prospect of opportunity discovery that access to the pooled contributions of others provides, scaled by their own probability of capturing it, which is a function of how many others are also contesting it. The agent's priors about the shape of the distribution, the number of other agents, and her own assessment of the value of their contributions to the commons will condition agents' entry or exit decisions and the level of cooperation they extend. This *rational cooperation* will also be strategic, in that the agent will expect that other agents are also behaving the same way. Unlike the status competition mechanism, agents need not engage in strategic deception but will seek to communicate their true intentions to engage in entrepreneurial action.

A further strategic play—consistent with enthusiastic cooperation and honest communication in the commons—is when the agent's intention extends beyond opportunity discovery and seeks to render the innovation commons a permanent mode of production. Open-source operating systems such as Linux, open-source browsers such as Firefox, and open-source web server software such as Apache (Lakhani and von Hippel 2003) are prime examples of such initiatives to create large-scale computational infrastructure in the commons that are institutionally protected by the creative commons licensing system (Benkler 2006). This institutional strategy seeks to limit or foreclose downstream opportunities for subsequent capture or control of the benefits of a new technology by private agents (e.g., corporations exploiting intellectual property rights) or governments (through regulated access). Interestingly, this institutional form can produce powerful incentives for cooperation because it mimics the competitive structure of a patent race (Fudenberg et al. 1983), incentivizing the fast development of a high-quality product that captures a market or establishes a dominant user base and thereby limiting the rents available to market competitors.

Problem 3: Consent

A third problem the innovation commons must solve is how to make rules—that is, the institutional arrangements of the innovation commons—such that they have consent. The content of such consent to the "constitution of the commons," as it were, will generally be in relation to understandings of expected contributions and costs, procedures for allocation of the benefits of the innovation commons, and rules for bargaining across these processes and outcomes in relation to special circumstances or changed conditions. Consent helps ensure the rules that govern the commons are singular and legible, and that acts of monitoring and enforcement of rules, or procedures for changing rules, are undertaken from a prior position of presumed agreement about what those rules are, what they mean, and willingness to follow those rules unless particular special conditions arise. The generalized presumption of consent lowers transaction costs of operating such rule systems, minimizing costly side bargaining or use of force.

Unanimous consent is an ideal scenario for collective action under conditions of zero transaction costs (Buchanan and Tullock 1962). However, unanimous consent can be achieved in an innovation commons by making it an implicit condition of membership: in other words, consent by joining. In this way, consent in an innovation commons is not the outcome of a collective choice, but of a *supraindividual choice*. To the extent that an innovation commons has club-like properties of membership—that is, the possibility of exclusion through denial of entry—consent is at least implicitly guaranteed among all who have attained entry. In practice, this will largely work through whatever costly screening mechanisms are in place, such that willingness to pay the cost required by the screening mechanism is an implicit consent to the rules of the commons. These may indeed be embodied in the screening mechanism itself, such as in the expectation that members of the Homebrew Computer Club would freely present their work to other members of the club.

Unanimous consent gives the rules of an innovation commons the properties of a *constitution*, and is in an important sense concerned with matters similar to those of the constitution of a nation-state, namely the expression of individual rights, the distribution of wealth, and the mechanisms of power and executive decision-making (Buchanan 1990). A constitution is in essence a political *exchange* in which a group of individuals mutually agree to impose constraints on each other (to mutually constrain the set of their own actions) in return for a share of the gain produced by the group through that mutual constraint. Obviously, this requires unanimity, such that the gains from the group only go to those who agreed to be so constrained "along the boundaries of private spaces and within the confines of acknowledged public spaces" (Buchanan 1990, 4), and not to those who never entered into the political exchange in the first place by agreeing to constrain themselves (i.e., so-called free-riders).

Consent is maintained in an innovation commons as a private order, generally requiring regular "performances" of the constitutional order so as to continually remake and reinforce the cultural and social norms of the innovation commons. Hackerspaces will often have biweekly meetups, and the innovation commons of the cryptoeconomy is continually enacted on social media platforms, such as for instance Reddit member community forums (r/Bitcoin, r/btc, r/CryptoMarkets, r/CryptoCurrency) and reported on digital media sites such as Coindesk.[7] What these rowdy and popular yet ostensibly democratic sites create is legitimacy for an underlying constitutional agreement that is emergent from anarchy (Leeson 2014). The rules of the innovation commons need to be embodied in observable mutual action and regularly publicly performed in order to maintain consent. Such public performativity is essential to the prospect of participation in decision-making, or in influencing the community, which in turn maintains group cohesiveness.

This sense of mutual participation and inclusivity is central to the politics and moral ethics of the innovation commons. An innovation commons is fundamentally an egalitarian community under a veil of ignorance about the future prospects of the technology or idea that is being explored through pooling of resources and information. The rules of the innovation commons must be such that they produce an acceptable order to all "constitutional citizens" regarding what is what is just, efficient, and fair (Rawls 1971). It is not of course impossible that some citizens may have special rights or privileges owing to the mutually recognized or known value of the special resources or prospects they bring into the community. Indeed, as Buchanan and Tullock (1962) long ago pointed out, such side payments will often be an efficient political exchange solution. This will often privilege founding members of the commons (e.g., Richard Stallman in the open-source community), or those who have made unusual or notable sacrifices to maintain or grow the innovation commons (e.g., Larry Lessig in the Creative Commons community). Yet whatever special considerations are reached, it is implicit that these too are established by as close as possible to unanimous consent.

Problem 4: Monitoring

A fourth problem an innovation commons must solve is how to track who is contributing what and who is taking what. In a standard common-pool resource this involves monitoring who is contributing what resources to the pool, and often more importantly, who is taking what resources from the pool, in order to detect free riding, that is, taking from the pool without contributing. Monitoring serves two purposes: (1) gathering information to ensure integrity in the system, including knowledge that monitoring is occurring, which will in turn condition individual behavior; and (2) to detect rule violations, which instigates the need to deal with problems of punishment, as well as dealing with dispute resolution and conflict, which we discuss next.

Because an innovation commons is a species of knowledge commons, in which a resource is produced and not only consumed (Frischmann et al. 2014), there is a particular concern with monitoring contributions to, and not only takings from, the pool. Yet an innovation commons is a somewhat special case owing to the value of the pool as a resource for discovery of opportunity emergent from patterns observed in combined distributed information. Participants in the pool have strong individual incentives to actively monitor new contributions to the pool to assess whether the latest information or innovation resources added to the pool are high-value bits (knowable only ex post) that furnish some kind of gestalt, completing the pattern and revealing the opportunity.

In a natural common-pool resource, such as a fishery, there is an underlying stock resource that can be sustainably harvested at some flow rate, but subtraction beyond that rate will collapse the stock. Monitoring of takings by all of the commoners is essential to ensure that the total use will not endanger the stock. But in an innovation commons, taking from the pool of innovation resources and information does not deplete a rivalrous resource per se. Instead, the stock is expected to collapse at some point once the necessary and sufficient resources are pooled. The difference is that ex ante no one knows what those necessary resources will be. Once they are sufficiently assembled, the value of the stock is collapsed when one or several of those commoners perceive the opportunity and race to the exit to exploit it. This is where the true rivalry lies, at the point of catastrophically unsustainable consumption at the moment of fundamental transformation from proto-entrepreneurial potential to entrepreneurial action. Yet this collapse is not a tragedy of the commons, but its raison d'être. It is why people are in the commons in the first place.

The collective action problem is not weak incentives to monitor contributions and takings. Rather, it is weak incentives to report that monitoring to others. Each participant has strong incentives to monitor contributions and takings (where a taking is a commoner switching from a proto-entrepreneur to entrepreneurial action). Such action indicates that the common-pool resource has been completed and the opportunity is revealed to any who will piece the parts together, making the collapse of the innovation commons liminal. A commoner who perceives this opportunity has little incentive to broadcast that message to others, because such cooperative behavior would immediately create competition. But they might also be mistaken in their perception of the opportunity, and there will be value in having this verified. Such is the situation in the knowledge commons of science (Mokyr 2016), for instance, where the race to the door is the race to publication—free revealing in exchange for a property right that buys status (Dasgupta and David 1994)—but there is both private and public value in having such discovery claims confirmed, as facilitated by the institution of double-blind peer review.

Innovation commons will tend to be intensely privately monitored but only weakly publicly monitored. The problem is to provide incentives to induce public revealing of private discovery and private monitoring. Successful innovation commons solve this problem through the deeply atavistic institution of the tribal gathering: the periodic *conference* and its variations (the festival, meetup, forum, conclave, competition, colloquium, bake-off, and so on). Innovation commons usually require some kind of institutional variation on the conference in order to solve the problem of collective monitoring of progress in building the common-pool resource by creating cultural norms of sharing private information reinforced with status incentives to the sharing of high-valued information or, especially, reporting on claims of discovery of opportunity. While this has obvious value to the community, there is also private value to those making such claims in having them reviewed, critiqued, and verified by others who are in an expert position to do so.

Participants in a traditional scientific conference travel and meet in the same place, sharing ideas and information over several days, then depart. One of them, usually of high rank, organizes the conference (a costly undertaking that confers prestige within the group). This task circulates among the group in order to minimize accumulation of power. In innovation commons that occur around new sports (such as mountain biking in the 1970s, or drone racing today), colocation in time and space is an essential part of information sharing, as competitive matching needs to occur in order to evaluate the new ideas or developments. However, there are other institutional mechanisms—such as the moderated public forum, whether as a periodic newsletter or magazine (as in the past), or as is now common as an online community—that achieve similar aims without commoners needing to gather at the same place or time. Ideas can be demonstrated via blogs or YouTube clips, and forums can exist in moderated comments or subthreads. The costs of providing such institutional infrastructure for an innovation commons have fallen significantly in recent decades and have greatly increased the scale at which an innovation commons can operate.

Problem 5: Punishment and Conflict

A fifth suite of problems a successful innovation commons must solve is punishment for rule-breaking (and monitoring rule violations), as well as providing dispute resolution between commoners who may have different interpretations of those rules, or find themselves in situations where the rules are ambiguous or missing.

On the whole, innovation commons tend to be rather poor at endogenously dealing with punishment and conflict. There is an obvious reason for this, in that innovation commons are neither by design or expectation intended to be long-lived institutional entities, and the rules that govern them tend to be culturally enforced social norms. In many cases these sanctions are judged and administered at a peer-to-peer level through social feedback (e.g., criticism, gossip, and shaming) on norm violations, the most extreme form being excommunication, or banishment from the commons. Bargaining and due process are costly, so when cooperative norms break down and rule violators appear or when conflict arises, an expedient option is simply *banishment*, or, where it is a group and not just an individual that has violated rules or is in conflict, then what we will tend to observe, in proportion to the costs of remediation, is breakaway *exit*.

A clear example of this phenomenon can be observed in open-source software, where the use of the group exit option in consequence of community conflict is known as *forking*. The word derives from phylogenetics, where at a point of macro-mutation an evolutionary lineage branches or splits (or forks) along two or more distinct evolutionary pathways. In software engineering, a project forks when developers copy the source code to start a new line development, often as a result of a fundamental disagreement or schism within the developer community about basic principles of the project or its aims.

In an innovation commons the key resource is the knowledge community itself. For this reason, fundamental disagreement within the community, or the breakdown of the social cooperative norms of the community, will tend toward group exit more often than attempts at justice and reconciliation. Punishment of small individual defection can realign wayward members, requiring perhaps little more than a veiled threat of banishment from the group. But where norm violators themselves form a group, punishment can be extremely costly and ineffective. Furthermore, there can be gains to both the extant and the exiting groups from secession, in that both are no longer devoting resources to conflict and are free to focus their energies entirely on the project at hand. Exit, as Hirschman (1970) explained, can be efficient.

Problem 6: Independence

The sixth suite of problems an innovation commons must solve is to create legitimacy and autonomy for the group to protect it from external forces that seek to weaken or exploit it, or who would otherwise free-ride on its actions or gain from its failure. Independence is crucial for an innovation commons, yet can be difficult to achieve.

Independence serves to protect the integrity of the information and resources pooled within the innovation commons. Integrity of information and resources is important because the quality and unbiased nature of this pooled resource, such that the information accurately reflects the true reality of the situation, is sine qua non for discovery of genuine entrepreneurial opportunities. If the information in an innovation commons is distorted or resources are degraded, then the innovation commons will be worse than a failure; it will be a wasteful distortion that will yield false opportunities. This situation is analogous to science with flawed methodologies, corrupted experiments, or false data. Only error can come of it, but worse, that will only be revealed ex post, when action tries to build on those seeming results. The value of an innovation commons is directly proportional to the quality of the information and resources pooled within it, and independence is a prophylactic to protect that pool from outside corruption and infection. A discovery engine must value truth.

Independence is necessary because the nature of an innovation commons is to be disruptive, and as Schumpeter (1942) realized, this will impose costs on those who get disrupted. To the extent incumbents can organize, they will have a strong incentive to resist or block development of new technologies that threaten their position and the rents they enjoy (Juma 2016). In consequence, an innovation commons is vulnerable to attack by whatever or whoever feels threatened by its rebellious existence. The Republic of Letters, for instance, was broadly under attack from the Catholic Church, due to the existential treat it posed to its monopoly on the authority of knowledge. What we now know as the august institutions of science were in the beginning a ragtag network of free-thinking heretics. Innovation commons around hobbyist drones and amateur rocketry and space clubs are broadly under attack from civil aviation authorities because of the threat they pose to its domain of control and tied funding arrangements. It is relatively easy to paint them as enemies of public safety, bent on reckless endangerment for their seemingly pointless amateur enthusiasms. The early history of the cypherpunk movement (e.g., May 1994 on the "Cyphernomicon") is essentially that of an outlaw gang of hackers, not the pioneers of computer security and global electronic commerce we now understand them to be. Independence affords protection because it limits the ability of enemies of innovation to attack the innovation commons by directly lobbying its sources of support or control. Elite research universities, which have evolved robust institutions to protect themselves from corrupting external influence (e.g., seeking independence of funding, independence of hiring), for this reason can often provide effective cover for an innovation commons.

Innovation commons also need protection from innate conservative or reactionary forces within that might otherwise constrain the search space of discovery of opportunities. While innovation commons tend to be club-like at their boundaries, they function best as an open community, with maximum freedom (or implicit permissions) to explore ideas within the space of the commons, subject, of course, to complete transparency in doing so, reporting all successes and failures. This playful "hacker" attitude thrives on deliberate rule-breaking and pushing boundaries in order to learn about the limits of the technology or idea in question, secrets that often only yield under imaginative probing or extreme testing (Graham 2004). The radical egalitarianism of an innovation commons helps preserve this freedom. But the innovation commons itself must nurture a culture of openness to exploration, resistance to self-censorship, and protection of deviance. For this reason, innovation commons tend to be culturally, politically, and socially tolerant spaces (aka inclusive domains) that value their independence from the local political, cultural, social, or economic milieu.

Economic Problems the Rules Must Solve

The innovation commons is really a series of nested economic problems. At the highest level, the innovation commons is a solution to a *collective action problem* that requires the creation of incentives to effectively induce mutual cooperation over a common pool of information and resources. The value of this common-pool resource lies in its value to reveal entrepreneurial opportunities.

But to solve that overarching collective action problem requires solving (at very least) a suite of subproblems—namely, as above: (1) identity, (2) cooperation, (3) consent, (4) monitoring, (5) conflict, and (6) independence. These six problems of the innovation commons are solved with *rules of governance* that address each aspect. From an institutional perspective, an effective innovation commons is a complex and somewhat modular system of rules that is variously adapted to solve these problems. Consider the varieties of economic problems that these rules of the innovation commons need to solve.

The subproblem of *identity* is really a species of *coordination problem*, in that distributed individuals need to be able to find each other and communicate on the same topic, through the same channels, and with the same understanding of what they are contributing to and to what end. But all of this has to be done without the centralized benefits of an ostensible leader or hierarchic organization. The resolution of the identity problem, as a coordination problem, is also a contribution to solving the *knowledge problem* of innovation, in that the pool of distributed knowledge (the innovation commons) facilitates mutual adaption among the individual plans of proto-entrepreneurs.

The subproblem of *cooperation* is really a species of *incentive problem* that works by creating an efficient signaling system for status and prestige based on a *property rights* system that renders contributions to the pool socially fungible. Cooperation is rendered a form of investment, with an expected payoff in the social currency of status and prestige.

The subproblem of *Consent* is really a problem of minimizing transaction costs involved in subsequent bargaining and exchange. The context of consent is that the innovation commons is a voluntary, albeit temporary, association. It is not a permanent group like a tribe or nation-state, but an ad hoc group like a hunting party or a committee. Yet all who enter into it and who submit to its constitutional restrictions undertake this action as a voluntary exchange.

The subproblem of *monitoring* is really an information problem of inducing optimal public disclosure of private information. This is, in other words, a local public goods problem coupled to a mechanism design problem.

The subproblem of *punishment* is also a problem of private provision of a (local) public goods problem (Bergstrom et al. 1986), or equivalently of incentivizing altruistic punishment (Fehr and Gachter 2000). The subproblem of *conflict* in turn is really an *optimization problem* of exit and of dynamically determining optimal group size (i.e., coalition formation [Olson 1965]).

The subproblem of *independence* is really a species of institutional or mechanism design problem of boundary formation and maintenance to constrain the externalities that one group can impose upon another, and particularly to prevent these from washing into the innovation commons. But boundary construction and maintenance is a club good (i.e., a local public good [Buchanan 1965]) and its provision is therefore also a collective action problem. But an effective boundary also makes a coherent group that can interact with other groups, revealing a problem of exchange and contract.

6.5 Origin of Rules

An innovation commons is an institutional complex—a modular suite of rules—that solves these problems. But where do these rules come from? Consider three answers: (1) they evolve through selective processes on naturally occurring variation; (2) they are designed; or (3) they emerge through a combination of design and evolution. I want to make the case that the origin of the rules of the innovation commons is invariably the third option—a complex system of top-down and bottom-up rules. But to see why this is necessarily so it is instructive to think about what it would mean, and how it would be possible, for the rules of the innovation commons to emerge purely from the bottom up, or to be imposed purely from the top down.

First, how might an innovation commons spontaneously evolve as an ordered set of rules that no one deliberately designed, such that it just appears? The basic scheme of an answer is differential selection acting on natural variation in the "rule-pool" (Dopfer and Potts 2008). In this world, suppose there are N agents, each carrying a random suite of rules for social interaction propensity and sharing information and resources for innovation (call this i), as well as an endowment of innovation resources (call this j). Each agent is an N-tuple {ij}. Suppose these measures are distributed: cooperation (i = H, L); endowment (j = H, L). Now randomly match agents pair-wise. Let a payoff function be when two agents {HH} meet = 1, else 0. Allow that when two HH agents meet, the positive payoff forms a meta-agent (a 4-tuple, as the origin of a commons) HHHH, which is now returned to the pool. Let the payoff to an LH match with an HHHH = 1, else 0. This makes a 6-tuple LHHHHH. As a simple replicator model, cooperation (H alleles of high cooperation) will spread in the population. This is a far simpler model than even the presumption of just six subproblems—identity, cooperation, consent, monitoring, conflict, and independence—but the general principle still applies when limited just to a binary measure on cooperation.

This simple model outlines the evolutionary process by which an innovation commons could emerge, starting from random rules coupled with random pairwise interactions. This model is entirely abstract and hypothetical, but illustrates the general principle that an innovation commons could evolve to arbitrary rule complexity from entirely random rule initial distributions provided there was sufficient variety in the initial pool, and differential payoffs to cooperative group formation among agents who carried innovation resources. Of course, this says nothing about the likelihood of such evolution or the stability conditions or other dynamics. For that we would need a formal modeling approach and some calibrated estimates of the distributions of traits and endowments, and of the strength of selection effects. But in principle an innovation commons could evolve under standard Darwinian evolutionary mechanisms (à la Hodgson and Knudsen 2010).

Second, how might an innovation commons be deliberately designed, such that its existence is, as it were, engineered? The basic scheme of an answer here is that a person would create a particular set of rules that govern membership in a club, where the purpose of the club is to pool and share innovation resources and information, for example in a hackerspace. In this situation, the rules are created first by the "formateur" (to borrow a term from Congleton [2011]), referring to an entrepreneurial agent who makes an organization). The rules—which would be expected to cover at least the six problems above—are then adopted by each new member of the club, who upon joining the club becomes a carrier of the rules, creating a "meso" population of rules and rule carriers (Dopfer and Potts 2008).

Yet in reality both the random evolutionary selection model and the top-down designed model are unlikely to manifest in pure form, and any actually observed innovation commons will be a complex combination of both processes. The random evolutionary process is too slow. However, its quality is that it facilitates distributed learning and adaptation through feedback. The design approach, while quickly proposing rules that target the particular problems an innovation commons is expected to face, is also constrained by bounded rationality and problems of adaptation to local conditions and circumstance. Innovation commons will emerge as entrepreneurial agents (formateurs) propose rules to govern the commons—specifically, rules for making group identity; rules to facilitate cooperation; rules for manufacturing consent in relation to the allocation of the costs and benefits of the commons; rules for monitoring free riding (seeking benefits without paying costs); rules for managing conflict; rules for establishing and maintaining autonomy—but those rules then adapt and evolve.

The design rules and the evolutionary selection processes that are variously deployed and harnessed by an innovation commons are not ex nihilo. They are, for the most part, repurposed rules from other domains of the organizational economy or society, or are what evolutionary theorists call "exaptations."[8] The reputational economy that works in an innovation commons is borrowed and repurposed from other peer production reward systems of knowledge, such as science (Merton 1973). The identity-making systems in innovation commons that facilitate in-group cooperation are a deep part of the human evolutionary lineage (Bowles and Gintis 2011). The rules for managing conflict in an innovation commons borrow from similar rules in other peer production communities (Ostrom 1990; Frischmann et al. 2014). This raises the question of whether the rules of the innovation commons are arbitrary adaptations, or whether they conform to more general principles of effective design rules for collective action. Specifically, we now consider the extent to which the rules of the innovation commons align with Ostrom's eight design principles of the commons.

6.6 Core Design Principles

North (1990) conceived of institutions—"rules of the game," he called them—as mechanisms to reduce uncertainty in complex, ambiguous environments. Institutions coordinate because agents use mutually adopted behavioral decision rules, and they adopt similar rules because of contexts of uncertainty, an idea long understood in organizational studies (Heiner 1983; Cyert and March 1963). An innovation commons is an institution to enable a group of people to coordinate on a set of mutually adopted rules to create and govern a common-pool resource. The purpose of that resource—the basis of its value—is to facilitate the discovery of entrepreneurial opportunity associated with a new idea or technology by pooling information in order to reduce uncertainty.

Prior to Ostrom's (1990) breakthrough work (see Dawes et al. 1986; Ostrom et al. 1992; Tarko 2016), it was widely believed that private-ordering solutions to common-pool resource problems through complex local institutions of self-governance were generally inferior to externally imposed and expert-sanctioned government solutions (regulation or public provision), or to solutions that sought to create clear individual property rights (privatization). By gathering and analyzing a large number of case studies of successful and unsuccessful common-pool resource institutions in use, Ostrom showed that beneath the complexity of successful institutions were eight underlying design principles.

Why these particular constellations of institutional rules worked, while others didn't (Cox et al. 2010), was explained in terms of behavioral characteristics of social dilemmas, the biophysical characteristics of common-pool resources, the distribution of useful knowledge about the properties of the resource system, and the modular structure of effective decision-making with feedback.[9]

Ostrom's (1990) eight core design principles can be summarized as such (see also Wilson et al. 2013, 522):

1. *Identity and boundaries*. Clearly defined and delineated boundaries, within which it is clear what the resource is (and what it isn't) and who has access to it (and who does not). This need not be legible to outsiders, but it is usually crucial that the commoners know who they themselves respectively are, and the resource domain of their jurisdiction.
2. *Proportionality between costs and benefits*. Expected contributions to the common-pool resource and benefits drawn from the commons are proportional. Particular benefits require particular contributions, and these must be arrived at through consensus bargaining. Inequality is only tolerable in a commons when it is universally understood to be fair.
3. *Inclusive collective-choice*. The rules of the commons must be arrived at through an inclusive group process, including rules for changing rules. Successful common-pool resource arrangements tend to have a supermajority constitutional aspect.
4. *Monitoring*. Commons are vulnerable to free riding (Hardin 1968) and require active monitoring of contributions to the pool, and takings from the pool, to detect such exploitation. Efficient monitoring often exploits distributed group efforts.
5. *Graduated sanctions*. When attempted free riding is detected, successful commons tend to punish in proportion to the scale of exploitation. Mild transgressions are punished lightly at first, with more severe punishments, including banishment, reserved for serious offenses. Free riding is costly, but so too is punishment, and needs to be economized on.
6. *Conflict resolution*. Conflict among commoners about any of the preceding aspects will arise, and the successful group will need an efficient and effective way to resolve this. Successful commons often tend to be small for this reason.
7. *Local autonomy*. Successful commons must be able to make their own rules (principle 3), which means that they need to be able to make rules independent (or at least quasi-independently) of local prevailing institutions.
8. *Appropriate relations with other groups*. Principle 7, however, must be balanced with recognition of the commons embedded in a broader social and institutional system (aka polycentric governance).

Ostrom (1990) argued that successful self-governing groups that can effectively solve social dilemmas are likely to follow, whether implicitly or explicitly, the eight core design principles sketched above. A meta-analysis by Cox et al. (2010) of 91 studies of these design principles in common-pool resources broadly supports Ostrom's original findings, and proposes some modifications to principles 1, 2, and 4 (see table 6.1). The evidence of the types of problems that the innovation commons is trying to solve in sections 6.4 and 6.5 indicates a reasonably close overlap between Ostrom's eight principles (Ostrom 1990; Stern 2011), or their generalized modifications by Cox et al. (2010) in table 6.1, and the rules of the innovation commons.

First, consider user and resource boundaries. In a natural resource commons, such as a watershed or grazing pasture, the resource preexists and at issue are its boundaries or definitions of what (subtractable, rivalrous) resources are specifically included or excluded. Clarity about resource boundaries also reciprocally defines the users (clarity of the "what" defines the "who") by whether they do or do not make a claim on those resources. Each component helps to internalize the positive and negative externalities produced by participants, so they bear the costs of appropriation and receive some of the benefits of resource provision. This becomes trickier in a cultural commons or knowledge commons (Madison et al. 2010; Frischmann et al. 2014), in which the users themselves coproduce the common-pool resource. With such a dynamic resource, the boundaries of the innovation commons themselves will be culturally constructed and maintained, cocreating insiders and outsiders.

The process of boundary creation—broadly identity discovery in relation to who and what: "Who is this for? Who is involved in making this?" and "What are the elements of this technology? What are its applications?"—is a key part of the value creation in an innovation commons. This proceeds as the identity of who and what cumulatively becomes less uncertain and protean to become sharper and more defined. Indeed, the resolution at which the resource is fully created (triggering the collapse of the innovation commons, à la the "fundamental transformation") occurs when the resource loses its ambiguity and opacity, becoming lucid as the opportunity is fully revealed.

Boundary creation and maintenance is a core design principle of the innovation commons. The process by which boundaries around users and resources are identified, staked out, and maintained is not necessarily done with fences and ramparts, as one might with a herd of pigs, but rather with their social and cultural equivalent, that is, names (Lotman 2009). Boundaries are semiotic in order to define social groups with respect to which your identity is that of an insider or an outsider (what Hartley and Potts [2014] call a "deme"). These can develop into sociological and institutional norms that transform into reputational assets (Baker and Bulkley 2014), intellectual property (O'Mahony 2003), or private-group property (von Hippel and von Krogh 2003; von Krogh et al. 2003).

Table 6.1 **Elaborated design rules**

Principle	*Description*
1A	User boundaries: boundaries between legitimate users and nonusers must be clearly defined.
1B	Resource boundaries: clear boundaries are present that define a resource system and separate it from the larger biophysical environment.
2A	Congruence with local conditions: appropriation and provision rules are congruent with local social and environmental conditions.
2B	Appropriation and provision: the benefits obtained by users from a common-pool resource, as determined by appropriation rules, are proportional to the amount of inputs required in the form of labor, material, or money, as determined by provision rules.
3	Collective-choice arrangements: most individuals affected by the operational rules can participate in modifying the operational rules.
4A	Monitoring users: monitors who are accountable to the users monitor the appropriation and provision levels of the users.
4B	Monitoring the resource: monitors who are accountable to the users monitor the condition of the resource.
5	Graduated sanctions: appropriators who violate operational rules are likely to be assessed graduated sanctions (depending on the seriousness and the context of the offense) by other appropriators, by officials accountable to the appropriators, or by both.
6	Conflict-resolution mechanisms: appropriators and their officials have rapid access to low-cost local arenas to resolve conflicts among appropriators or between appropriators and officials.
7	Minimal recognition of rights to organize: the rights of appropriators to devise their own institutions are not challenged by external governmental authorities.
8	Nested enterprises: appropriation, provision, monitoring, enforcement, conflict resolution, and governance activities are organized in multiple layers of nested enterprises.

Source: Reproduced from Cox et al. 2010.

Second, consider congruence with local conditions and proportional appropriation and provision (Agrawal 2002). An innovation commons is a cooperative, egalitarian space. What it gives up in the centralized benefits of control hierarchies it gains in its institutional ability to use local knowledge and adapt to local conditions. But to achieve this cooperative dynamically efficient outcome, an innovation commons must be understood to be fair. Fair does not necessarily mean equal: inequality is tolerable, and even desirable, to the extent that it is just. And justice means proportionality between effort and reward (à la Adam Smith: higher contributions to the group effort allow higher takings from the group product), or proportionality between capability and opportunity (à la Karl Marx: from all according to their abilities, to all according to their needs). These mappings of proportionality are social rules about joint production that account for local circumstances both of the individual people and of the social, cultural, technological, and physical environment. Such rules of governance make cooperation safe under robust conditions where you don't necessarily need to know too much about the other people or the environmental conditions, only whether the rules are in place, and are clear, respected and enforced. When cooperation is safe for you under such institutional conditions, you also know (by expectation) it is safe for others too, for the same reason, driving mutual expectation toward coordination on a cooperative equilibria. Common knowledge of general rules, widely respected, makes cooperation safe.

An innovation commons is an institutional outcome in which individuals strategically cooperate because they expect others to do so as well, resulting in mutual coordination on a cooperative equilibria. Technically, the mathematical structure of an innovation commons is therefore a *coordination game* (Coyne 2008) or a *stag hunt game* (Skyrms 2003; Tomasello 2009) and not that of the prisoner's dilemma (PD), because if you expect others to cooperate, your dominant strategy is also to cooperate (in the PD, your dominant strategy is always to defect, irrespective of what you expect others to do). This is why trust and communication matter so much in the stag hunt game, but not in the PD. Such mutual cooperation, however, is not necessarily altruistic, but can be powered by competition, specifically nonprice competition through status or reputational hierarchies in which individuals compete to be seen as valuable members of a community (Sigmund and Nowak 1998). As observed in previous chapters, there is ample evidence that this evolutionary mechanism operates in innovation commons, and with the effect of drawing local information and knowledge into the pool and promoting social learning and dissemination of that resource through the pool.

Third, consider collective choice arrangements, in which the rules of the commons need to be arrived at inclusively, nominated by, and with as close as possible to unanimous assent from, the group. The reason why supermajority consent matters is that, as a private ordering, an innovation commons fundamentally lacks coercive ability through which to enforce rules. Strong ex ante and publicly confirmed agreement to the rules therefore significantly increases the likelihood of rule-following and the efficacy of distributed monitoring, as well as reinforcing the mutual expectation of rule-following, which in turn lowers transaction costs of interaction within the innovation commons.

Mechanisms for collective choice arrangements often depend upon group assembly (e.g., townhall-type meetings), or on some proxy representative mechanism (e.g., a governing board that takes instruction from and reports back to the relevant community). For a common-pool resource that is fixed in place or potentially exists in perpetuity if well managed, collective choice arrangements can develop and adapt with the community around the resource. The problem with an innovation commons, in which the resource itself is what the community is producing, a community that is by nature temporary, is that collective choice arrangements do not necessarily have time to evolve and adapt to reflect a condition in which "most individuals affected by the operational rules can participate in modifying the operational rules" (Cox et al. 2010, 8).

Yet innovation commons can function remarkably well when individual commoners have a sense that decision-making processes are accessible through open invitations to participate, and transparent and legible through open forums with auditable trails. The open-source software community, for instance, functions with relatively centralized decision-making among a core of elite developers by making explicit a high level of transparency in such decision processes and open-access rules for community lobbying (O'Mahony and Ferraro 2007; Harhoff and Lakhani 2016). In turn, problems arise in such contexts when they depart from these principles.

Fourth, consider monitoring of users and resources. Any collective action problem presents a social dilemma (Hardin 1968) in which resolution will require monitoring the state of the resource and individual contributions to and takings from the pool. Monitoring needs to occur over the resource itself, and over the producers and users of the resource.[10] "Who" and "what" needs to be monitored: that is, the state of the resource as a *stock* (the what) and of the *flows* into and out of the stock (the who). Monitors can be commoners themselves, or they can be agents of the commoners who gather and report information on the state of the resource and behaviors of the resource users. Ostrom (1990) showed that community monitoring, or situations where the monitors were directly accountable to the community, produced the best outcomes. In contrast, situations where monitors were appointed by and reported to third parties (e.g., the local government) performed poorly because of weak or distorted incentives. Ostrom (2005, 259) further explained that monitoring works best when polycentric (i.e., nested and overlapping governance), so that the domain and method of monitoring are appropriate to the scale and local context of the resource. Efficient and appropriately incentivized monitoring is essential to resolve collective action problems in the commons.

Ostrom's predictions hold in the innovation commons too, but in an interesting way. Specifically, there are in an innovation commons powerful private incentives to monitor both the state of the resource and the continuous contributions made to it because of the unusual nature of the resource as a *prospect*—namely something that is of relatively low value (or, rather, subsidiary value) until it reaches a certain state of completion or maturity, namely the point at which the entrepreneurial opportunity is revealed, upon which it suddenly has very high value.[11] Marginal contributions to the pool can have outsized value, but no one knows which marginal contribution will be the final piece that completes the puzzle.

There are several models we might use. The simplest and most familiar is a model in which the supply curve for "opportunity discovery" (i.e., the commodity that is jointly produced in the innovation commons) is basically flat, until an ex ante unknown contribution x is made, at which point it becomes vertical. The probability of making contribution x is independent of the value of previous contributions, and because it is a unique event, it has an unknown distribution. Another model descriptive of the innovation commons as a joint but sequential production process is the self-organized critical sand-pile model (Bak et al. 1987), also known as the power-law model. In this conceptual approach, the probability of a marginal contribution revealing the entrepreneurial opportunity is analogous to the probability of a single grain of sand dropped onto the pile (each x) triggering a large "avalanche" in a complex system—in a power-law model, the probability of an "avalanche" of size x is basically $1/\log(x)$.

In a model of joint production of a *prospect* with an unknown probability distribution, private monitoring is not the problem because each agent has a strong incentive to continually scan the pool looking for the marginal contribution that completes the puzzle (recognizing that the person who made that contribution might himself not recognize it because, assuming bounded rationality and scarce attention, he might lack knowledge of other relevant information in the pool). Rather the problem is to create incentives to publicly reveal that private monitoring so that the monitoring itself becomes, as a common-pool resource, part of the pool.

A key part of Ostrom's (1990) breakthrough in understanding why the Hardin (1968) model of the tragedy of the commons and Olson's (1965) suspicion of interest groups might be misleading as a guide to policy action in escaping social dilemmas came in recognizing that communities are not institutionally stuck with the given "rules of the game" (North 1990) but can organize to create their own rules in relation to the bundle of rights associated with the common-pool resource in order to solve particular incentive problems (Tarko 2016, ch. 3). They can see the looming tragedy of the commons and then, as an ad hoc civil society, collectively devise institutions to mutually constrain and monitor each other's behavior so that the tragedy can be averted.

One such institution that is particularly important in an innovation commons is the development among the emergent community of *rules of revealing*, otherwise known as the meeting, workshop, seminar, colloquium, symposium, festival, tournament, or conference. This is an ancient institution (for instance, the seminar [from *seminarium*, Latin for seed plot], which took place in the agora, αγορα, meaning "gathering place, or assembly" in ancient Greek, was a key institution in Greek civilization), critical to any situation of joint knowledge production under uncertainty. The rules of revealing in an innovation commons, like those of a seminar, are designed to make what could risk being a prisoner's dilemma into a stag hunt game by furnishing an institutional expectation of coordinated mutual revelation of your information and knowledge combined with comment (sometimes critique) of other's information and knowledge, also revealed, and to set up systems of social reward (prestige, reputation) for those who share and contribute the most. The rowdy criticism and sometimes vain posturing of an academic conference, as with the ancient agora that gave us modern democracy as well as the modern university, is the outcome of an ingenious system of institutional rules to prevent secrecy and to incentivize the public revealing of private monitoring. An innovation commons, when effective, runs on the same institutional rules.

Fifth, consider graduated sanctions, which Ostrom (1990) discovered were a widespread feature in successful governance of common-pool resources that related monitoring rule violations to effective punishment. The key idea is proportionality between infractions and punishments, which is important both for efficiency (free riding is costly to the group, but so too is punishment) and also for perceptions of fairness and justice. Agents in the commons may violate rules for complex reasons, not all of which will be unambiguously opportunistic, and some may be a result of error or misunderstanding of the rules. Graduated sanctions also allow the technology of punishment to be adapted to the scale of the transgression, with social communication technologies, such as gossip or shaming, deployed in a distributed and low-cost manner (Fehr and Gachter 2002), with organizational technologies, such as exclusion from group events (such as meetings) deployed in more severe cases, and use of legal technologies (such as lawsuits) threatened in the most extreme cases. Obviously, while the cost and objectivity of the sanction rises along this graduated continuum, so too does the extent to which the innovation commons community needs to coordinate in order to deliver the sanction. Gossip and shaming for low-level norm violations can be delivered largely without coordination, although they gain strength when they are communicated or coordinated. By contrast, a full legal banishment requires a high level of community consensus in order to carry force.

The further significance of graduated sanctions is that by maintaining the reserve option of low-level distributed punishment, delivered by citizen monitors, the rules of the innovation commons become manifest rules-in-use, rather than more abstract rules-in-form. Graduated sanctions in this sense are also elements of community maintenance, ensuring that small trespasses do not escalate into group-threatening actions and response. This is particularly important in an innovation commons, which will often be an ad hoc temporary commons, the governance of which can be especially vulnerable to unraveling (due to backward induction—if I think the end is imminent, I might as well defect [i.e., withdraw cooperation] soon, but if I think that, then it is reasonable that I think that you are thinking it already, and so I should defect now).

Again, this points to the significance of the performative agora to the innovation commons (the public gatherings as meetings, meetups, workshops, seminars, colloquia, symposia, festivals, tournaments, or conferences) in which pooling, communication, and monitoring take place, but also community norms and values can be observed and enacted and public punishments can occur. Some of these may be ritualistic, such as a collective denunciation, but they can be subtle, such as observing the conspicuous absence of a particular party or simply as an efficient opportunity to gossip. Online forums, which can be quasi-anonymous, can be particularly efficient communication mechanisms for gossip, and therefore as vectors for punishment. An example is the cypherpunk community, an effective innovation commons from the 1990s. The Cypherpunk Electronic Mailing list was started by Timothy May in 1992, and with its constitution laid out in the *Cyphernomicon* (May 1994), was a forum for several thousand at its peak in 1997. While rightfully known as a powerful community that was able to galvanize a movement around the importance of online privacy, including issuing lawsuits against alleged unconstitutional actions by the US government, what is also striking, as discussed in Rid (2016) (and fictionalized in Neal Stephenson's 1999 novel *Cryptonomicon*) is the intensely strong community bonds that formed within the group, and the high frequency and robustness of its internal communication.

Sixth, consider conflict resolution mechanisms. In Ostrom's (1990) meta-analysis, an essential institutional feature of a successful commons is low-cost arenas for timely and effective resolution of inevitable conflict among users of a common-pool resource, or between users and those monitoring and governing the resource. Because conflict resolution is organizationally intensive and tends not to scale, Ostrom recognized that this aspect tended to limit the size of effective commons.[12]

However, many instances of knowledge commons (Hess and Ostrom 2003; Ostrom and Hess 2006b; Frischmann et al. 2014), such as open-source software communities, are by design global in scope but nevertheless need to develop adjudicating forums for conflict resolution. What tends to happen in globally scaled knowledge commons is that rather than a centralized or hierarchical mode of dispute resolution, they have much more polycentric or network-based modes of dispute resolution in which the dispute is allocated to the lowest level on the network at which it can be addressed, but passes to higher-level forums through a distributed network process of "up-voting" that occurs as many members of a community recognize and signal the importance of the conflict, or in which many members of the community find themselves having the same conflict (Lessig 2001; Benkler 2006).

Innovation commons, as a species of knowledge commons, tend not to be particularly good at dealing with conflict, as indicated in section 6.3, because the exit option is always looming and many types of conflict are not about the allocation of a finite resource, but about directions for future development and therefore the best deployment of the shared resource. Conflict does not necessarily have a resolution in *justice* (i.e., as the outcome of wise arbitration) but may only be resolved in time by *experiment*. Irresolvable conflict may therefore represent an efficient mechanism of subdividing the search space, with different communities following different hypotheses. A recent example in the bitcoin/blockchain community is the block size debate, with one group wanting to retain the existing 1 MB block size, with another coalition seeking a much larger block size. Innovation commons tend to fork at the point of conflict (i.e., with two different versions of the blockchain going forward with different block sizes, and then letting economic selection decide.

Seventh, recognition of rights to organize (local autonomy) is an essential and necessary feature of the relation between a commons and its sociopolitical, cultural, and legal environment. A commons is a civil society action in which a group of people *makes their own rules* in order to govern a common-pool resource. Except in trivial instances these rules will be different to the prevailing milieu of rules, reflecting the idiosyncratic and particular details of the resource, the context, the community, and other such "local conditions of time and place" (à la Hayek 1945). These characteristic differences will also reflect the positive creations that have been made by the group in order to create property rights where none previously existed, or to modify existing rights to better fit the needs of the community (à la Demsetz's [1967] and Alchian and Demstez [1972] notion of property as a bundle of rights). It therefore matters whether and to what extent these governing rules and their reinterpretations of property rights are recognized and legitimated by external authorities and prevailing institutions, and at what cost.

Local autonomy to create a collective choice arena is a necessary constitutional principle for any successful commons. While the seventh of Ostrom's eight core design principles, it is in a very basic sense the foundational principle: it is the rule that creates the possibility of rules for governing the commons. Yet this abstract ideal (viz., the right to organize) actually has very specific two-part meaning in practice: first, it means a mutual decision by the prospective commoners to, as it were, *secede* from an existing arrangement and to *reform* with a new arrangement of rules with respect to the common-pool resource; and second, it also means and requires *external recognition* of that secession and reformation, thus granting legitimate local authority.

Unlike nation-state secessionist movements, however, where a group seeks to redraw a national boundary (e.g., usually resulting in a civil war conflict), the emergence of a commons is a type of nonterritorial secession (MacDonald 2015) where a group seeks to change the governance arrangements for a particular resource or property within a territory, leaving other property and boundaries unchanged. The emergence of a commons is a collective action by the group of commoners, but it also needs to be, in a sense, permissioned by the residual society and polity. It one sense this is the *subsidiarity principle*[13] stating that matters should always be handled at the smallest or lowest competent level of authority. This will often be resisted by higher-order authorities (e.g., local and national governments) who, swayed neither by the moral argument from social philosophy nor by the argument from economic efficiency, may nevertheless rightly perceive the reformation of property rights and locus of decision-making as a costly loss of authority and domain of control. The impetus for self-governance over local resources is a hardy perennial that breaks through the cracks of each and every site of inefficiency in private property and public provision.[14] But it is continuously vulnerable to top-down disruption through harassment or outright hostility (Leeson 2014).

An innovation commons will not tend to meet these issues in jurisdictional disputes about land boundaries access rights to watersheds, or the rights of communities to self-organize to educate their children. But innovation commons do tend to run into very specific employment contract disputes and what is permissible while earning a salary at a private or publicly funded organization, and to what extent the things done while in those contracted roles can be rereleased into the commons. Private firms, public corporations, universities, and public science institutes tend to have systematically different attitudes to these in general, as well as differences through time and between nations. Innovation commons therefore tend to look and behave differently through time and space as they seek out viable niches they can occupy (temporarily) to maximize institutional support and minimize institutional harassment and molestation.

Traditionally, universities have provided the most fecund and secure home for innovation commons. This seems to be for two reasons. First, university employment contracts are generally loose enough that they can permit the allocation of time and local research resources (e.g., laboratories, libraries) and organizational infrastructure (e.g., for seminars, workshops). Second, universities have traditionally worked hard to create enclaves that resist influence from government priorities and thus retain independence that can shelter an innovation commons. It has often been observed in the economic geography of innovation literature (e.g., Audretsch and Feldman 1996) that clusters of new industries tend to begin in regions dominated by high-quality universities. This is usually attributed to knowledge spillovers. But an alternative explanation is that the institutional cover created by a high-quality university also creates a fertile environment for innovation commons to form.

Eighth, relatedly, consider *nested enterprises*, which is an expression of the *polycentricity principle* in which "appropriation, provision, monitoring, enforcement, conflict resolution, and governance activities are organized in multiple layers of nested enterprises" (Ostrom 2005, 259). This recognizes that the independence of the commons granted in core design principle 7 (local autonomy) is not absolute, but is conditional upon effective embedding of that commons and its rules of governance in broader social, technological, legal, cultural, and economic systems. No commons is an island. Every commons needs appropriate relations with other groups, groups that will invariably exist at multiple different scales.

So it is with a successful innovation commons. An innovation commons will need to have effective relations with other groups and systems at scales different from its own, for several reasons. An obvious need is to acquire resources, much of which acquisition occurs not through trade and exchange, but through inducement to join, which in turn means that appropriate relationships are really about managing the commons' external and collective reputation, and in particular its prestige, or reputation for quality. (Note that a university has a similar challenge, and for similar reasons; further indicating the basis of the natural symbiosis between an innovation commons and a research university.) A further reason is specialization and, in a sense, the ability of the commons to exploit the surplus resources afforded by other higher-order organizational forms. An innovation commons will often seek to pool information and resources that have been created and controlled by other organizations, such as research from private firms or public science organizations. The innovation commons benefits from its ability to pool, or to broker access to, this information. The Homebrew Computer Club meetings, for example, were originally held in Gordon French's garage in Menlo Park, but soon moved to an auditorium in the Stanford Linear Accelerator Centre, operated by Stanford University. This gave this fledgling innovation commons access to the considerable electrical engineering and programming resources gathered at Stanford University.

A further development is bridging institutions that enable an innovation commons to interact with the broader world on its own terms. An example is Creative Commons licensing, a copyright licensing institution that emerged in 2001 from Harvard University's Berkman Centre for Internet and Society, championed by Larry Lessig. The Creative Commons license for open sharing was based on the Free Software Foundation's GNU General Public License.

Creative Commons is a way for someone to put something into an innovation commons, and to ensure that it stays there through subsequent iterations and developments. It's a way for an innovation commons to interact safely with other institutions by expressing its values in legible outward-facing legal terms.

In section 6.1 we saw why cooperation occurs in the innovation commons, namely uncertainty. In 6.2 we saw how an innovation commons harnesses this evolved human behavior, and in 6.3 how an innovation commons can be an efficient institution for solving the problem of pooling knowledge under uncertainty for discovery. In 6.4 we looked at the problems the innovation commons needs to solve, and in 6.5 and 6.6 we explored the origin of these rules and mapped them to Ostrom's core design principles. Considered individually, the core design principles closely map to the rules of governance observed in the innovation commons. Before concluding this chapter, I make one further extension to this line of analysis, which is to position the innovation commons in a broader evolutionary framework, an idea first proposed by Wilson, Ostrom, and Cox (2013), who noted the similarity between Ostrom's CDPs and the tenets of multilevel selection theory. To what extent can the innovation commons be explained not as institutional entrepreneurship, but as the outcome of an evolutionary process?

6.7 Can Evolution Explain the Innovation Commons?

The innovation commons is an outcome of a collective action to resolve a social dilemma in which players—the commoners—by pooling their innovation information and resources are choosing to mutually *cooperate*. For an innovation commons to emerge and function, such mutual cooperation must prevail. Economics is almost notoriously a study of individual action resulting in emergent group-level phenomena, such as the output of a firm, industry, or macroeconomy, or the order of a market. There is not much in the way of a theory of *groups* in economics (cf. Frijters and Foster 2013), nor for that matter in innovation studies, which take the innovating firm as the individual unit, and whose behavior is to be explained. So where do cooperating groups of innovators come from? Interestingly, a near identical question, mutatis mutandis, stalks biology in the puzzle of how to explain *altruism*—or individually costly behavior that is good (i.e., has a selective advantage) for the group. I want to suggest that the same theory that evolutionary biology uses to explain cooperation can also be used to explain the origin of the innovation commons, namely *multilevel selection theory* (Wilson et al. 2013).

Evolution of Cooperation

Cooperation is an evolutionary puzzle because it is unstable. A population of pure cooperators can be invaded by a mutant defector, who receives the benefits of interacting with cooperators (i.e., suckers) but pays none of the costs of cooperation. With such a payoff advantage, defectors will increase in frequency in the population: that is, under evolutionary selection pressure, cooperation will collapse in the population (Williams 1966). The first major advance in the evolutionary theory of cooperation was the theory of *kin selection*, developed by Hamilton (1963, 1964), and popularized in Richard Dawkins's "selfish gene" formulation. Kin selection theory said that altruism (cooperation between phenotypes) was not a puzzle at all from a genetic perspective, and that cooperation could be explained as a function of genetic relatedness. The study of social insects (a colony of bees, for instance, is mostly made of sisters) confirmed that theory. But that theory didn't really explain the broad swathes of mammalian and human cooperation, which extends well beyond nonkin.

The next advances in the evolutionary understanding of cooperation were the theories of direct and then indirect *reciprocity* (Trivers 1971). The idea that reciprocity could explain cooperation came from the study of cooperation in a social context, and specifically that of a repeated game (Maynard Smith 1976; Nowak 2006b). Repeated games were an old mathematical model being newly studied using computer simulations (Axelrod and Hamilton 1982; Axelrod 1984). Direct reciprocity harnesses strategic interaction with learning, in which one player has the opportunity to punish a defecting player by defecting herself in a subsequent round of repeated play.[15] Strategies of mutual cooperation can evolve through reward-and-punishment feedback processes. This was a key element in Ostrom's explanation for how a commons can escape the tragedy predicted by Hardin (1968), an argument she learned from Reinhard Selten, an economist and game theorist (and fellow Nobel laureate). *Indirect reciprocity* (Nowak and Sigmund 1998) extends this to third parties, such that A cooperates with B because A observed B cooperating with C, and thus infers that B is a cooperating type. The mechanism of indirect reciprocity requires honest communication and accumulation of reputation signals that can be "read" by third parties. This attention to conspicuous cooperation and monitoring, and to the accumulation of reputational currencies, is widely observed in human social interaction (Bowles and Gintis 2005, 2013), and is thereby an unsurprising component of the innovation commons.

But the story I want to focus on here concerns the role of *group selection* (known these days more accurately as *multilevel selection*) as an evolutionary explanation for cooperation. Group selection is actually the original model of altruistic behavior as argued by the Russian prince and early evolutionary theorist Peter Kropotkin, by the zoologist V. C. Wynne-Edwards, and the pioneering evolutionary animal behavioralist Konrad Lorenz. However, as John Maynard Smith and William Hamilton argued in the 1960s, they were all wrong to the extent that they did not account for individual selection within the group. In short, a cooperative group could be strategically invaded.[16]

For the next several decades, it seemed that group selection theory had been firmly ejected from evolutionary thinking.[17] But in the past decade or so it has made a striking comeback under the heading of multilevel selection theory, broadly led by zoologist and evolutionary biologist David Sloan Wilson and colleagues (Wilson and Sober 1994; Wilson and Wilson 2008), and the mathematical biologist Martin Nowak and colleagues (Nowak 2006b, 2011; Nowak et al. 2010).[18] The basic argument, as succinctly explained by Peter Turchin (2015, ch. 4), is that "competition within groups destroys cooperation, but competition between groups creates cooperation."

Multilevel selection models are a way to represent the conditions under which a trait (A) will evolve in a population by decomposing the costs and benefits of the trait into two covariance terms that relate individual fitness to group fitness (Price 1972). In this formulation $A = 1/r[\mathrm{Cov}(r_j A_j) + \mathrm{Cov}(r_{ij} A_{ij})]$ in which A_j = group-level average of characteristics; A_{ij} = individual value of characteristics; r_j, and r_{ij} = population and group average reproduction coefficients. The trait of interest here is cooperation, and the first covariance term in the Price equation predicts that this costly trait will be selected out in a single population. However, the second covariance term indicates that if there is sufficient variance in the levels of cooperation between groups, then a cooperative trait will evolve in a population if

$$A\left(\frac{\text{between group variance}}{\text{within group variance}}\right) > A\left(\frac{\text{selection strength on individuals}}{\text{selection strength on groups}}\right).$$

When variation in cooperation is concentrated at the group level, selection will strongly favor cooperative groups, and cooperation (the trait under selection) will evolve. The more cooperators are able to assortively match, which in turn leads to greater variation in group-level cooperation (cooperation evolves when groups are as different as possible), the stronger will be selection for cooperation.

The early proponents of group selection (e.g., Wynne-Edwards, Lorenz) failed to understand how important between-group variation is, or how difficult it is to maintain group difference in face of migration and free riding (Turchin 2015). But *Homo sapiens* are very good at maintaining cooperation in the presence of incentives to defection through culture and institutions (Henrich 2015). Multilevel selection works powerfully on cultural animals, because they can make groups (Hartley and Potts 2014). This is the essence of the eusocial model of evolutionary selection of cooperative behavior (Nowak et al. 2010).

Multilevel selection can in this way illustrate the conditions under which the innovation commons, as a cooperative social technology of alertness—that is, a group trait—can outcompete individual alertness by revealing deeper opportunities for innovation. The main game theoretic findings are that group selection can favor individually costly (cooperative) behavior only when the underlying game is not prisoner's dilemma and when groups are assortive (Bergstrom 2002). Both conditions apply in the innovation commons. This model predicts that societies and cultures that can marshal this form of institutional cooperation in order to discover opportunities to subsequently compete in markets will be more economically successful than societies with only individual-level entrepreneurial alertness.

Multilevel selection is the idea that competition and differential selection operate not only between individuals, but also between groups (Wilson and Sober 1994; Sober and Wilson 1998; Nowak 2006a, 2006b; Wilson and Wilson 2007). The theory explains how cooperation evolves when the selection force operating between groups is stronger than the selection force operating within groups. *Lower-order selection* operates within groups, predicting that selfish individuals will outcompete altruists. *Higher-order selection* operates between groups and predicts that groups of altruists (cooperative agents) will outcompete groups of selfish agents. The evolutionary success of cooperators therefore depends on the relative strength of competitive selection operating within groups (lower-order selection) versus selection between groups (higher-order selection). When between-group selection dominates within-group selection, we will tend to observe an evolutionary transition and the emergence of a higher-level organism (Maynard-Smith and Szathmary 1995; Wilson et al. 2007). This usually requires powerful mechanisms to suppress conflict or competition within a group—using, for example, docility (Simon 2005), punishment (Bowles and Gintis 2005), morality (Haidt 2007), or coordination on an external threat (Van Vugt 2006; Turchin 2015; Taylor 2016). As Traulsen and Nowak (2006, 10952) explain: "Group selection is an important organizing principle that permeates evolutionary processes from the emergence of the first cells to eusociality and the economics of nations." It also explains the emergence of innovation commons.

Evolution of Cooperation in the Commons

Wilson, Ostrom, and Cox (2013, 23) noticed that the Ostrom's (1990) eight core design principles (CDPs), "when viewed from a multilevel evolutionary perspective . . . provide an ideal social environment for the evolution of group-level adaptations in any social species and for a wide range of contexts in our own species." They used this argument to search for evolutionary adaptations consistent with the predictions of the CDPs, finding a wide range of empirical and theoretical support for the evolution of group-making cultural adaptations (Boyd and Richerson 1992; Gintis et al. 2001; Fehr and Gächter 2002; Boehm 2012).

The evolution of group-making cultural adaptations enables group-selection mechanisms to gain purchase. Wilson et al. (2013, 27) explain that "when a group possesses the core design principles, the opportunities for some members to benefit at the expense of others become extremely limited. Succeeding as a group becomes the only remaining option." When you are in a group that is protected by the CDPs it becomes safe to be cooperative and empathetic: the rules of the commons protect members from exploitation by defectors. Cooperation and its mutual expectation are themselves common-pool resources.

Rules of governance are in this sense group-making adaptations that coevolve with the products of those groups. This is the theory of cultural evolution (Bowles et al. 2003; Richerson et al. 2003; Henrich 2004; Mesoudi 2011). This is, in essence, is the logic behind Hayek's theory of cultural evolution and cultural group selection (Hayek 1960, 1973). While there are multiple genetically inherited cognitive and behavioral adaptations that facilitate group formation in humans, the cultural ability to make and use rules for social coordination and group formation is the gateway to modern economic evolution (Dopfer 2004; Doper and Potts 2008; Hartley and Potts 2014). The innovation commons is a continuation of that same evolutionary process of institutional rule-making and rule-using to create a self-governing group in which cooperation for innovation is made safe.

When task complexity exceeds individual capability, cooperation is an adaptive response. But cooperation is not free; it is costly and requires special conditions for cooperative groups to emerge.[19] The evolutionary function of culture is to make groups. In game theory, institutions are modeled as solutions to coordination problems (Aoki 2007), but they are also group-making rules that can, when they incentivize cooperation, increase the success of groups.

Is Cooperation for Innovation the Institutional Equivalent of War?

How did humans evolve to be such a highly cooperative species?[20] The surprising answer is war (Turchin 2007, 2015; Bowles and Gintis 2011). Intertribal war requires high within-group cooperation. Cooperative groups can outcompete less cooperative groups, take their resources, and expand. While it remains true that individuals compete for resources within tribes, in which cooperators will generally lose to free-riders, it is also the case that tribes compete against other tribes. The more cooperators within a tribe, the more likely it will defeat a tribe with fewer cooperators. This is an evolutionary process in which cooperative traits evolve under conditions of intertribal war, which is descriptive of the human ancestral environment.[21]

Now translate this argument into the space of innovation. Innovators compete within a nation (e.g., patenting discoveries, forming private companies, and so on). Innovators that cooperate by sharing ideas will generally lose to those who free-ride, exploiting these ideas without paying the costs of discovery of opportunity and research and development. But nations also compete on innovation (the Schumpeterian hypothesis), and nations with more cooperators will discover more opportunities for private exploitation, and thus could outcompete nations with fewer innovation cooperators. Strong competitive incentives for innovation within a nation could actually lower innovation because those same incentives constrain group-level discovery of new opportunities. A more cooperative group could outcompete a more competitive group. The key to resolving this seeming paradox here is the Price equation $(A = 1/r[Cov(r_j A_j) + Cov(r_{ij} A_{ij})])$, and recognizing that there are two selection forces operating simultaneously (within group and between group) and which force is strongest will determine the net outcome. Under global innovation competition, cooperative innovators (with efficacious rules for governing the innovation commons) will likely outcompete competitive innovators!

The role of institutions for innovation, then, is not simply to incentivize investment in R & D that would otherwise be undersupplied in a competitive market. Rather, the role of institutions of innovation is to furnish the institutions to facilitate cooperation in pooling and sharing information and other discovery resources from behind the veil of ignorance about the proximate shape of the entrepreneurial opportunity.

The Innovation Commons as Higher-Order Discovery

This multilevel-selection argument makes a specific claim about the nature of entrepreneurial opportunity discovery that, interestingly, suggests a refinement of Kirzner's (1973) model of entrepreneurial discovery. Kirzner's approach is methodologically individualist and oriented within market institutions. The entrepreneur is alert to new information in relative prices and price movements, and it is from this information that plans for entrepreneurial action emerge in a newly conceptualized innovation design space.

However, as Lavoie (2004, 34) explains, "Markets are an extension of language," and entrepreneurial action depends upon an extraction of meaning from a context. For Lavoie (2001, 12), "The 'seeing' of an entrepreneurial opportunity is best understood not as perception, but as a kind of reading of a meaningful situation in a language-constituted world." An innovation commons is not a market institution (there are no prices). But like a market, it is a mechanism to facilitate entrepreneurial discovery of opportunities in the Kirznerian sense of reading the opportunity in the messages and meanings generated by the institution. These opportunities are not revealed by alertness to relative prices or price changes, but by alertness to the constructed meanings that emerge from the pool of information and knowledge in the innovation commons, and by the meanings discerned and inferred from within the community.

The innovation commons *augments* the institutions of market discovery with a higher-order discovery mechanism to pool and create information that would otherwise not be available to any potential entrepreneur. The information and messages generated by the innovation commons have a higher order of complexity than information created or read by an individual entrepreneur (Foster 2005). An innovation commons is in this sense an emergent *cooperative social technology of alertness* that complements competitive individual alertness in markets, but is also, under conditions of high uncertainty, a more computationally complex and adaptively efficient institutional technology.

In the standard economic model of innovation a single level of selection operates over firms, leading to differential growth at the population level of the industry. Innovation is competitive, modeled through the metaphor of competitive selection, or a competitive race or tournament (Alchain 1950; Loury 1979). No other levels of selection are at work, nor are there collective action problems to resolve. Even open innovation is framed as extensions of firms—implicitly conceived as the locus of innovation—into networks of exchanges (Dahlander and Gann 2010) rather than as Coasean inquiry into the relative efficiency of different institutions for innovation (Ostrom 2005; Ostrom and Hess 2006a). The standard model elucidates neither the logic nor the distribution of cooperative and competitive institutions of innovation.

A multilevel selection model shows how the innovation commons, as a cooperative social technology of alertness, can outcompete individual Kirznerian alertness. An innovation commons is an institutionally evolved or more complex emergent form of Kirznerian pure entrepreneurial alertness. It extends beyond simple arbitrage opportunities to process distributed knowledge requiring coordination and governance to reveal deeper opportunities for innovation.

The "innovation commons as higher-order discovery" model predicts that societies and cultures that can marshal this form of institutional cooperation (as a "social technology of alertness") in order to discover opportunities that will subsequently compete in markets, will likely be more successful than societies with only individual-level entrepreneurial alertness (which in turn are more successful than societies without entrepreneurial alertness). In itself, this suggests that the emergence of institutions for cooperation in innovation, even among small groups, would have marked the origins of the modern economy (Mokyr 2016).

6.8 Conclusion: We Innovate Together

Innovation benefits from cooperation because it pools innovation resources (including information) under uncertainty. This promotes discovery of opportunity, an outcome that is good for the group as well as for individuals in that group. But that cooperation requires rules in order to solve collective action problems. The sorts of rules that can induce such cooperation tend to have a structure that Ostrom (1990) mapped out in terms of eight core design principles. This appears true in the innovation commons too. Innovation begins as a group activity, and it is the origin of these groups, or more specifically the institutions that construct them, that innovation scholars should seek to understand.

The origin of these groups—the innovation commons—can be explained as an evolutionary outcome of a multilevel selection process. The central idea of multilevel selection theory is that groups matter. In any generalized population, selfish actors will always defeat cooperators because cooperators pay the price of cooperation but don't get the exclusive benefit, while defectors gain the benefit without paying the price. This is the tragedy of the commons, which is a competitive Nash equilibrium. Multilevel selection theory explains how cooperators can win when they form functional groups. This group must solve the same problem, namely suppressing the free-riding payoff, by whatever means. When it can do this and the solution is stable, a cooperative group can outcompete a competitive group. Evolutionary theory uses this logic to show how cooperation can evolve (Wilson and Wilson 2007; Nowak 2011; Turchin 2015), and multilevel selection theory similarly shows how the innovation commons can emerge. Societies with this cooperative social technology of alertness will outcompete societies that depend on individual Kirznerian alertness. In other words, just as there is higher-order capital (Harper and Endres 2010), and societies with it are richer than societies without, there can also be higher-order institutional mechanisms of entrepreneurial discovery, and societies that can harness this technology will be at an entrepreneurial discovery advantage over societies that have not yet evolved to this emergent complex state.

From an evolutionary perspective, innovation commons will likely form unless blocked (Juma 2016). The scale and effectiveness will depend upon communication and coordination technologies, and the constraints of resources and substitutes. Economic forces point in the direction of innovation commons forming, because they are generally more efficient than alternative institutions. Sociocultural forces also point in the direction of innovation commons forming, because we are broadly a cooperative species. And innovation commons do form repeatedly, engendering economic evolution across multiple scales of time and space. Yet innovation does not happen everywhere. Though global history, innovation has not happened at all times. If my thesis is correct, this is because innovation commons have failed in these times and places. Why is that? We consider this in the next chapter.

Notes

1. Mirowski (2001) furnishes a superb narrative history of "how economics became a cyborg science," including the germinal role of Hayek's metaphor of the market mechanism as distributed computation.
2. A catallaxy is "a special kind of spontaneous order produced by the market through people acting within the rules of the law of property, tort and contract" (Hayek 1973, 109).
3. http://www.thingiverse.com/. See Moilanen et al. (2014).
4. Differences in ex ante valuation are not necessarily a barrier to pool formation where the rules of the commons permit differential classes of contribution and access, but that still requires mutual recognition of those differences.
5. Prestige economies work by biasing social learning of new entrants toward those with prestige, where prestige is a form of noncoerced status granted in social learning contexts (Henrich and Gil-White 2001).
6. Perhaps enhanced through self-deception (Trivers 2011).
7. http://www.coindesk.com/.
8. Exaptations are adaptations that, evolved for one function, are ex-adapted for a new purpose, as feathers adapted for thermal insulation on dinosaurs were selected for flight on birds. See Buss et al. (1998).
9. This approach is known more broadly as the Bloomington school of institutional economics (Aligica and Boettke 2009; Tarko 2016).
10. "Monitors may not perform satisfactorily if they do not directly benefit from improved resource conditions. Thus, it may be important that monitors are accountable to those who most depend on the resource" (Cox et al. 2010, 9).
11. Like a model of self-organized criticality, or a tipping-point model (Schelling 1978, as popularized by Gladwell 2000).
12. This is analogous to Olson's (1965) recognition that the optimal size of effective rent-seeking groups will tend to be small because unresolved conflict leads to breakaway actions or otherwise licenses or is resolved with free riding.
13. A doctrine of Roman Catholic law, from Pope Pius XI's 1931 encyclical *Quadragesemo anno*.
14. A useful resource to provide an overview of the range of commons and common-pool resources is the Digital Library of the Commons: https://dlc.dlib.indiana.edu/dlc/.
15. This is a simple strategy called "tit-for-tat," as entered by the mathematical psychologist Anatol Rapoport in the first of Axelrod's computer tournaments. Tit-for-tat emerged as the clear winner against far more complex strategies. The only way to beat tit-for-tat is not to punish at all (Dreber et al. 2008).
16. A type of equilibrium first described by the mathematician and economics Nobel laureate John Nash.
17. A movement popularly associated with Richard Dawkins and the framework of universal Darwinism.
18. Multilevel selection is an extension of the replicator equation in which selection operates on variety within a population and between interacting groups (Lotka-Volterra-type coevolutionary models) (Bowles et al. 2003).
19. Jones (2015) finds that people who do well on IQ tests tend to be better at being cooperative, a phenomenon he calls "Coasian intelligence," reflecting the win-win outcomes

that tend to arrive when people are free to bargain and negotiate, regardless of starting positions.

20. We are one of only a handful of *eusocial* species in all of nature, along with the Hymenoptera (bees, wasps, ants), termites, and the naked mole-rat.
21. Pinker (2012) explains this as occurring when selection on groups is stronger than selection within groups (see section 6.1).

7

Life Cycle of an Innovation Commons

Consider an innovation commons over the full course of an innovation trajectory, from the emergence of a new industry to maturity. Innovation commons resolve the collective action problem that enthusiasts and proponents of a new technology face in figuring out the shape of the entrepreneurial opportunity, the design space for innovation. The relevant information needed to resolve the opportunity is partial, distributed, and shrouded in uncertainty. Each individual faces not only uncertainty, but what Kirzner (1973) calls "sheer ignorance." However, the situation is usually better within a group because each person will have different specializations, experiences, and perspectives; therefore, pooling that information will help resolve ignorance and uncertainty.

The theory of the innovation commons claims that any such pool faces a collective action problem and will require *governance* to facilitate cooperation in order to pool the distributed information and resources. Two predictions follow: (1) innovation commons occur at the origin of all Schumpeterian innovation trajectories; and (2) innovation commons collapse when entrepreneurial firms emerge.

Now consider what happens to an innovation commons after the collapse. When an innovation commons collapses, it does not disperse but, under certain conditions, will transform into a different and more club-like institutional form. Moreover, this new form serves a new evolutionary function, no longer expressly concerned with information pooling for entrepreneurial purposes, but with the new function of industrial *niche construction*. I propose a new theory of the origin of industry associations as an outworking of the life cycle of the innovation commons.

Both functions—innovation commons for pooling entrepreneurial information for industry discovery, and industry association for industrial niche construction—are governance solutions to collective action problems associated with technological dynamics. These institutional and organizational forms are largely neglected in standard models of technological trajectories and industrial dynamics, which tend to ignore private orderings and institutional governance. In chapter 5 I developed the idea of the innovation commons as the missing "zeroth phase" of the three-phase Schumpeterian innovation trajectory. One reason this zeroth phase has been analytically overlooked is it has a different governance structure (the commons, a private ordering) than subsequent phases (firms, markets and governments). Private orderings are often opaque and institutionally illegible (Scott 1998) because they tend to be visible to and valued by only those involved in them.

The governance of a technological trajectory—a private ordering of rules to solve collective action problems—evolves as a historical process (and thus we can think of it as a *life cycle*), the first phase of which is the innovation commons. The second phase is the industry association (broadly understood as private, voluntary, industry-level cooperation), and the third phase is sociocultural embedding. This *evolutionary governance approach* to the technological trajectory elucidates several distinct institutional phases of coordination that occur as a technology develops in response to different critical problems at each phase of the trajectory. The life cycle of the innovation commons also emphasizes the complexities and challenges of innovation policy, which must adapt to these institutional dynamics, a theme I explore in chapter 8.

7.1 Institutions of Collective Innovation

The innovation problem is actually two distinct economic problems: an allocation or investment problem (over society's scarce resources), and a coordination or collective action problem (over groups of people). *Collective innovation* describes the institutional space of the second formulation of this problem, namely the institutional variety of private ordering (as opposed to public ordering or government) solutions to the innovation problem. In this view, the innovation problem is really how a group of people can figure out how to work together to create a local public good. The scale of this "group of people" ranges from a small group coming together to make a firm, to a large group coming together to make an industry, to an encompassing group coming together to make a national innovation system.[1]

Institutional Varieties of Collective Innovation

In modern economic literature, the principal and predominant institution of collective innovation is Schumpeter's *innovating firm*: a hierarchical governance structure built on an entrepreneurial vision to organize resources into innovation capabilities. At the other pole, at the level of government policy, are the institutions of *national innovation systems* (Lundvall 1992; Nelson 1993; Freeman 1995). Between innovating firms and innovation policy, many other institutional forms of collective innovation have also been identified. These include: collective invention; user innovation; open innovation; private collectives; innovation networks; common innovation; the sharing economy; and, as the latest specimen within this institutional bestiary, the *innovation commons* and its subsequent transformation into *industry associations* (see table 7.1).

In the simple textbook model of the innovation problem, the institutional ecology consists of just firms, markets, and governments. Innovating firms engage in Schumpeterian competition in markets, but because of externalities and indivisibilities in private investment, there is a role for government policy to correct the expected market failure (Arrow 1962b; Dasgupta and David 1994; Martin and Scott 2000). What table 7.1 profiles is the broader range of institutional variety in collective innovation governance beyond firms and governments, and into which we locate the broad subject matter of this book—innovation commons—and the subject matter of this chapter: the dynamics of an innovation commons over the course of an industrial or technological trajectory, or what we call here the *life cycle of an innovation commons*.

The variety of institutional forms of collective innovation forms a *complex evolved institutional ecology* in the sense that all of these institutional forms exist simultaneously and interdependently. Moreover, the interdependence relationship will be dynamic, or coevolutionary. The innovating firm will exist in, and be in part dependent upon, an environment of user innovation and open innovation, while at the same time user innovation and open innovation will depend upon the existence of innovating firms: each will be the selection environment for the other.

There are varieties of forms that compose the institutional ecology of innovation, with relative populations and differing significance of each. Ostrom (2005) emphasized that analysis of institutional diversity is central to the study of natural resource economies. This is also true for "artificial resource economies" (or knowledge economies) for the same reason, namely that institutional variation is an adaptive response to environmental variation. Hodgson (2015) makes this same point in a more general context, namely that the economic institutions of capitalism are complex and an outcome of evolutionary adaptation. This is also true of the institutions of innovation.

Evolved institutional variety also implies variation in the *incentive mechanisms* and payoff functions that guide and shape economic behavior. The innovating firm is a profit-maximizing incentive system, and the national innovation system, as planned and implemented by a government, is a vote-maximizing incentive system. But the incentive systems of the other institutional varietals of collective innovation—collective invention, private collectives, user innovation, as shown in table 7.1—are more complex and protean.

In this broader view of the institutions of collective innovation, the process of innovation happens not just within firms but also between firms (viz., open innovation, innovation networks), and between firms and other economic

Table 7.1 **Institutional varieties of collective innovation**

Institution	*Literature*	*Description*
Innovating firm	Schumpeter 1942; Penrose 1959; Nelson and Winter 1982	Firm invests in R & D for innovation. With hierarchical contractual organization. With intellectual property. With government correction of market failure.
Collective invention	Allen 1983; Nuvolari 2004	Competing firms share technological knowledge, usually of plant designs and equipment in context of industry expansion. Without patents or prohibitions on copying.
Private collectives	von Hippel and von Gachter 2003; von Hippel and von Krogh 2006; Gächter et al. 2010	Combines private investment plus collective action model. Private firms benefit from process of supplying public goods. Without government.
User innovation	von Hippel 1986, 1998, 2005	Users develop innovations in process of using goods in novel contexts or to meet specific needs. Firms assist.
Open innovation	Chesbrough 2003a; West and Lakhani 2008	Firms seek to share their innovation with other firms or users, expecting reciprocity. Open licensing of intellectual property.
Innovation networks	Freeman 1991; Powell et al. 1996; Osborn and Hagedoorn 1997	Firms seek specific collaborations with other firms on innovation, exploiting specialization and competence. Innovation between firms.
Common or mass innovation	Leadbeater 2008; Swann 2014	Contribution of ordinary people to innovation. Without firms. Without intellectual property. Without government.
Community innovation/ sharing economy	Benkler 2006; Shirky 2008; Sundararajan 2016; Langlois and Garzarelli 2008	Collective ownership or mutual reciprocal exchange of surplus resources. High trust. Without firms.
Innovation commons	Allen and Potts 2016; Potts 2018	Pooling innovation resources to solve collective action problem of opportunity discovery. Without firms.

Table 7.1 **Continued**

Institution	*Literature*	*Description*
Industry associations	Thomas and Potts 2018; Potts and Thomas 2018	Governance networks to coordinate industry-level innovation systems and other industry-level public goods. Evolve from innovation commons.
National innovation systems	List 1841; Lundvall 1992; Freeman 1995; 2002, Nelson 1993	Firms form networks with other economic institutions, including universities, research institutes and governments.

actors (viz., private collectives, innovation systems). Innovation is not only a planned process within a firm, but also an emergent process (viz., collective invention, private collectives) involving households and users as well (viz., mass innovation, user innovation), shaped by complex motives and incentives. High-powered profit incentives and market competition will tend to be only indirect incentive mechanisms in this broader space, and hierarchic organization will often be a costly governance mechanism to coordinate innovative activities. Expectations and reputational mechanisms instead will tend to predominate.

Consider, moreover, the origin of the rules governing each institutional variation. In the case of the firm or the government, these rules usually originate from the entrepreneur or the policymaker. But with other institutional varietals some similar such "institutional entrepreneur"—or what Congleton (2010, 28ff.) calls the *formateur*,[2] that is, the agent that makes an organization—must exist, and if not then there must exist some emergent process of institutional origination. These institutions of collective innovation, even when ostensibly made of network linkages between organizations, are fundamentally reliant upon the social governance mechanisms of small groups, including gossip, costly signaling, coalition building, and reputation.

This has four broad consequences. First, owing to the speed and efficiency through which information moves through them, such institutions can be agile and adaptable, affording a margin of comparative advantage over firms and governments.

Second, because of these social mechanisms, some of these values will attach to the people involved, particularly the formateurs, who will tend to persist through institutional changes, that is, the same people reappearing across multiple institutional forms. In the next section I suggest that the origin of the institutional rules of industry associations will be adaptations of the institutional rules of the innovation commons, often carrying many of the same people through the transition.

Third, institutional forms of collective innovation evolve under selection pressure for adaptive self-regulation. They generally do not require external regulation because they simply would not have emerged in the first instance if not already functionally self-regulated. The implication is that external regulation will substitute for existing self-regulation, rather than imposing *ab nihilo* a regulatory order. However, the adaptive quality of this self-regulatory regime may be crucially dependent upon the particular people and social mechanisms extant in the system.

Fourth, there is the issue of the stability of the resultant private ordering of the institutions of collective action, and the mechanisms by which the order persists through time. Considering the inherently social nature of these institutions of collective innovation, the key analytic issue is the sociological, game-theoretic, and political-economy logic of *interest group coalitions* and their formation and stability (Olson 1965; Becker 1983; Granovetter 1985, 1995; Knoke 1986; Van Winden 1999). These models make specific predictions about the circumstances under which such groups will be stable and effective, or otherwise, in the context of the emergence of new industries and industrial dynamics. We can use these models to help understand the comparative efficiency of the various institutions of collective innovation.

A comparative institutional approach to the study of collective innovation enables us to locate innovation commons, as one institutional form, and also industry associations as another within this space of institutional variation. Innovation commons and industry associations are both *private orderings*. However, they have different functional purposes. An innovation commons pools distributed information to discover entrepreneurial opportunity from behind a veil of ignorance. An industry association is also a private ordering between organizations to create a local public good, namely institutions for industry development. Both are institutional mechanisms for cooperation, or the private organization of trust and coordination in order to create local public goods by effective rules of governance. They are different institutions for different purposes yet are interconnected to the life cycle of an industry and its unfolding technological trajectory.

Industry associations have long been analyzed as solutions to coordination problems in industrial dynamics, beginning with the institutional context of industry creation and organizational legitimacy in the "institutional ecology" literature (Hannan and Freeman 1989; Aldrich and Fiol 1994). Industry associations furnish governance for technological coordination and industry self-regulation (Gunningham and Rees 1997; Papaioannau et al. 2014) and resolve collective action problems in market-supporting and market-complementing activities (Doner and Schneider 2000). The theory of the innovation commons suggests a new theory about the origin of industry associations in which they evolve from innovation commons, and that their technological and innovation coordination role is an adaptation of the atavistic opportunity discovery role. To see this, it will be useful to review these institutions of collective innovation over the course of an innovation trajectory.

Institutional Transformations over an Innovation Trajectory

In evolutionary economics, the concept of an *innovation trajectory* (Schumpeter 1939; Freeman and Louca 2001; Perez 2003) represents technological change as a historical process or "long wave" that unfolds in the developmental and institutional context of firms and industries. The trajectory of technological change is shaped by institutions that structure how knowledge is organized and grows. Dosi (1982) called this a *technological trajectory*. The characteristic pattern of entrepreneurial discovery, firm entry, consumer adoption, and market selection over the new technology gives rise to what Klepper and others have called an *industry life cycle* marked by (usually three) distinct phases of development.[3] The technological trajectory over an industry life cycle maps out a three-phase *meso trajectory*, as the path of a generic rule (a new idea) from the point at which it enters the economic system, through its adoption and adaptation, to its complete embedding and retention within a complex structure of complementarity with other technologies and industries (Dopfer and Potts 2008; Dopfer et al. 2016).[4]

An innovation trajectory (or technological trajectory, or industry life cycle, or meso trajectory—we shall treat these concepts as synonymous here) is modeled within the analytic context of the broad institutions of market capitalism. This assumes a kind of dynamic institutional invariance over the course of any particular trajectory. This makes analytic sense: the logic of the trajectory is that a new idea of technology is changing against a constellation of evolved but within the relevant time-scale more or less invariant "institutions of market capitalism" (à la Williamson 1985a; Hodgson 2015). An innovation trajectory is a model of (fast) technological dynamics in an (invariant or slowly changing) institutional environment.

But from the comparative, ecological institutional perspective, we can invert this analytic image and instead seek to understand the changing composition of institutions-in-use over the course of an innovation trajectory. In other words, if we take the innovation trajectory as the invariant unit of analysis, we can inquire into the dynamics of institutions over the course of the innovation trajectory. What we observe are some characteristic sequences and orderings of institutional prominence.

The logic of these institutional distributions over an innovation trajectory relates to the changing problems—particularly collective action problems—that need to be solved at different phases of an industry life cycle. Different institutions have different effectiveness in resolving the different coordination problems that arise over the different phases of a trajectory. At the origin of an innovation trajectory, the collective action problem is opportunity discovery, and the best institutions for that problem are not necessarily the same that work best for collective action problems of regulatory lobbying, or complementary investment coordination, that occur in subsequent phases of the industry life cycle. An innovation commons and an industry association are different developmental phases of the same institution, but expressing themselves at different phases of the innovation trajectory to resolve different types of coordination problems.

7.2 The Origin of Industry

The concept of an industry, in Alfred Marshall's sense of it, is a curious analytic concept in economics, because strictly speaking industries don't exist. Firms exist, products exist, markets exist, factors of production and technologies exist, but an industry refers to a grouping of activities or an aggregation of various units (whether statistical, geographical, conceptual, administrative, or bureaucratic). From an existential perspective, an industry is a sum of parts, and so an industry really exists only retrospectively. In the beginning is a new technology, a new firm, and a new market, and it is only once these have developed somewhat that we may look upon various firms in similar (i.e., competitive) markets, producing a similar product (substitutes, from the consumers' perspective) using similar technologies (substitutes, from the producers' perspective), and identify an industry. In this sense it is somewhat meaningless to speak of the origin of industry.

In economic theory, an industry is defined as an aggregation of firms in the same market or field. This is a useful construct for economists because it defines a space of *competition* between firms supplying a particular market. But it also defines a space of *externalities* in those markets, where, for instance, the spatial clustering of these firms creates other markets, for example, for labor or ancillary services, as well as externalities for consumers due to colocation and competition (e.g., what Alfred Marshall called an industrial district). In this sense, an industry is a particular structure of economic organization of firms and markets around a particular product or technology, often with a spatial aspect. The modern game-theoretic definition of an industry refers to the space of *strategic interaction* (on pricing, entry or exit, collusion, etc.) between a set of firms that are mutually in each other's reaction functions. These definitions are geared to explain economic behavior and coordination in the context of an industry that is already presumed to exist. These definitions and models, however, provide no account of the origins and emergence of the industry.

The Schumpeterian or evolutionary model of an industry does seek to account for industrial dynamics through the life cycle of a suite of firms, technologies, and markets through entrepreneurial origination, competitive growth, and mature oligopoly (Klepper and Grady 1990). The Schumpeterian model also seeks to account for the dynamics of an industry as affected by innovation systems and government institutions (Dodgson et al. 2011). However, the evolutionary model has little to say about the origins of a new industry (the Schumpeterian origin story is entrepreneurial, not institutional) and like the neoclassical model tends to pick the story up some way into act 1.

What the neoclassical (Marshallian industrial, organizational, and game-theoretic) and evolutionary (Schumpeterian and industrial dynamic) conceptions of an industry have in common is that both supervene on the prior existence of multiple firms in the same market. This is a coherent and logical administrative and statistical definition: an industry is a grouping of economically similar activities. As a temporal ordering, first there is entrepreneurial activity in markets associated with a new technology or opportunity that will variously involve new firms or existing firms branching into new markets. Subsequently, an industry is said to emerge. This will usually occur through a process of self-identification (e.g., proposing a new name based around a new product type or service classification) followed by administrative legitimation (e.g., the creation of a new industry code). In the beginning are new entrepreneurs, firms, and markets, and subsequently a grouping of these is agreed upon as a new industry. This industry then develops through the evolutionary dynamics of firms and markets. To a rough approximation, the neoclassical approach is a largely synchronic analysis, and the evolutionary approach is a diachronic analysis. In both frameworks, the origin of new industries has basically the same answer: new industries are caused by the entrepreneurial actions that create new firms or new markets.

But the approach developed in this book suggests a different answer. It suggests a longer view in which the industry exists before the emergence of new firms or markets, and in which the emergence of new firms and markets is a developmental phase of the industry life cycle (the main phase, to be sure). Rather than thinking of an industry as an artificial, post hoc creation of economic bureaucracy and administrative statecraft, we think of it as a natural economic object in the dimension of *coordination*.

The life cycle of an industry is, in this new view, a series of transitions in the institutional resolution of the coordination problem of developing a new idea. An innovation commons is the first stage of institutional coordination of an industry. The public-ordering model of coordination through industry planning, industry regulation, or industry policy is usually the entire focus on what is meant by an industry. In the public-ordering model there is no role for an innovation commons, which is a species of private ordering. But in the private-ordering model the subsequent phase of industry coordination after the collapse of an innovation commons is an *industry association*, or some other governance institution for collective action.

In this view, the origin of industry is seen from the perspective of the resolution of collective action problems through various private governance institutions of coordination. The first collective action problem is the discovery of entrepreneurial opportunity, resolved through the institutions of the innovation commons. This gives rise to new firms and markets (as in the Schumpeterian story). But now there are new collective action problems associated with the legitimacy of these new firms and markets and economic activities. The resolution of this collective action problem can proceed through the creation of an association.[5]

Our concept of an industry is Schumpeterian in being developmental over an industry life cycle, but expands the prior range of that life cycle to begin earlier than in the public-ordering definition of industry. In the public-ordering definition, an industry emerges subsequent to the originating firms and markets, as in figure 7.1. I propose instead a *private-ordering* model of industry that begins in the institutions of the innovation commons that resolve collective action coordination problems and then transform into industry associations that continue with the same capability but over different coordination problems. In this institutional-governance-centered view, the concept of industry relates not to a common product or field, but rather to a continuous economic coordination problem. This is closer to the model of industry developed by Aldrich and Fiol (1994) through a process of institutional legitimation that is market-focused on consumers and firms making complementary investments, and also government-focused on policymaking attention through regulation and public expenditure. The collective action problem in this very early period is that there

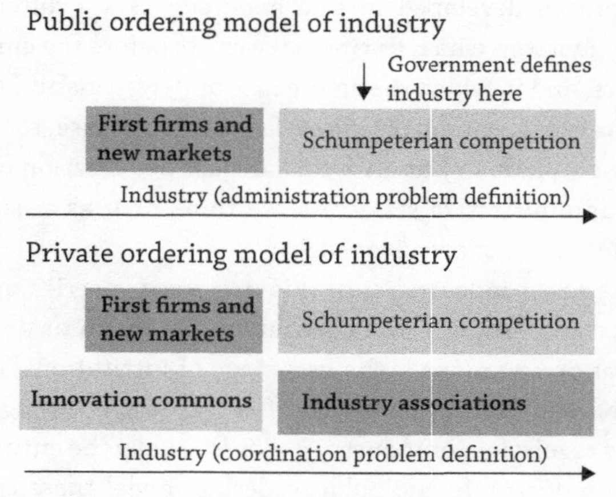

Figure 7.1 Public- and private-ordering definitions of industry

are substantial liabilities to newness and benefits from coordination to institutionalize an industry.

7.3 The Standard Model of Industry Associations

Industry associations—also known as trade associations, professional associations (in the case of professional services), business associations, or sector associations, but excluding the broader associative notion of business groups[6]—are economic and political institutions that engage in collective action (Olson 1965; Salisbury 1969; Knoke 1986; Barnett et al. 2000). As a quasi-independent, not-for-profit organizational coalition or consortium (usually funded through membership fees or levies, although sometimes through patronage), an industry association represents the industry's collective internal and external interests (Dalziel 2006).

Internal to the industry, these collective interests range over a number of specific economic coordination problems to internalize positive externalities between firms, including collusive behavior:

- Information sharing and learning (Sako 1996; Benner 2003)
- Coordination on technical standards, grades, and consumer-facing branding (Swan and Newell 1995; Damsgaard and Lyytinen 2001)
- Creating and enforcing industry-level self-regulation (Shaked and Sutton 1981; Gunningham and Rees 1997; King and Lennox 2000; Ogus 2000)
- Collective funding of industry-specific local public goods and corporate political activity, including training, public relations, issue lobbying, infrastructure (Foray 2003; Hillman et al. 2004)

These associations, however, are more commonly outward-facing, seeking to represent the industry's collective interests in bargaining with external parties. They tend to aggregate into so-called peak bodies in order to

- lobby for favorable regulation to raise barriers to competition (e.g., occupational licensing, regulation of industry practice, or trade barriers);
- pass private industry costs onto the public, for example by subsidizing training or industry-specific infrastructure (Potter and Sloof 1996);
- function as employer associations to present countervailing power against other coalitions or collective organizations (e.g., labor unions);
- represent a collective interest for political lobbying for legislative or regulatory rents (Stigler 1971); and

- facilitate the development of market-supporting and market-complementing institutions, particularly those that require or benefit from specific legislative actions and public support (Doner and Schneider 2000).

Industry associations are a private ordering, a voluntary coalition, and therefore the central economic problem they face is free riding on collective action. The two standard predictions, both following Olson (1965), are (1) that smaller groups or more concentrated industries will be more successful in forming effective associations (Lohmann 1995); and (2) that industry associations can overcome these problems through the design of specific mechanisms. A common strategy is to mix private information-sharing benefits, such as an industry conference, with industry-wide public goods, or what Olson called "selective incentives" (Knoke 1986, 6). Another method is compulsory fees collected through a sales levy. A further problem is aligning the incentives of the industry association (the agent) to the preferences of the levy-paying firms (the principals) in the presence of monitoring costs.

The free-riding problem predicts that industry associations are inherently unstable and that the existence and stability of collective action can only be explained by appeal to some additional factor that otherwise explains group coherence. Addressing this concern, Olson (1965) proposed the "byproduct" theory of group formation, in which the lobbying capabilities of a group such as an industry association arise as a byproduct of group formation for some other purpose:

> The common characteristic which distinguishes all of the large economic groups with significant lobbying organizations is that these groups are also organized for some other purpose. The large and powerful economic lobbies are in fact the by-products of organizations that obtain their strength and support because they perform some function in addition to lobbying for collective goods. (132)

My claim is that Olson's byproduct theory can be applied to industry associations when "innovation commons" are recognized as that "some other purpose."

Becker (1983) argued that the supply of industry associations, as an instance of "pressure groups," should be relatively elastic in proportion to the group's costs of organizing because the market for political influence is competitive. If there are industry rents to be gained from political influence, then we should expect to observe those rents being competed away (Barnett et al. 2000). An interest group forms as a function of its expected value to its members, conditioned by the costs of some mechanism that coordinates, monitors, and enforces the collective action. Where the benefits from group formation exceed the costs of the mechanism, we expect a positive supply of interest groups. But the mechanism needs to generate these benefits in a way that is compatible with individual incentives to participation. But the argument here is that the cost of the mechanism will be substantially lower if such groups preexist in a different form, thereby preserving trust relationships, pooled information, or embedded reciprocal cooperative investments. Instead of forming *ab nihilo*, an industry association might emerge from transformation of a previous organizational form, for example, an innovation commons.

The market-complementing functions of an industry association—which include vertical and horizontal coordination, lowering of information costs, setting of standards, and upgrading of quality (Doner and Schneider 2000, 265)—may evolve through specialization and division of labor. To lower information costs, for instance, it is common to see the development of a trade press or industry magazine covering such things as opportunities for used capital sales; reviews of new products or information about new technologies; information about upstream suppliers and downstream buyers, emerging markets, and industry-wide threats that might require coordinated or strategic action; and general gossip that helps manage reputations and facilitate coordination. Another example is the trade fair or expo. Standard setting can also develop as a specialized business to create standards for interoperability and connection for an industry's output as an input into other systems, and to develop product grades and labeling standards as information for consumers. Such standards and labeling can act to enforce minimum quality standards in an industry—and thus to manage potential externality problems arising from opportunistic producer exploitation of consumer ignorance (Akerlof 1970), and to coordinate industry reputation management, which is a common-pool resource vulnerable to social dilemmas.

Industry associations may also be run for the benefit of the association's own employees, as agency problems, asymmetric information, and monitoring problems combine to facilitate the creation and capture of rents.

In standard economic models, industry associations are a *countervailing power* (e.g., an employers' union, or a counterparty to regulators [Martimort 1999]), or a rent-seeking *distributional coalition*. The latter idea goes back to Adam Smith (but was subsequently refined by Olson, Stigler, and Becker) and emphasizes that where rents can be captured, they will be captured. An example is when industry associations lobby to raise the cost of new rivalrous technologies that threaten the industry's extant business model (Cavazos and Szyliowicz 2011; Juma 2016; Theirer 2016). Industry associations, in this view, are variously defensive or parasitical consequences of imperfect competition. But from the perspective of the life cycle of an innovation commons, an industry association is a further phase in the private governance of innovation discovery and coordination (Thomas and Potts 2018).

7.4 A New Model of Industry Associations: Private Governance for Discovery of Public Goods

Industry associations, I argue, are a subsequent developmental phase of innovation commons. Both are private-ordering institutions for resolving coordination problems associated with discovery problems in innovation and new technology. But where the adaptive function of an innovation commons is entrepreneurial opportunity discovery, the adaptive function of an industry association is a different sort of opportunity discovery problem, namely opportunities for public goods.

I present a new model of the origin of industry associations (they evolve from innovation commons) that is also a new account of the economic nature of industry associations (as institutions to coordinate discovery of opportunities for public goods). There is a notable symmetry to these different phases of the life cycle of an innovation commons: in the first phase (innovation commons) the discovery problem is about pooling collective resources to reveal a *private opportunity* that can be exploited through entrepreneurial action; but in the second phase (industry association) the discovery problem is about pooling collective resources to reveal a *public opportunity* that can be exploited through government action. In the first phase, a commons enables private entrepreneurship in markets. In the second a club enables public entrepreneurship in government.

There are at least three broad classes of public goods that can be discovered in the innovation context. First are opportunities for direct or indirect investment, for example, in R & D or infrastructure. This is sometimes known as industry policy when it is sectorally focused, or technology policy when it is technology focused. A second class of innovation-centered public goods are opportunities for regulatory or legal changes, or new public organizations and institutions, whether creating new coordinating regulations to reduce uncertainty or facilitate coordination, or though deregulation or design of experimental regulatory regimes that facilitate investment (Thierer 2016). A third class of public good comes from bargaining possibilities to mitigate the harmful or disruptive effects of an innovation by compensating (through public side-payments) those whose prior investments are devalued by the new technology or idea, and thus would otherwise seek to block the innovation through political or sociocultural interventions (Juma 2016).

Think of these three classes of innovation-based public goods as broadly corresponding to (1) *positive investment* (in infrastructure, R & D, skills, innovation networks, etc.), (2) *institutional environment* (regulations, laws, property rights, public institutions, etc.), and (3) *Coasian political bargaining* (e.g., side payments to those negatively affected by creative destruction, or positive inducements to support the new technology when market incentives are still weak).

These three classes are the menu items in the modern kitchen of innovation policy. It is normal for economic and policy analysis to be concerned with choosing well from this menu, carefully considering the expected value of these different policy options and accompaniments, or with degustation bundles of these options (e.g., innovation systems policy, triple helix policy, and so on). The modern view of innovation policy is customer-centric, where innovation economists and policy wonks prepare an exciting range of menu options, and governments choose the innovation policy mix that suits their political preferences and their budget. In this formulation there is no discovery problem, only a choice problem.

But an alternative way of seeing this problem is to start with the knowledge problem: namely how do you figure out whether there are specific opportunities to create public goods in the context of the new idea or technology? This is a situation structurally similar to the information as a public good model of Hausmann and Rodrik (2003), discussed earlier in this book, in which they represent the process of economic development as self-discovery of comparative advantage. Hausmann and Rodrik's key insight was that the comparative advantage that matters is at the six-digit Standard Industrial Classification (SIC) level rather than the two-digit level—think "cut flowers (tulips) airfreighted to Belgium in September" rather than "agricultural products." In the two-digit case it might have been obvious that a region had a comparative advantage in agricultural products, but there is no entrepreneurially valuable information in that. The six-digit discovery that that particular configuration is a profitable opportunity for trade is, however, the sort of useful information upon which entrepreneurs can act. It is contextually specific detailed information that is relevant to a particular time and place that is of value. This was also the key insight that I leveraged into analysis of the economic logic of the innovation commons, as the pooling of distributed information in order to discover specific entrepreneurial opportunities associated with a new technology.

An analogous concept applies to public goods associated with innovation. The two-digit equivalent is the recommendation to "invest in researching the new technology" or "build public infrastructure to support the new innovation," with the supposition that the difficult question is to determine the socially optimal level of investment. But what, specifically, should be built or invested in? What particular regulations should be tweaked or rescinded? Who specifically should be compensated and how?

These questions of mechanism and detail are usually relegated to the footnotes or appendixes of innovation policy analysis, but I argue that this has it almost completely backward. Innovation-focused public goods are veritable case studies in the knowledge problem. There are really two parts to furnishing technology- or innovation-focused public goods: (1) figuring out opportunities to create a public good and (2) doing it. In the standard analysis and policy framework, the second part is the entire focus of analysis (When should we do it? How much should we do it? What other policies should we complement with doing it? How should we finance doing it? If others are already doing it, should we do it more or less?). But I maintain that because new technologies are *new*, and because the economic context into which they enter is *specific*, and because the matrix of people and firms and markets and contracts that will be disrupted is *unique*, figuring out the exact shape of a public good opportunity is a significant information problem. The discovery of policy opportunities for public goods is no less complex and difficult, and no less a knowledge problem of information discovery, rather than the problem of entrepreneurial opportunity discovery.

Ainsworth and Sened (1993) proposed a game-theoretic analysis of the *interest group entrepreneur* (or lobbyist) as resolving an information problem for two audiences simultaneously: members of an associated group (such as an industry group), and government officials. Ainsworth and Sened's signaling game model shows how lobbyists' actions (to lobby or not to lobby) play an important coordination role by reliably signaling to government officials the existence of a potential public good. This enables individual members of the association to coordinate on a "good equilibrium" with positive member contributions, thus providing a focal point to enable the association to avoid the "undesirable equilibrium" of mutual free-riding. "The lobbyist provides information in the context of both a collective action problem and a coordination problem" (Ainsworth and Sened 1993, 835).

Building on Riker and Sened's (1991) political theory of the origin of property rights, Ainsworth and Sened's (1993, 835) starting assumption is that "a government may not recognize an opportunity for gain" due to incomplete information on the side of the government, and due to collective action problems on the side of the association that would cause it to fail to identify and communicate its concerns. The result is missed opportunities for political exchange. Ainsworth and Sened show how the introduction of an interest group entrepreneur (lobbyist) into this exchange provides crucial coordination information to both sides of the exchange about the existence of an opportunity to create a public good.[7] The economic logic of lobbyists is that they have "a comparative advantage in gathering information" (Ainsworth and Sened 1991, 847).[8] The lobbyist may acquire that specialization through experience, through investment in information, or by position in a network or creation of a network (Ramo 2016). We can generalize that point to recognize that an association (as a governance institution) can have some measure of capability or competence in gathering and processing such information. This may be due to a particularly talented individual (the interest group entrepreneur or lobbyist), or it could be an emergent property of the association, a capability embedded in the organization or a key team itself.

Whether attributed to an individual agent, or as an emergent property of the organization, this perspective requires an entrepreneurial view of an industry association in the innovation context. In our model, the industry association is alert (in the Kirznerian sense) to opportunities for gain. And it finds these opportunities by studying the data of its world and using entrepreneurial imagination to create possibilities for gain from civic and political trade (Schneider and Teske 1992). But the basic problem is fundamentally the same as in the innovation commons context, namely pooling distributed information in order to discover an opportunity, with the information about the opportunity being the "public good." These opportunities may derive from any or all of the three classes of innovation public goods previously mentioned—positive investments, changes in the institutional environment, or Coasian political bargains—reflecting the relative needs for them at particular junctions, and moreover these opportunities may emerge and shift quickly or be highly context dependent.

Our life-cycle model suggests a new approach to innovation policy. The central economic problem across the entire innovation trajectory is discovery of opportunity and design of the design space of innovation. What differs is the sequencing of what those opportunities are and to whom they are relevant. An innovation commons is a private-order institution that solves the collective action governance problem of pooling distributed information to reveal opportunities for entrepreneurial action. An industry association is the solution to a subsequent collective action problem that arises—quite possibly for *exactly* the same group of people, although not necessarily so—in which the discovery of specific information about what public goods exist in the innovation context and who benefits from them is of value both to governments, which can provide them in return for political gain, and to the industry constituents, including consumers and owners of specialized innovation specific assets, including human capital, physical capital, and intellectual property. We will pick up this issue again in the subsequent chapter on new innovation policy.

While the Ainsworth and Sened (1993) model locates the interest group entrepreneur in a two-sided market between associational constituents and government officials, a similar logic of opportunity discovery and coordination can also be constructed with respect to industry *self-governance*. An example of this is the problem of "innovation overshooting," as developed by Earl and Potts (2004, 2013, 2015), who proposed an evolutionary model of unstable dynamics in technological competition in duopolistic markets in which technological innovation imposes adoption and learning costs on consumers, disproportionately raising the entry costs for new consumers. However, Schumpeterian competition for market share leads firms to invest heavily in developing new frontier technologies that are often very good for elite performance, but expensive and difficult to use for beginners. But entry of beginners into a sport is an industry-level local public good that can be ruined by innovation overshooting. In this model, the absence of effective governance in technological coordination can lead to rational but destructive technological competition, resulting in industry collapse. Potts and Thomas (2018) showed that this mechanism is observed in some sports industries, and also that effective institutional governance by some sports organizations—which are in effect industry associations—can mitigate overshooting and collapse. This is an example of the discovery of a public good in the context of industry self-governance.

Another specific context of opportunity discovery of public goods relates to the "liabilities of newness" that Aldrich and Fiol (1994) emphasize in the institutional process of industry-making, and the overcoming of institutional resistance to technological change and innovation for which Juma (2016) furnishes multiple case studies. It is worthwhile putting this into the context of the theory of economic clusters, the geography of innovation, or the spatial economics of comparative advantage. In these broadly factor-based models of positive externalities (e.g., natural advantages in the supply of resources, or emergent path-dependent advantages due to colocation) the role of government is to seek to create through public investment such a local comparative advantage that will pay for itself through higher tax revenue from growth in economic activity.

In this model, public infrastructure creates a comparative advantage that induces economic activity. But in the model I have proposed here, causality works the other way. In the beginning is the discovery of entrepreneurial opportunities from the innovation commons. Then there is a subsequent induced demand to coordinate discovery of information about the value of public goods to facilitate transforming that nascent entrepreneurial activity into an industrial trajectory. The comparative advantage here might not be a resource advantage at all, but the absence of institutional barriers to adoption of the technology, or the absence of continued public support for the displaced technology (e.g., consider how different countries and cities have responded to the arrival of Uber and Airbnb, and how they will respond to automatic vehicles, drones, etc.). It may also consist of dedicated public policy to make effective side-payments to those negatively affected, in order to dampen resistance. Public policy support does not necessarily imply supporting entrepreneurs and innovating firms directly; it can also mean protecting them from their enemies, as we will discuss in chapter 9. The discovery of effective ways to do this is an innovation-specific public good that can be supplied by an industry association.

Consider what we might expect the ecology of industry associations to look like over the strategy space of generalist versus specialist services. From a competitive perspective, we would expect to observe that each niche collective good is furnished by the association most specialized in its provision. This would predict a rich and competitive ecology of specialist providers: generalist organizations would be outcompeted on every margin. However, Barnett et al. (2000) propose an evolutionary model of collective organizational actions as the outcome of a social search and matching process under bounded rationality. Firms seek to join organizations to solve collective problems, but under the satisficing condition (Cyert and March 1963), they stop searching when they find a satisfactory means. Generalist collective organizations are more likely to meet this satisficing criterion, and where contagion effects due to *ambiguity* about the worth and value of collective action and *network effects* (where the value to joining depends upon the extent to which others have joined) take hold, this will induce path dependency in the evolutionary process.

The ecology of collective organizations in an industry setting will likely be dominated by a small number of generalist organizations, rather than many more specialized interest groups. This evolutionary ecological model makes sense of why we would expect to observe multiple and sometimes even conflicting industry association goals, only some of which relate to coordination of industry discovery problems, bundled within a dominant industry association.

A final observation relates to the nature of the industry association in the context of innovation from the perspective of the Coase-Williamson-Hart theory of the firm in terms of the value of residual decision rights to deal with externalities and collective action problems. Langlois (2018) proposes a Smithian (as opposed to Arrovian) view of the innovating firm in which residual decision rights for dealing with coordination problems within an industrial market context matter more than incentives. In essence, a hierarchical, vertically or horizontally integrated firm can solve coordination problems through its claim on residual decision rights in the context of technological innovation that would not be efficiently resolved through market transactions. Langlois gives the example of Westinghouse, which was able to coordinate the technology standards for electricity across modular products (networks, appliances) because the structure of the firm gave it residual control over modular interfaces. This capacity facilitated investment.

But the same argument applies to an industry association, whereby association members voluntarily cede to the association residual control rights under specific governance conditions.[9] Industries that can resolve these collective action and coordination problems endogenously through self-governance do not create conditions or incentives for exogenous solutions through government action, whether through competition policy, industry policy, or regulation. From a comparative institutional economics perspective, we expect that an endogenous (governance) solution is likely to be more efficient than an exogenous (government) solution (Ostrom 1990), but only where collective action problems can be solved.

7.5 Industry Associations Construct Niches

The evolutionary ecological model of industry associations is a fertile one. We can also extend it to the idea that an industry association—as a civil society or private ordering—is a group of people coming together to solve a collective action problem related to the *niche construction* of the new industry (Luksha 2008). I have emphasized the discovery problem of information about public goods. But we can also frame this as a collective action problem in shaping the local economic environment to fit the needs of the incumbent species.

The particular group of people involved in creation of the industry association will likely also be the early players in the new industry. They will often be the same group of people who realized the opportunity and exited the innovation commons for exactly this reason. But there will likely also be others who enter through imitation; they will be less trusted from the perspective of the insider group, but may bring compensating differentials in specialized and valuable resources.

An industry association has a different purpose than an innovation commons. An innovation commons' purpose is to pool distributed information to reduce uncertainty, making possible entrepreneurial action that starts the industry. An industry association picks up where the successful innovation commons leaves off, and now has the purpose of constructing the environmental *niche* that the industry will occupy. "Niche construction" is a term from biology. It refers to the actions of a species to reshape the local environment to increase its fitness (Laland et al. 2016). The beaver dam is the classic example, but most all animals engage in niche construction. So too do economic species.

The niches that an economic species (such as an emergent industry) will need to shape are many, including market acceptance, institutional familiarity (Aldrich and Fiol 1994), legislation and regulation, private and public infrastructure, supply of factors, public perception (or so-called social license to operate), public support (i.e., subsidy, tax breaks), and so on. Such a niche is not something that just naturally appears, because it is unlikely that the space into which a new technology/industry moves is completely unoccupied (and therefore uncontested), or that it meets extant institutions that are perfectly well designed. It is sometimes the case that a new firm is the only firm and will take this task on entirely itself, internalizing the cost, and presumably expecting some monopoly reward. But the general case is that several firms undertake this, or that imitating forms soon enter, or that specialization emerges in the industry, creating a symbiotic imperative. Industry niche construction is a collective action problem, just as the innovation problem was for the incipient entrepreneurs.

Niche construction means retrofitting and newly constructing the economic and institutional infrastructure of an emerging and growing industry so that it is adapted to the business models, market imperatives, and technological plans of the industry. It happens in conjunction with the entrepreneurial contestation unfolding in the creative destruction of the industry development (Baumol 2001), and in parallel with the growth-of-knowledge development of the technological trajectory of an evolving industry (Dosi 1982). Industrial niche construction is a local public good in this respect. But it is also a collective action problem in that under perfect competition it will be suboptimally provided, or there are opportunities to free-ride. The function of the industry association is to furnish collective organization to create this local public good, which is equivalent to the creation of a common-pool resource when some exclusion mechanism can be extended.

This is a change in organizational form, but not in institutional function. Previously it focused inward, on pooling distributed information in a knowledge commons. Now, as an industry association, it is focused outward, on reshaping its environment (niche construction). Some of the same individuals might move through this transformation, shifting roles and responsibilities, but with the same focus on the development of the technology, now as a commercial opportunity. It is likely that there will be accumulated and earned trust among that insider group, given the fights and uncertainties they've already survived. There will also likely be effective social and cultural norms in the form of behavioral and institutional templates to draw upon in crafting the new constitutional form of the industry association. This is likely to be far more successful than any *ab nihilo* organization, both in transaction costs and in effective compliance and coordination. An industry association that transmogrifies from an innovation commons will likely defeat any competitor ad hoc industry association, even where the external incentives remain the same, because of internal efficiency.

But does an industry association always follow the collapse of an innovation commons? Can niche creation be achieved directly from the commons? One prospect is that the commons may be extended through a considerable period of time, possibly indefinitely, so the collapse of the commons never occurs, and the technology remains a common-pool resource (not the same as a public good, because there are private contributions, and the technology remains quasi-excludable owing to learning costs). An innovation commons can maintain viability when the technology is what Kealey and Ricketts (2014) call a "contribution good." The benefits to a technology staying in the commons for an extended period of time include a larger run of experiments on use under different conditions and applications, giving greater chance of shaking out any deep flaws or risks that may be very costly to remedy once the technology is developed to scale in the industrial trajectory. We should also expect that a longer period in the commons will lead to a greater trial of alternative uses and functions, thus avoiding the costs of lock-in. A longer commons should deliver a more robust and well-adapted technology, at the cost of delayed commoditization and the benefits that accrue to production under competition.

The force pulling a technology out of a commons and into the market is the ability to develop some advantage that can be exploited for profit, whether built on claims of intellectual property over some design or process, or from embedded use in a good or service. To keep a technology in the commons therefore requires actions that constrain that ability, which in some cases will require a mechanism of mutual restraint (a constitution, in effect) (Raymond 1999).

Another such strategy is pre-emptive public release, in effect making the technology public to such an extent that it cannot subsequently be enclosed. The public release of the polio vaccine by Jonas Salk is an example, as is the public creation of HTTP (the World Wide Web) by Tim Berners-Lee. This does not necessarily foreclose for-profit business development where what is kept in the commons is a platform. The Linux OS is an example, which is in an innovation commons, surrounded by a competitive ecology for for-profit businesses (e.g., Redhat).

By considering how innovation commons transform into industry associations, this approach also furnishes a theory of the persistence of industries due to niche construction, and why innovation slows down in consequence of the increased barriers to further or competing innovation commons.

New Evolutionary Themes

Note four distinct evolutionary themes to this discussion of emergent institutions of innovation cooperation and coordination that solve the innovation problem over a technological trajectory.

- *Symbiants*. An innovation commons is competitors that evolve to share the same body and thus become locked into ongoing cooperation. But, as in the evolution of symbiosis, this is not necessarily unexploitative.
- *Metamorphosis*. This starts in one form (of collective action), the commons of technology enthusiasts, and transforms at some point (I define the onset of the industry by the collapse of the innovation commons) into a new form: the industry association, but now focused on reshaping the economic and institutional environment to meet its needs.
- *Niche construction*. This occurs as the industry association reshapes its institutional environment to adapt to its specific needs, creating a new institutional niche.
- *Remnants*. The old form of the innovation commons is remnant as a political mechanism. Innovation policy becomes mostly about clearing away remnants. The industry niches form the structure of sociocultural embedding.

7.6 The Demic Phase of an Innovation Commons

In the life-cycle story developed here, an innovation commons collapses and an industry association emerges, continuing to resolve collective action and coordination problems. But we argue that an industry association is not the final phase, but rather the phase that carves out the industrial niches and identifies and coordinates innovation specific public goods. The next phase in the life cycle of an innovation commons is that the technological innovation continues a process of social and cultural embedding through the final phase of *demic concentration* (Hartley and Potts 2014).

In *demic concentration*, the technology transitions from an economic institutional embedding to a sociocultural institutional embedding. It becomes embodied in individual uses, beliefs, habits, and so on, embedded as education, politics, religion, and so on. This process is usually studied in the "social construction of technology" literature and the cultural studies and sociology of technology domains. However, this literature does not examine this process as a distinct evolutionary phase (demic concentration) within a total technological trajectory as subsequent to an economic trajectory, but views it as an independent sociocultural process. Furthermore, and parsimoniously, the cultural science model does not require the concept of the social (cf. Latour 2007), but works through cultural group-making.

The cultural science model of demic concentration (Hartley and Potts 2014) offers a unified account of the process of cultural embedding of technology consistent with the preceding phases of the technology trajectory of an innovation commons and an industrial trajectory of adoption and diffusion. The theory of demic concentration emphasizes that the function of culture is to make groups, and that it is groups that make and carry knowledge, and that this knowledge is tested against other groups and develops at that boundary (Ruef 2009). The innovation commons forms the industry associations that construct the industry niches that structure the sociocultural embedding that in turn coevolves with everyday use and cultural practices. Technologies in this way evolve into cultural groups (demes) that become the vehicle by which that technology replicates and further develops.

This approach also integrates with the evolutionary models of technological dynamics (e.g., Ziman 2000; Arthur 2009). The technology-centered approaches emphasize the evolutionary dynamics of technology as driven by recombination (recombination = heredity, in which a technology has fitness value because it harnesses some natural phenomenon), forming a model of what Kelly (2010) calls the "technium." Technology is made of recombinations of existing technologies, applied to new applications and domains. Humans are the vectors of this evolutionary dynamic, yet culture and society are not parts of the model.

However, from the cultural science perspective these technology-centered models miss the significance of cultural group adoption in making and sustaining cooperation at the level of the technology-adopting group, and therefore of the replication of the technology becoming hitched to the fitness of the cultural group, or deme. A technology is in this crucial way not eventually a public good, available to anyone, but rather is a demic good as part of the identity and boundary definition of a cultural group. This is the path to studies of technology and civilization (including cooperation and conflict).

In the demic phase the technology is now completely "publicly owned" or culturally embedded, which is to say that it has institutionally passed from an original commons good (phase 1), to a private good (phase 2), to a public good (the third and ultimate phase). This is the natural trajectory of any technology. What now occurs is that the technology becomes organized and coordinated socially and culturally (of which political action is one mechanism, but so too are social learning, habituation and enculturation, and so forth). This form of cultural coordination is mostly about group formation. In essence, a technology becomes part of a group's identity: "This is our knowledge, we do this, they do not." The "we" and the "they" can form any boundary you can think of, including seemingly arbitrary distinctions based on consumption patterns and technology use. A technology in this way becomes embedded in a deme (and in strong cases, as a deme), which is a culture-made unit of knowledge based on group identity.

7.7 Conclusion

The organization of trust and governance to develop a new technology requires institutions for collective action and coordination. The innovation commons is the originating institution, but also the seed for subsequent institutions, including industry associations. The collapse of the innovation commons and the onset of the Schumpeterian phase of firms and markets will also be accompanied by the emergence of the industry association. Industry associations are not de novo organizations, but arise from a previous form in the innovation commons. The properties of the innovation commons may carry over to those of the industry association. The function of the industry association is different from that of the innovation commons: it is not a mechanism to pool distributed information, but rather a mechanism to shape to their advantage the environment in which the firms within the industry function. This can include regulatory or legislative environment and public provision of complementary assets and inputs, including infrastructure, market-making, public relations, trade agreements, industry-level wage bargaining, coordination of industry standards, developing self-regulation, and providing protection against competing technologies or other industries. Such industry *niche construction* is a common-pool resource and is invariably subject to free riding; hence the same governance institutions that were effective for the innovation commons can be expected to also operate in an industry association.

An innovation commons and an industry association are different organizational and governance forms with different objectives. An innovation commons forms under extreme uncertainty to pool distributed information for the purpose of discovery of entrepreneurial opportunity, but from behind a veil of ignorance about exactly who will benefit from it. Nevertheless, it is a cooperative endeavor made possible by the emergence of effective rules of governance. This is also the case for what follows, namely the formation of an industry association with a different task, namely that of discovering opportunities for public goods and for shaping of the industrial environment (called niche construction in evolutionary biology) to increase the fitness of firms within the industry. However, this also raises the barriers to subsequent innovation commons emerging from within the industry. Industries thus tend not to be continuously self-transforming, but require external disruption. Indeed, this approach also clarifies the definition of an industry in relation to its point of origin (defined by the collapse of the commons), and the endogenous origin of industrial regulation as part of niche conduction.

This approach to the total technological trajectory (i.e., an innovation trajectory, from its creative origin to its cultural embedding) elucidates the several distinct institutional phases of governance that occur as a technology develops in response to the different types of problems that are critical at each phase. This highlights the natural complexities and challenges of innovation policy, which must therefore also be adapted to these institutional dynamics. Of course, trade and industry associations might not be the only organizations that form after the collapse of the commons. That is, there might be other organizational forms for developing research on a technology that also eschew markets and firms. We might also observe the formation of universities / fields of research / research departments / foundations (e.g., agriculture and mining universities). Maybe it is not about industry associations per se, but about the organization of trust to develop technology.

Notes

1. "Activity can only be regulated by a group intimate enough with it to know its functions" Durkheim (1933, 5). "Nothing, in my opinion, is more deserving of our attention than the intellectual and moral associations of America. . . . In democratic countries the science of association is the mother of science; the progress of all the rest depends upon the progress it has made" (Tocqueville 1840, ch. 5).
2. "Individuals or groups that found an organization will be called 'formateurs' and the persons recruited by formateurs will be called 'team members'" (Congleton 2010, 29).

3. Key references developing the theory of the industry life cycle are Gort and Klepper 1982; Winter 1984; Klepper and Graddy 1990; Audretsch and Feldman 1996.
4. Meso trajectories are thus embedded within the institutions of innovation systems (Freeman 1987; Lundvall 1992; Nelson 1993).
5. An association may not be necessary where a single firm dominates the space of activity sufficiently that these problems can be internalized entirely within the organization.
6. Granovetter (1995, 99–100) points out the paucity of attention to meso-level analysis of intergroup organizations and institutions in economics and sociology.
7. While they do not cite Ainsworth and Sened, drawing on a different literature, Hausmann and Rodrik (2003) essentially employ the same logic regarding the existence of the first-mover entrepreneur, who by entering the market profitably credibly signals to others the existence of a comparative advantage, and therefore a viable entrepreneurial opportunity. In Hausmann and Rodrik's model, the credible entry information is the public good, and being a public good is subject to market failure.
8. They build on the work of John Hansen (1991), who argued for the value of the political intelligence about preferences and technologies gathered by lobbyists and associations.
9. At the time of writing, an interesting example of this is currently playing out in the space of cryptocurrency platforms in relation to debates about crucial technological parameters, such as block size and platform interoperability.

8

Innovation Policy for the Commons

Modern innovation policy, which is based on neoclassical and Schumpeterian economics, seeks to resolve market and systems failure problems through government interventions. It attempts to resolve Arrow's (1959, 15) famous summary of the problem:

> We expect a free enterprise economy to underinvest in invention and research (compared with an ideal) because it is risky, because the product can be appropriated only to a limited extent, and because of increasing returns. This underinvestment will be greater for more basic research. Further, to the extent that a firm succeeds in engrossing the economic value of its inventive activity, there will be an underutilization of that information compared to the ideal allocation.

Yet modern innovation policy might benefit from new institutional economic foundations too, derived from the theory of the innovation commons. However, this leads to a different type of innovation policy, one that seeks to facilitate private-order and emergent governance solutions. It is also one that focuses on a different type of innovation problem, namely the knowledge problem of discovery failure. The innovation problem is really a knowledge problem—a discovery problem, which is a class of coordination problem—and this has an institutional solution through private governance.

So what should government do, in order to promote long-run economic growth and human flourishing?[1] Or more specifically, given our new understanding of the innovation commons—including its development from a broader theory of knowledge commons and private governance institutions, acknowledging how this weaves entrepreneurial discovery into the Schumpeterian theory of innovation, assuming that the objective is to develop a best-practice innovation policy, and recognizing that innovation policy is basically code for "all the conceivably different ways you can spend money on technology and the future"—what should a smart, capable, and well-intentioned minister of a government department with innovation somewhere in its name seek to do?

In the theory of innovation commons, the quality of innovation trajectories is a function of the quality of innovation commons. So there should be a high incentive and payoff to developing effective innovation commons policy. But innovation commons do not emerge from government. They are products of civil society as group-made sociocultural institutions to govern the pooling of resources, under conditions of high uncertainty, in order to discover entrepreneurial opportunities to create new value (Waguespack and Fleming 2009). It is not policy that delivers effective innovation commons, it is *expediency*, or what Victor Hwang (2012) has called "the rainforest," as a combination of factors that all have to come together as an ecosystem—an evolutionary, complex system (Colander and Kupers 2014)—for value to be created. As such, there is seemingly little that direct policy intervention might do to foster an innovation commons.

Accordingly, innovation commons policy is not a specific set of interventions but refers to institutional design principles that need to be respected and understood. Interestingly, this is the same policy conclusion reached by Ostrom (1990) with respect to natural resource commons, and by North (1990) with respect to long-run economic growth. The policy is about getting the institutions right in order to get the incentives for cooperation right.

8.1 A History and Critique of Modern Innovation Policy

Theory of Innovation Policy

Long-run growth is an outward shift in the aggregate production function. Only changes in knowledge (or total factor productivity) can explain such continuous outward shifts. This theoretical economics argument is central to all modern growth economics, including endogenous growth theory and Schumpeterian economics. Economic growth is caused by the production, adoption, and diffusion of useful new knowledge and ideas in the economic system, a process collectively known as innovation (Mokyr 1990, 2016b; McCloskey 2016).

Innovation policy refers to government actions to facilitate such economic growth processes by dealing with market failures in private investment in new knowledge and with systems failures in the networks of organizations and institutions by which new knowledge is adopted and diffused into the economy. Innovation policy is the overarching rubric of a range of policy frameworks—including research policy, technology policy, science policy, and advanced industry policy—all ostensibly products of the post–World War II period, when national governments came to realize not only the military advantage, but also the massive benefits to the civilian economy, of large-scale public support and investment in new knowledge creation.[2]

The idea that government has an active role to play in fostering research and innovation in order to promote long-run economic growth derives from a mix of information economics and Schumpeterian economics, the latter being an evolutionary theory of economic growth centered about entrepreneurial firms, new technologies, and market dynamics (Nelson and Winter 1982; Nelson 1993). The underlying economics of innovation policy is based on the idea that new information (including new technologies and science) have *public good* properties that are associated with *market failure* in their production (Martin and Scott 2000). This is based on the theoretical claim that, under perfect competition, private investment in research and innovation will, from an aggregate social welfare perspective, be suboptimally low (Nelson 1959; Arrow 1962b). As discussed in chapter 2, the innovation problem is normally defined as an allocative efficiency problem caused by competitive market prices (and associated profit incentives) misallocating resources by failing to incentivize private investment. Consequently, aggregate social welfare can be improved by public interventions to redistribute resources into research and innovation.

An addition justification for modern innovation policy stems from economic theory critiques of a market system from a development perspective. Much of modern innovation policy is a reconstructed form of what used to be called industrial policy (Rodrik 2004). Industry policy endeavored to create favored primary and manufacturing sectors as part of an economic development plan, often with the goal of advancing industrialization. Modern innovation policy has adapted many of these methods and approaches with the goal of strategically developing (cf. "planning") particular high-technology sectors. The best expression of this model is the science-and-technology policy approach embedded within the concept of national innovation systems (Freeman 1995; Box 2009), which in the European Union is a regional development policy called "smart specialization" (Foray et al. 2009; OECD 2013).

Mechanisms of Modern Innovation Policy

As an application of both neoclassical and evolutionary economics, innovation policy establishes a role for government to correct both market failures and systems failures (see Martin and Scott 2000; Aghion et al. 2009; Dodgson et al. 2011; Bleda and del Rio 2013; Tassey 2013) through a suite of institutions that include intellectual property rights (e.g., patents); the tax system (R & D tax credits); differential industry support (infant industry, strategic industry, defense contracting); direct public subsidy (national science laboratories); indirect public subsidy (research universities, government purchasing); government support (departments of science and innovation); and regulatory and legislative means (licensing and trade barriers, bankruptcy provisions).

In practice, innovation policy is really a suite of policies across different government departments and operating through various instruments. A range of policy instruments are brought to bear on this task, including legislative actions (e.g., intellectual property, trade barriers, licensing); supply-side spending (e.g., public science); supply-side incentives (e.g., R & D tax credits); demand-side spending (e.g., industry and technology policy through government contracting); demand-side legislation (e.g., industry and technology policy through protection); indirect subsidy (e.g., research policy through university or military support); programmatic support (mission-orientated policy); and so on. These policies operate through property law (e.g., intellectual property), tax policy (e.g., R & D tax credits), regulation, direct and indirect public spending (e.g., public procurement, military contracting, public universities, and science agencies), industry policy (e.g., favoring industry champions, or factor market support), and government ownership. In the market failure approach, the particular instrument of intervention depends upon where the alleged market failure originates and with respect to the government organizations or levels of government best placed to act on that failure (Jaumotte and Pain 2005). Innovation policy eventually touches all aspects of government.

There are many different institutional forms innovation policy can take (e.g., intellectual property, R & D tax credits, industry policy, public science, factor market support), and these operate through a variety of policy mechanisms and instruments (property law, tax policy, regulation, public spending). All, however, are different institutional approaches to solving the same broad "innovation problem": namely underinvestment in private innovation in a market system compared to an optimal level from the social welfare perspective.

These interventions create artificial rents (intellectual property law, tax credits, industry support) and do so in various ways. At one extreme, these interventions seek to induce private actors to invest more in innovation than they otherwise would through regulatory intervention (changing the rules of the game). At the other extreme, they autocratically direct public finance toward providing new ideas as public goods. The institutions of innovation policy, however, are a politically and institutionally varied set that includes private collectives (e.g., open-source communities); intellectual property (e.g., an artificial monopoly); tax policy (e.g., R & D tax credits); industry policy (e.g., favoring industry champions); public procurement (e.g., defense contracting); and public science (e.g., public universities or science agencies). In all cases rents are created, but the institutional way they are created differs substantially from a political economy perspective.

In Schumpeterian innovation policy, analysis is less focused on market failure per se (Cowen 1992; Zerbe and McCurdy 1999) than on "systems failure" (Freeman 1995; Niosi 2010). This in turn invites a broader notion of institutional correction rather than just market intervention. Because each technology or innovation prospect suffers different types of failure—for example, in incentives, information asymmetries, appropriability, financing costs, demand uncertainty, public risk—no single institution will suffice. Effective innovation policy requires a suite of coordinated institutional interventions that compose a complex innovation system (Nelson 1993; Dodgson et al. 2011). Innovation systems are classified and studied at different levels and focal scales including national, supranational, regional, local, sectoral, and technological. That some are more privately oriented and some more publicly oriented is generally treated as irrelevant in this richly textured multi-institutional mosaic framework (Box 2007).

Evolutionary approaches to innovation policy[3] more broadly emphasize the role of evolutionary mechanisms of variation, selection, and differential replication operating through processes of firm entry and exit, or technology adoption and diffusion, in what can be usefully conceptualized as an ongoing collective learning process in an "experimentally organized economy" (Witt 2003; Metcalfe 1994; Eliasson 1991; Hanusch and Pyka 2007). Evolutionary policy seeks to guide a process of decoordination of existing structure of knowledge and to facilitate the recoordination of the meso structure of a macroeconomy (Dopfer and Potts 2008; Dopfer et al. 2016).

Innovation policy institutions as various government interventions span the range of comparative economic systems, but with different emphasis. Publicly funded science was a significant part of command economies, and technology-focused industry policy was and remains a significant intervention in socialist and mixed economies. This transmogrified into science and innovation planning through the concept of national innovation systems (Freeman 1995). Nominally more market-focused economic systems tend to devote greater resources to interventions through the tax system (e.g., R & D tax credits) or through the legal system (intellectual property rights).

Nevertheless, in modern innovation economics the list of institutions that seek to solve the "innovation problem" is often expressed in no particular order, and without reference to whether these institutions are more naturally part of a command economy or a market economy. In the market-failure-based "science-and-technology policy" approach favored by the Organization for Economic Cooperation and Development (OECD), for example, the particular instrument of intervention depends upon where the alleged market failure originates (e.g., in factor markets, financial markets, regulatory markets, final goods markets) and with respect to the government organizations that are best placed to act on that location. Jaumotte and Pain (2005, 5), for example, identify five principal policies to address market failures in private sector innovation: direct fiscal policy (tax or subsidy), public research, intellectual property, finance provision, and human resource support. They find no reason to order these policies by any institutional criteria of political economy; it's just a list. In contrast, table 8.1 offers a classification of innovation policy along a planning or market focus.

Furthermore, it is widely recognized that the degree of competition differs over the course of a technological trajectory, thus affecting optimal policy (Aghion et al. 2005), and also that for historical, cultural, and political reasons

Table 8.1. **Innovation policy ranged between private and public instruments**

Innovation Policy					
Private	*Semiprivate*	*Mixed*	*Semipublic*		*Public*
Market focused			*Planning focused*		
Intellectual property rights	R & D tax credits, innovation vouchers	Targeted public procurement, research infrastructure	Targeted industry support, regulatory exemptions	Public research universities and cooperative investment	Public science institute

(e.g., trade treaties) different technologies will find themselves developing under different institutional forms, making it problematic to evaluate these institutions with respect to economic efficiency considerations.

Innovation policy is politically popular. Every government does it because it services many core constituents and voting blocs (universities, scientists, businesses in high-technology sectors, and so on). Few governments lose support by proposing to spend money on science, research, "jobs of the future," high-technology industries and other technology-centered drivers of growth. It is hard to find a political constituency opposed to innovation policy. But while the market failure line on innovation policy—as applied growth and development policy—has obvious appeal to politicians, bureaucrats, and voters and is broadly consistent with textbook neoclassical economics (à la "the Pigou club" [Trajtenberg 2012]), critique of the market failure model of innovation policy from Austrian, public choice, and new institutional economics has started to grow. The upshot of these critiques is that incentives and institutions matter, and that governmental attempts to design and plan innovation are plagued by the same sorts of problems that arise when governments attempt to intervene in other parts of the economy.

Critique of Innovation Policy

Despite the popularity of innovation policy, there is little clear evidence, from a cost-benefit perspective, that it actually affects aggregate economic growth rates (Box 2009, 6). To the contrary, the OECD (2003) actually found evidence that public science expenditure reduced the economic growth rate. Furthermore, there is a growing number of studies of "control group" industries, technologies, sectors, or nations that did not receive innovation policy treatment and nevertheless prospered (Kealey 1996; Mokyr 2001; Boldrin and Levine 2004, 2007; Diamond 2006; Moser 2005, 2012; McCloskey 2010, 2016). Those outcomes are inconsistent with the market failure model of research and innovation.

Then there are basic economic theory counterarguments to innovation policy. One approach simply denies that any market failure occurs, or when it does occur that it is inconsequential. Davidson and Spong (2010) argue that innovation spillovers have been misdiagnosed and do not form a sound basis for innovation policy. In addition, private provision of a public good (i.e., research and development) is individually rational under a wide range of circumstances (Allen 1983; Bergstrom et al. 1986; Lindsay and Dougan 2013). Innovation might actually be misdiagnosed as a public good and better understood as a contribution good (Kealey and Ricketts 2014) or a club good (von Hippel 1998; Lerner and Tirole 2002). Appropriation can be addressed by means other than the legal creation of a monopoly rent, such as secrecy or norms (Fauchart and von Hippel 2008; Raustiala and Sprigman 2006). In short, the theoretical foundations of innovation policy are contested.

A different line of argument is that innovation is really an entrepreneurial discovery problem, not a scientific, engineering, or technical problem. This denies the very logic of market failure (and government correction) and replaces it with a market process theory (e.g., Foss and Klein 2012). Hausmann and Rodrik (2003), however, argue that this entrepreneurial information can actually be understood as a public good, so converting it back into innovation policy (Bakhshi et al. 2011).

A further approach, consistent with both Chicago political economy and the public choice school, acknowledges market failure but emphasizes that government failure, including the incentives to rent seeking, will likely be a worse problem. Goolsbee (1998), for instance, finds that the benefits from big-science funding are largely captured in researcher salaries. Dourado and Tabarrok (2014) explain how intellectual property creates enormous opportunities for rent seeking, while ignoring the possibility of private-ordering institutional solutions, that is, the commons. Greenberg (2001) catalogs the enormous rents created by US science and technology policy.

These and similar arguments emphasize two points. First, there is weak empirical evidence for market failure in scientific and technological investment, and considerable counterevidence of entrepreneurial market adaptation to opportunities. Second, government interventions to correct these supposed market failures largely result in economic distortions and rent-seeking behavior—in other words, government failure. The upshot is a sustained case against operational-level innovation policy based on reallocating resources and strategic planning, and greater attention to the quality and effect of different economic institutions on entrepreneurial action and innovation outcomes (Baumol 1990).

Political Economy of Innovation Policy

Beyond the direct interventions model of neoclassical and Schumpeterian innovation policy are broader political economy considerations that examine the trade-offs and complexities between the objectives of government (analyzed from the perspective of the private incentives of government agents and voters) and the evolutionary dynamics of a market economy.

The basic Austrian economics and public choice critique (collectively the political economy critique) of modern innovation policy is that it neglects the supply side of innovation policy and thereby fails to account for the distortions and inefficiencies that arise though rent-seeking competition for innovation policy spending (Witt 2003). Austrian economists have explicitly modeled evolutionary policy as the artificial devaluation of the market opportunity set as "strangled catallaxy" (Wegner 1997).

One line of this public choice argument targets the political supply of market regulation as a kind of anti-innovation policy that is popular because it is sellable to voters as consumer protection and to incumbent industries as market protection by raising the costs of new knowledge discovery and adoption. Thierer (2016) argues that deregulation is an effective innovation policy when it aims to foster a legal regime of "permissionless innovation" that is broadly in favor of experimentation and seeks to limit the ability of incumbent firms to lobby for market protection (and therefore rents) associated with entrepreneurial competition from new and uncertain technologies. We examine this problem in chapter 9. Furthermore, Cowen (2017) argues that public risk aversion (present in what he calls "the complacent class") also constrains innovation by reducing the demand for radically new products, and withdrawing social license to experiment with such. In both cases the political economy framing of innovation policy seeks to position government so as to avoid harming innovation.

Rules as Policy

Modern neoclassical and Schumpeterian innovation policy is based on intervention (e.g., public spending) to solve a resource misallocation problem. An alternative policy model is one of rules to solve a coordination problem.

From the Smithian perspective, in which an economic order is a complex process-structure of knowledge, the foundational source of order is the *institutional governance* that furnishes rules to facilitate coordination and change. This order has multiple, and sometimes simultaneous, sources, variously arising from shared culture (a commons), organizations (hierarchy), networks of organizations (an industry), institutions of exchange (markets), institutions of voluntary collective action (civil society), and institutions of collective force (governments). Normally only the last of those is associated with policy—that is, government, utilizing the institutions of collective force to transfer resources or legislate actions. But what matters are the rules that furnish the generic order of knowledge—that is, governance. Consider the nature and origin of the rules that furnish the order of an evolving economy.

The growth of knowledge requires effective coordinating rules. The institution or mechanism that creates these rules (whether from emergent culture, networks, organizations, markets, or government) is performing the governance role of policy. This is how policy can emerge from the bottom up (Colander and Kupers 2014). Policy can emerge from private orderings as well as from public mechanisms. There are many ways this can happen, and policy is the creation of rules for purposeful collective action in which government is only one of several possible sources of such "policy." The rules that facilitate, enable, and constrain this process are emergent policy. They issue from culture, networks, organizations, and markets as well as from governments. Governments in particular are often major institutional forces blocking new ideas through their support or protection of existing industries (chapter 9). However, at the same time, they can facilitate transitions through social welfare nets, public subsidy of retraining, lowering transaction costs of markets, and reallocating resources within an economy.

Innovation Policy as a Public and Private Goods Problem

In the standard economic model of just private and public goods, in which the innovation problem is diagnosed as market failure, the solution is "policy," that is, some manner of government intervention. But if we also allow club goods and common-pool resources, both of which are private-ordering solutions, then the solution space for policy includes both public and private orderings.

These range from individual choice in markets to coercive action by governments, but also include collective action at the level of self-selected groups. For instance, information may be a public good in the "state of nature," but by adding intellectual property rights we can, in effect, make it a private good. If we undertake to use secrecy, we can make it a club good. When its exploitation will bring value proportional to the order in which people acquire it (e.g., financial market rumors) we can make it a common-pool resource. We should not therefore think of the innovation problem and innovation policy as synonymous, but rather that the innovation problem invites a range of institutional solutions, some of which come from markets, some from organizations, others from government, and yet others still from civil society. So innovation can be produced under different institutional configurations. It can be produced in *markets* (pure exchange [Gans and Stern 2010]), in *hierarchy* (firms in markets, under different degrees of competition [Nelson and Winter 1982]), or in *governments* (also hierarchy, backed by coercive force [Mazzucato 2013]). It can be produced in *networks* (e.g., open innovation [Chesbrough 2003a]) and in *clubs* (usually described in the spatial economics language of local spillovers, or innovation clusters). And innovation can also be produced in the commons (Globerman 1981; Storper 1996). A good example of innovation in the commons is open-source software. The innovation commons is, in this sense, a type of infrastructure, that is, a shared resource, but not necessarily a public or private good, but one that can be provided through the governance institutions of a commons (Frischmann 2012).

Innovation Policy and Its Discontents: A Summary

Modern innovation policy, based on neoclassical and Schumpeterian economics, argues that long-run economic growth (and the social benefits growth brings) is caused by innovation, but that the economic production of innovation suffers market and systems failure problems that require government intervention. It is implicitly a top-down planning and investment model. The basic critique of this economic theory diagnosis and policy treatment model is that it ignores a further class of problem, and solution, namely the discovery of opportunity and the private-ordering mechanisms (i.e., institutions of governance, or collective action solutions to coordination problems) for solving that problem. New innovation policy based on the theory of the innovation commons therefore seeks to solve a different, but logically prior, problem, namely discovery failure.

8.2 Discovery Failure

Market failure occurs when market mechanisms fail to maximize social welfare because of externalities, increasing returns, indivisibilities, information asymmetries, or uncertainty (Bator 1958; Arrow 1962b). Market failures are resolved with government interventions. *Government failure* occurs when these interventions fail because of knowledge problems, agency problems and incentive problems (Buchanan and Tullock 1962; Stigler 1971; Wolf 1979).

Market discovery is the process by which buyers and sellers, with free entry and the feedback of profit and loss, collectively discover the equilibrating prices that enable agents' plans to mesh (Hayek [1968] 2002; Buchanan and Vanberg 1991; Kirzner 1997). The corresponding failure concept is that government planning and interventions distort and corrupt the market discovery process (Mises 1949; Boettke et al. 2007). But another type of nonmarket failure can also derail market discovery at the outset, a phenomenon I will call *discovery failure* (as introduced in chapter 2, section 2.6).

When discovery failure occurs, it is the transition from invention of a new technology to realizing its value as an innovation that fails. Just as market failure describes departure from the analytic concept of a perfect market, and government failure describes departure from the analytic concept of a perfect government, so discovery failure describes departure from the analytic concept of a perfect discovery. So what is meant by perfect discovery? With *perfect discovery*, from the perspective of the alert entrepreneur, a new idea or technology will contain with it all necessary and sufficient information to realize the innovative opportunity. While drawing attention to the agency of economic dynamics and market coordination, Schumpeter (1911, 1942) and Kirzner (1973) both formulated an implicit concept of perfect discovery that begins with the entrepreneur. But when discovery failure occurs, the entrepreneur never arrives in the first place.

This is discovery in the Austrian sense of "price discovery," rather than in the scientific sense of a "eureka" discovery. The difference is that price discovery is the emergent result of collective action on distributed information. Furthermore, the cost of discovery failure is not a direct cost, as an unrecoverable investment in R & D or venture capital, that is, a production cost, but rather it is an opportunity cost, a benefit forgone. Discovery failure occurs when governance mechanisms to pool information—in order to enable opportunity discovery, which begins the entrepreneur-led process of market discovery—fail to emerge. Discovery failure is a risk whenever information necessary to reveal the entrepreneurial opportunity is distributed and requires cooperation between many agents to realize it (Singh 1998; Felin and Zenger 2009). That cooperation requires governance. Discovery failure, therefore, is a consequence of missing governance institutions. When discovery failure occurs, the process of market discovery never gets started, or is retarded or distorted. Discovery failure may subsequently manifest as market failure and then as government failure.

Discovery failure is due to governance problems arising under high transaction costs and extreme uncertainty. The concept recognizes that the "innovation problem"—formulated in terms of market failure, as a problem of allocatively efficient levels of investment in new knowledge under competition—has an entire other dimension that is a problem of transaction costs and institutions of governance. Perfect discovery is perfect in the institutional dimension, such that the path from invention to innovation stays on the institutional efficiency frontier (Djankov et al. 2003). Discovery failure occurs when institutional choice is suboptimal, resulting in the arrested development of the innovation trajectory.

The innovation problem that societies face—the resolution of which determines the wealth of nations—is rarely just market failure in the allocation of private investment, that is, the wrong answer to the question, What resources should we allocate to innovation and how? It is also, and indeed primarily, a coordination problem associated with opportunity discovery. This is equivalent to saying the innovation problem has an institutional solution in the supply of governance rules to resolve a collective action coordination problem. The true nature of the innovation problem, as I have argued throughout this book, is actually discovery of opportunity.[4] The economic problem is not invention. The economic problem is the entrepreneurial problem of discovery of value (Shane 2000b; Metcalfe 2004).

From the policy perspective, the relevant framing is not market failure (wrong prices) or systems failure (wrong coinvestment coordination) or even government failure (wrong incentives), but discovery failure (missing rules or institutions to facilitate common pooling of resources leading to the discovery of entrepreneurial opportunities (Hausmann and Rodrik 2003; Potts and Hartley 2015; Potts et al. 2016; Potts and Bakhshi 2011).

8.3 Efficient Institutions of Innovation Policy

The Comparative Institutional Approach

An alternative approach to innovation policy that acknowledges the basic empirical and theoretical critiques of the market failure models of innovation policy, while still recognizing the economic reality of the innovation problem, can be constructed from within the perspective of new institutional economics by building on the Djankov et al. (2003) model of the institutional possibility frontier (IPF). The basic idea is that innovation policy should be designed and evaluated from an *institutional efficiency* perspective rather than from an allocative efficiency perspective.

The application of the comparative institutional efficiency perspective to innovation economics is based around the idea that an efficient innovation institution will minimize the total social costs of a policy, trading off different types of social cost. To understand why this shift in perspective from maximizing social benefits to minimizing social costs is important, observe that political support for innovation policy largely comes from an argument that routinely ignores the cost side of the cost-benefit equation (Davidson and Potts 2016c). This results in an evaluation approach that tends to look at innovation policy through the lens of multipliers, spillovers, and externalities, where the worst-case scenario is simply that these are small, and therefore the policy had only low impact. The comparative institutional approach, however, adopts a consistent economic methodology by assuming that different innovation policies—say intellectual property versus tax credits versus publicly funded research—represent different types of trade-offs in terms of their costs. An efficient innovation policy achieves a given benefit while minimizing the social costs it incurs.

To arrive at this insight the innovation policymaker needs to recognize two crucial points: (1) that innovation policies do have social costs; and (2) that different innovation policies have social costs over different dimensions. The general framework for analyzing institutional efficiency in the presence of alternative institutional mechanisms for pursuing a specific social benefit (in this case, resolving the innovation problem) is the institutional possibility frontier. Different innovation policy interventions rarely consider comparative institutional costs. The different innovation policy interventions are each separately justified by instrumental recognition of the respective multiple points of failure and multiple opportunities for intervention. Innovation commons policy can be usefully seen through the lens of the new comparative economics of an IPF that maps the trade-off in any set of institutions aimed at social control in pursuit of some socially desirable end: such as seeking to regulate business activity to address negative externalities, or to incentivize innovation to address positive externalities.

The Djankov et al. IPF model assumes that a perfect institutional order requires a world of zero transaction costs, and therefore any real institutional order is always caught in the trade-off between the costs of freedom and the costs of control: or between the problems of *disorder* and social losses due to private expropriation on the one hand, and *dictatorship* and the social losses due to state expropriation on the other. They frame these social losses due to state and private expropriation as the *x* and *y* axes of figure 8.1, and with four institutional orderings for social control (private orderings, independent judges, regulatory

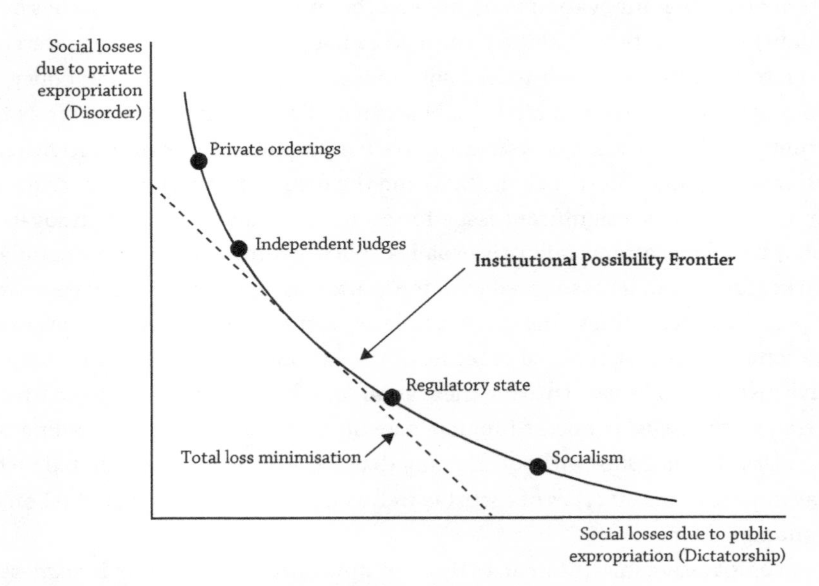

Figure 8.1 The institutional possibility frontier (source Djankov et al. 2003)

state, socialism) mapped along the IPF. Levels of "civic capital" determine the position and shape of the IPF in the relevant society by the relative transactions and governance costs of the various institutions. A 45-degree line represents points of total loss minimization, and the equilibrium tangency with the IPF therefore represents an efficient institutional solution.

Djankov et al. (2003) use this model to analyze historical and contemporary institutions, considering institutional transitions (e.g., Russia in the 1990s) as well as persistent institutional inefficiencies, for example economic development failures (Acemoglu and Robinson 2012). The model is well suited to this task, given its focus on the political trade-offs inherent in economic orders.

The Djankov et al. IPF model begins with a Hobbesian-Smithian recognition that all institutional forms impose social costs in some way. The risk of more freedom is disorder, and the risk of more government is dictatorship. Any attempt to address the problems of one necessarily imposes greater costs from the other, variously by considering more freedom or more control. The central idea of the model is to recognize this trade-off (and to assume convexity to generate an interior solution). This logic of analysis of the social costs of any institutional endeavor to solve a social problem makes clear that there is no such thing as a perfect or costless institutional form. Any institution represents some set of compromises between the risks of private expropriation (net of private benefits) and the risks of state expropriation (also net of possible benefits).

This same approach can be applied to the analysis of innovation institutions, which, for the most part, are not viewed from a perspective that represents inherent trade-offs or recognizes comparative institutional inefficiency. In different ways, the "innovation systems" and the "market failure" approaches both avoid this implication, making them somewhat agnostic about the preference given to the different institutional solutions in respect of innovation policy, or tending to regard them as historically accidental or path dependent. Yet as the Schumpeterian innovation system approach exemplifies, this comparative institutional ordering (Boettke et al. 2005) and the focus on social losses or costs are rarely regarded as a significant issue for economic analysis. Indeed, innovation policy based on systems failure is usually explicitly contrasted with the standard market failure model associated with innovation as a public good and generator of positive externalities. The market failure perspective also tends to overlook the comparative institutional ordering of the various solutions and the comparative institutional costs, treating them as all somehow equivalent. Alternatively, it frames the issue as one of fungible substitution and potential crowding out (e.g., David et al. 2000) without allowing that these different institutional forms may impose different *types* of costs (as well as the usual focus on benefits) on an economic order.

A comparative institutional analysis of innovation institutions is suggested where we can sensibly array the various innovation institutions by an ordering from those that are ostensibly private and decentralized to those that are essentially public and centralized institutional mechanisms. Some innovation institutions preserve the decentralized and private nature of innovation activities, involving little or no indirect government action (e.g., innovation commons and intellectual property). Others involve a full government takeover or socialization of the innovation process (e.g., public spending and public science) (see figure 8.2). The IPF represents a framework for analysis of the trade-off between the social costs of private versus public actions.

Consider these six institutional strategies—from innovation commons to public science—for the development and control of a technology and the innovation trajectory that develops from it.[5] Starting in the upper-left corner of the IPF is private action unencumbered by any public action, without law or legislation, regulation, or any public support or direction in private collectives of open innovation (von Hippel 2005; Chesborough 2003), or what we more generally call an innovation commons. The risk of disorder and private expropriation refers to ability of private agents, who develop technologies and can control them in such a way as to harm or impose costs on others. This may occur by the power this gives to extort or overcharge others who seek to use these technologies, or in other ways that enable private control to impose costs on others. It may also arise through powers of private agents to withhold ideas and innovations from others, or to block the development of an idea, using any resources available, if to do so benefits them, even at substantial cost to others.

The courts-based system of intellectual property can constrain the reuse of ideas, both because of the term of the monopoly rights granted and because of

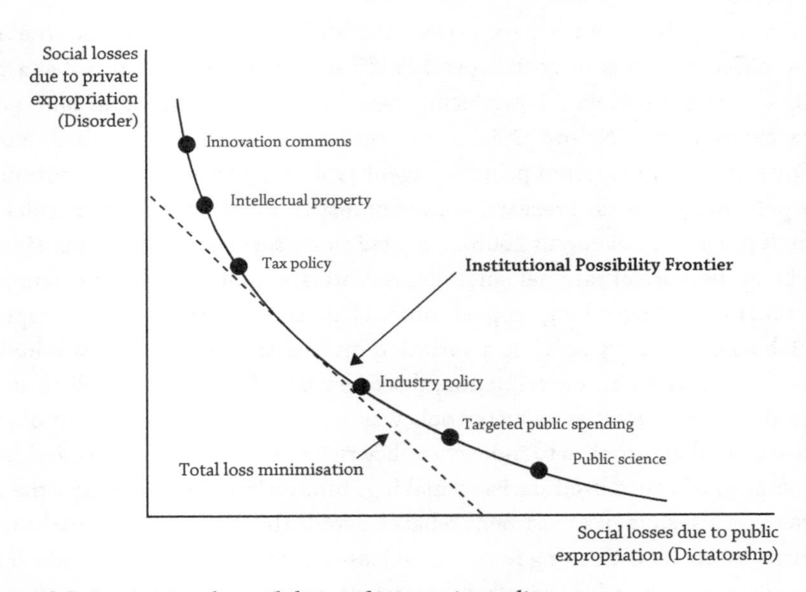

Figure 8.2 Institutional possibilities of innovation policy

the downstream control over use or rights to exclude (Boldrin and Levine 2004). As Wu (2006) elaborates, the economic effect of intellectual property is not just higher consumer prices. It also includes the centralization of industry structure and the loss of the dynamic adaptive benefits that accrue from decentralization. Moving toward a more centralized model of knowledge production enables some costs to be avoided or mitigated by creating institutional rules for property rights over ideas. Intellectual property rights, while privately contracted, nevertheless draw upon the powers of the state to grant the monopoly rights that enforce those claims. This limits the powers of private expropriation by requiring disclosure of the idea, thus reducing the extent to which the private individual can exert power over others through private knowledge. Tax policy is nearer to the disorder end of the IPF, whereas industry policy, which moves the decision locus toward the state, is closer to the dictatorship end. Both tax and industry policy provide substantial powers to the state to control the development of technology (Rodrik 2007b), particularly where that technology provides political benefit. These mechanisms are used for the development of "strategic" industries and politically favored sectors. Further along the IPF is direct public procurement or technological support (e.g., military, communications, or space technology) or public spending on, and public production of, research through government research organizations. Ideally, these will supply only research not produced by other means, but nevertheless crucial to industry development. The public system, however, is subject to capture by special interests, relies on a bureaucratic and risk-averse mechanism of resource allocation, and, not being market directed, can fail to create knowledge or solve problems in ways that add value.

From a public choice perspective, the various stations around the IPF have different forms of social costs. *Public science* is intended to solve a collective action problem in producing new knowledge with significant positive externalities (Nelson 2004). But the comparative institutional model emphasizes the prospect of principal-agent problems in the forms of capture by the personal interests of researchers and of institutional lock-in to particular research programs (Diamond 2006). *Targeted public spending* suffers from similar problems because of rational ignorance by voters, exploitable by politicians and coordinated by "log-rolling" opportunities (Tullock 1959) in the form of capture by lobbyists. *Industry policy* is a variation on this at the sectoral level. Rodrik (2007b) advocates an experimental, discovery-based approach in which innovation policy is recast as industry policy as an opportunity discovery problem. But standard approaches to industry policy risk a coordination failure and lock-in because of centralized decision-making. Innovation policy through the *tax system*, as a system of investment rebates, avoids this problem, and works with market incentives, meaning fewer social losses from dictatorship. But like *intellectual property*, it is dynamically inconsistent and induces rent seeking. Private collectives (von Hippel and von Krogh 2003) minimize social losses from dictatorship, but maximize losses from disorder due to weak cooperation incentives (von Krogh et al. 2012).

The relative costs of disorder and dictatorship will condition the economic evaluation of particular innovation institutions. There are plainly circumstances where the costs of dictatorship are low and the costs of disorder are high; for example, the development of radar and atomic weaponry during World War II. In situations with a well-defined problem and a targeted solution, dictator costs are low and disorder costs are high. The success of this experience gave substantial credence to the efficacy of publicly directed science (Bush 1945).

There are also circumstances where the opposite holds—where costs of disorder are low and costs of dictatorship are high. The development and globalization of internet commerce that emanated from US innovation institutions is a case in point (Greenstein 2015). In such situations, innovation commons and market-based institutions of innovation are generally superior because the social benefits of wide search over a space of technological and organizational opportunities are high, as are the costs of policy-induced lock-in and path dependency (Davidson and Potts 2016a). Information technology is the prime example, but a similar observation applies to the services sector as a whole. Here the social losses of dictatorship are very high. A similar argument can be made about blockchain, a next-generation web technology (Davidson et al. 2018).

The Low Social Costs (and High Private Benefits) of Innovation Commons

A market failure diagnosis of the innovation problem (à la Nelson 1959; Arrow 1962b) implies that the economic problem of innovation is one of weak incentives to private investment—because of free appropriability, indivisibilities (i.e., fixed costs), and marginal cost pricing—to be resolved with public investment and rent creation mechanisms collectively known as innovation policy. But a collective action diagnosis of the innovation problem (à la an innovation commons) implies that the economic problem of innovation requires a governance mechanism to incentivize cooperation and pooling of distributed information to facilitate opportunity discovery.

For many classes of technologies, and certainly for most civilian technologies, the innovation commons is an efficient institutional solution to the opportunity discovery problem in which disorder costs are low and dictator costs are potentially high. The more innovation commons are used to develop new ideas and technologies, the better quality the design space information, and the better will be the private and social decisions that follow (Storper 1996). Firms that start will be better because entrepreneurs will be acting with better information. There will be less failure (loss of resources), and less costly path-dependency (institutional failure). Because new ideas are exposed to wide and disinterested scrutiny, latent externalities will be revealed and realized sooner. This means more appropriate definition of the market and so more well-defined entrepreneurial bargains and contracts. It also suggests fewer overreaching and chilling regulations from government because of a clearer understanding of the actual "creative destructive" effects of the innovation. There will be fewer opportunities for rent-seeking protection by technology incumbents.

8.4 New Innovation Policy

Diagnosing the Innovation Problem

Innovation policy is based on innovation theory, which is an economic analysis of the innovation problem that economists have characterized as, in essence, a problem of market failure (Nelson 1959; Arrow 1962b). A policy suite of government interventions has been proposed and built to remedy this. But the central argument of this book is that this diagnosis and treatment risks being an instance of what I have termed "the innovation fallacy," which supposes that the innovation problem is solved when a new technology is produced. The implication is that that production also becomes the measure of policy success.

But the innovation problem is a knowledge discovery problem, and the range of that knowledge includes, crucially, not only technical information (i.e., the new technology), but also market information. The solution to the innovation problem is an information set that fully reveals the economic opportunity. This information set is often distributed and benefits from pooling, which requires cooperation, which requires governance. The significance of the innovation commons is that it is, often, an efficient institution to facilitate the production of that information set and therefore for the entrepreneurial discovery of new economic opportunities.

To overcome the innovation fallacy requires recognizing that the innovation problem is not an investment problem alone, but is also a coordination problem and a collective action problem, both of which have a governance solution. New innovation policy needs to solve not only the investment problem (an allocation problem) but also the collective action and coordination problem (a governance problem).

Innovation policy thereby consists of any governance rules, protocols, or institutions that lower the cost of opportunity discovery and facilitate cooperation leading to pooling of information and other resources that are inputs into opportunity discovery and realization. These governance rules can be cultural expectations and social norms, or they can be organizationally or legislatively defined. Innovation policy, in other words, does not issue exclusively from government, but also from organizational networks and from civil society. But this is still policy because there are aggregate benefits to a group from coordinated action.

Benefits to Groups, Regions, Nations, and the World

In the standard model of innovation policy, the cost and payoff accrues to the nation-state. The nation-state must fund the policy—that is, directing tax-financed resources to public investment in R & D, or public science, or industry policy expenditure, or operating intellectual property systems, and so on. The benefit accrues in increased innovation, and so productivity growth and economic growth. Economic growth increases private and corporate income, with new tax revenue on that additional income financing the original public expenditure on innovation policy. Innovation policy is a public investment. Obviously, there are distributional issues and consequences, but in the long run these should wash through (McCloskey 2016).

The innovation commons approach to innovation policy does not work like this because the nation-state is not the natural unit for policy. Rather, the relevant unit is the emergent community created by the new idea of technology. This may correspond to a nation-state in particular circumstances when there are corresponding nation-state investments in relation to infrastructure and education curriculum or for sociocultural reasons. But the relevant "policy unit" is more likely to be emergent over a region (e.g., a university, a district, a city), a technoculture (a *deme* [Hartley and Potts 2014]), or a social network (Mokyr 2016). The theoretical argument was made in chapter 6 using multilevel selection theory (aka evolutionary group selection) to show how individually costly private cooperation in the context of an innovation commons could evolve when it facilitated effective group-level competition. Innovation policy as governance rules emerges at the level of a self-organizing community. Benefits then spill over to the particular location, scope, and reach of that community, which may be a district, city, region, nation, or global network. Indeed, it makes sense to think of the policy space of an innovation commons as being simultaneously composed of a quasi-local network of cooperation, drawing on a potentially global set of actors and participants, while emphasizing the role of platforms and exchanges. Innovation commons policy therefore is most fundamentally constrained by the openness of communication and interaction, and the ease with which people can meet, talk, and exchange information and ideas.

This Comes from Civil Society

The innovation commons is a hypothesis about the nature of the origin of innovation. It argues that innovation begins, as the first time and each time anew, from civil society (Potts 2014). The relevant parameter here is community formation

(Potts and Hartley 2015). Innovation emerges from a self-interested and self-governing community that is attempting to solve an uncertainty problem by pooling information and knowledge.

What are these communities? One perspective is they are what eventually becomes industries (strong form: every industry starts this way; weak form: most industries start this way). Either way, the upshot is that new industry formation begins as an emergent process of community formation. Now, it is possible that government policy can facilitate this process in an effective way. But what needs to be understood is that what government is doing is engaging in information-pooling and community-building processes and seeking to do so under conditions of extreme uncertainty, which is to say without a clear ex ante plan for the eventual outcome.

Innovation policy for the innovation commons should focus on solving the problem of discovery failure, not of market failure. Market failure is an allocation or resource problem, whereas discovery failure is a species of knowledge problem and coordination problem. The goal is to minimize information costs for transaction costs and discovery costs, and this is achieved through the creation and facilitation of effective rules for making self-governing communities for knowledge pooling.

Innovation commons will likely emerge wherever innovation systems self-organize or are otherwise coordinated along the lines of communities of technology exploration (e.g., communities of enthusiasts) and market/industry lines (around coordinated development of technologies for particular market applications). This explains the role of industry or market associations over and above the need for collective action in bidding or bargaining situations with external parties (e.g., labor unions, government regulators, and others). It also suggests that public/state activity to facilitate innovation may work best by encouraging, or at least not crowding out, the commons solutions. It also means seeking to shift public funding of research, science, and knowledge discovery from direct production toward providing infrastructure for information brokering and sharing of the market commons.

The theoretical model also suggests that commons may yield a highly "polycentric" model of innovation policy of all different scales and scopes, with perhaps a good deal of messy overlap (Koppl et al. 2015). This may seem inefficient and disorganized, but that is what organized complexity may look like, and indeed such polycentricity may be a necessary condition for effective knowledge pooling across technological regimes or communities. There will still be a core set of common design principles (à la Ostrom 1990, 2005).

The Innovation Economy Cannot Be Planned

Innovation theory has sought to characterize a difference between *open* and *closed* innovation,[6] and between *user* and *producer* innovation (von Hippel 1986, 2005; Harhoff et al. 2003; Baldwin and von Hippel 2011; Gambardella et al. 2017), including hybrid concepts such as private knowledge-sharing networks and "private collectives" (von Hippel 1987, 2007; von Hippel and von Krogh 2003, 2006; Gächter et al. 2010; Haeussler 2010; Hienerth et al. 2014) and distributed innovation (Lakhani and Panetta 2007). These are useful distinctions. Yet by focusing on architecture and roles, they elide what is going on with information.

The lone-genius (autarkic) model of innovation is misleading. Because diverse and distributed information has to come together, innovation is always and everywhere a group activity (Wuchty et al. 2007; Muthukrishna and Heinrich 2016). This is not only true at the phase of *exploitation* of a new idea, when resources and tasks need to be organized by firms and governments, but also at the beginning, in the discovery phase, in the innovation commons. The notion that the beginning phase is characterized by individual genius, imagination, creativity, or alertness, rather than group action, is a remarkably persistent refrain of methodological individualism.[7]

Distinguish between two institutional modes of organizing innovation from the perspective of information (Gurri 2014): *hierarchy* and *networks*. Hierarchies are firms and governments. They are organizations of control and information. Plans and strategies form at the top of hierarchies, and actions are carried out at the bottom. Power flows down and information flows up. Hierarchies are generally associated with closed innovation and producer innovation, but even open innovation is often about creating horizontal nodes into hierarchies, or networks of hierarchies (Pisano 1991). They are still largely characterized by organized professional actions, based around strategic plans and programs, and coordinated through leadership, management, and systems in which the legitimacy of information is based on certification and rank.

A network, like a commons, is flat. There is no centralized control, but mutual adaptation and norm-guided behavior in groups that are the product of spontaneous self-organization about a common interest. These voluntary associations—civil societies in the Burkean language of Tocqueville—are more like an interested "public" of serious amateurs who come together under conditions of radical equality. The purpose of these groups is to focus attention and create information for mutual benefit. Such forms are often poor at undertaking planned and programmatic activity: hierarchy is better for that. But such groups excel at discovery and exploration, and in finding meaning and value through pooling information and distributed processing. New technologies and innovation need this function. But paradoxically, this function cannot be effectively provided through hierarchy.

The implication is a surprising prediction: an innovative economy cannot be planned.[8] Innovation policy can only work on a sociopolitical economic order that *has already solved the innovation problem in the commons*. An innovative economy can be planned from behind the technology frontier, or as adoption-diffusion catch-up. But planning, programs, and hierarchy are inefficient (in the institutional and transaction cost sense) for opportunity discovery. That has to come from civil society, from "little platoons," the vital communities of amateurs and enthusiasts.

The economic problem begins with a conjunction of the Hayekian knowledge problem (distributed information) and the Kirznerian problem of entrepreneurial discovery of opportunity. An innovation commons is, under certain conditions, a transaction-cost-minimizing institutional configuration for solving this problem. The economic problems that modern innovation theory and policy deal with do not actually begin until the primary innovation problem (discovery of entrepreneurial opportunity) gets solved.

An innovative economy requires more than innovation policy, or innovating firms, or even entrepreneurs. It requires an effective innovation commons. A key insight is that an innovation commons cannot be planned, cannot be produced strategically, as the result of a program. Innovation commons emerge from a healthy and robust civil society as a voluntary self-assembling group. Such groups can create quasi-public goods by pooling resources in the commons (Franzoni and Sauermann 2014), which, as Ostrom (1990, 2010) showed, can be efficient institutions for governance when these rules are well adapted to the context and conditions. By better understanding the bottom-up solutions to the innovation problem, we can hope to better understand how cities and cultures interact with the innovation process (Andersson and Andersson 2011, 2015).

8.5 Conclusion

The theory of the innovation commons proposes a fundamental challenge to the modern intellectual framework and government practices of innovation policy. It does not, to be clear, argue that the existing models and approaches are wrong. Rather, it claims that they are incomplete, and particularly that they have neglected the originating phase of the innovation process, namely opportunity discovery.

The policy model that the theory of innovation commons points toward emphasizes an institutional process of community formation to facilitate information pooling in order to facilitate opportunity discovery. Policy, in this framework, consists of the supply of governance rules to facilitate cooperation and collective action. When these governance rules work effectively, common-pool resources are created from which the basic conditions for entrepreneur-led innovation are supplied. What is most striking is that these governance rules can be expected to originate from civil society. However, as we will see in chapter 9, the role of government then shifts to creating the conditions under which such communities can form, and this often means providing protection from the natural enemies of such communities, namely established incumbent technologies and associated industries and markets.

Notes

1. "Little else is requisite to carry a state to the highest degree of opulence from the lowest barbarism, but peace, easy taxes, and a tolerable administration of justice; all the rest being brought about by the natural course of things" (Smith 1759).
2. See Bush 1945; Price 1963; Lundvall and Borras 2004; Bonvillian 2014. This argument traces back to List (1856) as a technology-based national economic development policy of industrial catch-up based on a form of technological mercantilism.
3. For an overview see Pelikan and Wegner 2003.
4. This is a central theme of innovation strategy developed by business economists advising companies on organizational design and innovation strategy, but usually proceeds under different label, such as von Hippel's (1986, 2007) "user innovation" (Oliveira and von Hippel 2011) or "democratized innovation" (von Hippel 2005) and Chesbrough's (2003a) "open innovation." A pioneer of this line was the economic historian Robert Allen (1983) on "collective invention" (see also Nuvolari 2004; Moser 2005, 2012).
5. Allen (2017, 134) explains: "Given that each individual economic activity within the innovation problem has a different cost minimising institutional solution, the IPF can be represented not at the level of the innovation system [or technology], but rather at the level of the individual economic problem. This enabled a focus on the earliest stages of new technologies, and in particular the proto-entrepreneurial innovation problem."
6. For example, Chesbrough 2003b; Dahlander and Gan 2010. A somewhat parallel discussion happens in science (Nielsen 2011), including the extent to which science is the private production of a public good (Kealey and Ricketts 2014).
7. This romantic conceit was popularized by Schumpeter, channeling Sombart and Nietzsche (Ebner 2006).
8. See Nelson 2004 on a similar point.

9

Inclusive Innovation Policy

Modern innovation policy addresses market failure and systems failure. Both focus on investing in innovation (solving a market incentive problem) and building infrastructure for innovation (solving an institutional coordination problem). An alternative approach to innovation policy, suggested by Juma (2016), is to focus on overcoming latent resistance through *inclusive innovation* (solving a sociobehavioral resistance problem).[1] I distinguish between innovation policy to "help its friends" and policy to "engage its enemies." I explore what an inclusive innovation policy approach might look like and how it would be developed.

9.1 Two Types of Innovation Policy

The purpose of innovation policy, it is often said, is to *support innovation*. And the value of supporting innovation is of course self-explanatory because innovation drives economic growth. Innovation policy is necessary, in this view, to solve the innovation problem that arises because of market failures and systems failures in the innovation process. Now if you like eggs, one way to get more eggs is by supporting chickens, say by building them a nest. But you can also support chickens by killing foxes. Maybe we don't kill the foxes, but relocate them, or rehabilitate them: the point is that under some cost margins, the most efficient way to get more eggs will not be to directly support chickens, but to be against the things that are against chickens.

So it is with innovation policy too. If you want more innovation, one option is to support innovators. But another option is to be against those who are against innovators. Which strategy is best will depend upon relative costs and elasticities. Yet the egg-maximization strategy of modern innovation policy is almost entirely about supporting chickens, rarely about fighting foxes.

When politicians speak of the need for economic growth to drive prosperity, they sometimes confuse cause and effect. Most economic growth is caused by innovation, by figuring out new and better ways to do things in pursuit of profit.

It is the adoption of these new ideas that causes the investment and capital accumulation that in turn causes the higher productivity that produces the effect of higher real incomes, which then causes higher consumption and spending. Note that spending and investment does not cause prosperity; rather they are consequences of innovation. Innovation is the driver of economic prosperity, and barriers to innovation are barriers to growth (Mokyr 1990; Parente and Prescott 1994). The confusion stems from supposing that the spending *causes* the innovation. But it's the other way around: it is the innovation (the new ideas) that causes the spending.

The politician's hopeful message is that governments can cause economic growth by allocating public investment spending to innovation (Mazzucato 2013). This is known variously as innovation policy, industry policy, or economic growth and development policy. Different types of public spending are sometimes labeled a push or pull approach: push when on the supply side of new technologies (e.g., public science); and pull when creating demand (e.g., military spending). But the basic idea is that public spending can cause innovation (and that innovation in turn causes growth).

There are two specific arguments as to how this mechanism works through innovation policy: a *market failure* rationale; and a *systems failure* rationale. The market failure approach (Arrow 1962b) emphasizes an incentive problem to private investment under perfect competition. Without some mechanism to create artificial rents, private investment in innovation will be too low from a social welfare perspective. The systems failure approach (Nelson 1993) emphasizes a coordination problem in the creation of complementary investments in the innovation infrastructure or ecosystem. In both cases, there is a strong role for public sector involvement in targeted market interventions and the creation of innovation institutions (Romano 1989; Romer 1990; Stephan 1996; Martin and Scott 2000; Bleda and Del Rio 2013).

Economists who study innovation argue about the optimal policy mix within this framework and specifically whether market failure or systems failure is the more significant concern (Dodgson et al. 2011), whether intellectual property should be stronger or weaker (Boldrin and Levine 2002, 2004), and whether R & D tax subsidies are appropriately targeted, and generally on the measure of the social return to public investment in R & D (Jones and Williams 1998). Indeed, what else could innovation policy be if not understood as different ways to support, promote, and protect innovation? And what else could an economics of innovation policy be but analysis of the comparative efficiency of these different innovation support mechanisms?

An alternative view of innovation policy starts by dividing the world differently. Instead of market failures and systems failures as a basis for policy, or supply-side and demand-side constraints, or pull forces and push forces,

I suggest an alternative but equally foundational classification of innovation's *friends and enemies.*

Friends of innovation are people engaged in doing innovation and who seek to benefit from it. They include, at a minimum, entrepreneurs, scientists, employees at (and contractors to) innovating firms, and early adopting consumers. Enemies of innovation (Juma 2016) are those who recognize or expect that they will be harmed by a specific new innovation and seek to stop its progress or mitigate its effect. Enemies of innovation are not necessarily or even generally anti-new technology or antiprogress, nor reactionary or conservative. Rather, they are against *this* specific new technology or innovation (e.g., horseless carriages, vaccines, synthetic biology, artificial intelligence, driverless cars, fracking) because of specific fears or concerns about the harms that *this* particular innovation will bring to *them* or those they represent. Friends of innovation focus on the benefits of innovation for the many. Enemies of innovation focus on the costs to the few.

The modern view of innovation policy is that it should help its friends. That is, those who engage in innovation should be protected and supported. This can mean direct (public research) or indirect subsidy (R & D tax credits), rent creation (intellectual property), legislative protection (trade barriers), or special treatment (preferential purchasing) through various and often high-level policy instruments (science and technology policy, industry policy, development policy, trade policy, etc.). Most innovation policy is of the "help your friends" type. This is an expected economic outcome of interest group politics (Olson 1965).[2] The "help your friends" approach also seems sensible from an aggregate public welfare perspective given the overarching net social benefit to innovation (Nordhaus 2004).

Yet a benevolent dictator (or central planner) seeking to maximize the innovation potential of her economy might yet prefer to pursue a different strategy, namely that of "engaging the enemy" (note: the enemy of innovation, not the enemy of the dictator). This is because while the average returns to supporting innovation (the "help your friends" approach) might well be high, what actually matters is the marginal benefit, and it is not a priori obvious which of the two pathways in figure 9.1 has the highest marginal return. This is the problem this chapter seeks to explore.

9.2 Innovation Seen and Unseen

Frederic Bastiat (viz., the "broken window fallacy") explained the concept of opportunity cost in terms of the difference between *things seen* (the repair of the broken window) and *things unseen* (the new suit the shopkeeper didn't buy, and the tailor who didn't make that sale, because the shopkeeper spent his

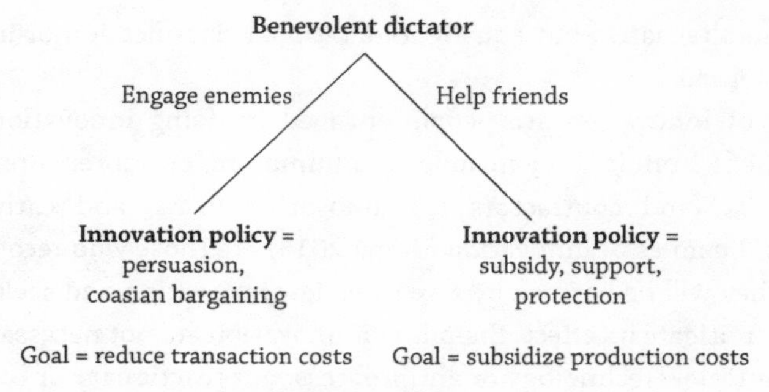

Figure 9.1 Two innovation policy approaches

money fixing the window). The same concept also applies to innovation policy. Innovation policy should be judged not only by the innovation seen (that which innovation policy directly promotes), but also by the opportunity cost of that particular innovation policy, namely the innovation unseen (the innovation that was successfully resisted because innovation policy wasn't there to defend it).

Innovation policy is justified in modern policy debates through cost-benefit analysis that measures the additionality or multiplier, say β, of the public expenditure over some range of target outcomes. Vastly simplifying things, for any $\beta > 1$, the expenditure is justified. Public spending on innovation can also be compared to other fiscal priorities (e.g., public health, environment, etc.) with this method.

But this method only counts things that happened: the expenditures made, and subsequent expenditures attributed to that support. This is good accounting but bad economics. The proper comparison is between the things that happened *and their opportunity cost*, that is, the things that didn't happen. Now obviously things that didn't happen are harder to count. But figure 9.1 can help us to see what these might be. The relevant comparison is not between public support of a supercollider versus a genomics laboratory, or between technology X versus technology Y, or technology company A versus B. The relevant comparison from the perspective of a benevolent dictator seeking to promote an innovation agenda is whether this is best done by supporting innovation (helping friends) or clearing away forces that retard innovation (engaging enemies). Resources devoted to one are resources taken away from the other.

Yet the economics of the innovation problem is usually stated in terms of allocating resource between "competing friends"—that is, supporting this or that technology, or between different mechanisms to help friends. It is rarely framed as a choice between, on the one hand, helping friends and, on the other, fighting enemies. Why is that?

The answer is given by public choice theory. The friends of innovation are an organized lobby group, whereas taxpayers who fund the support they receive are not (Olson 1965). On the other side of that ledger, enemies of innovation are not seeking to stop innovation in general, just to raise the costs or erect barriers to a particular innovation. They seek to inflict private harm, and the collateral damage that harm may cause to the public through higher prices or reduced market offerings—to consumer surplus and productivity (real incomes)—is diffuse and harder to see, and so able to be politically manipulated.

The benefits to political support of particular innovation projects are concentrated, enabling organized parties to capture the benefits, and from these rents to contribute to political campaigns, and for politicians to associate themselves with the particular, often highly visible and charismatic, successes or outcomes (such as the opening of a new research center, or to affiliate with a new technology). However, fighting against the enemies of innovation is the opposite experience. The costs are concentrated: in often highly contentious and visible public disputes with people with much to lose. Yet the benefits are diffuse: in clearing the way and lowering transaction costs for unseen others to improve their innovation offerings and opportunities, it is difficult to link the political action to the benefit created. So the incentives to direct innovation policy to help friends are much sharper than the incentives to engage their enemies. We should be unsurprised to observe that almost all innovation policy is of the "helping friends" variety.

One implication is that the tendency for mature sectors to be less innovative than new sectors may be an endogenous consequence not only of diminishing returns to R & D and market structure effects (Aghion et al. 2005) but also due to this political economy effect of the growth-retarding accumulation of special-interest regulations on innovation (Olson 1982; Mokyr 1994; Acemoglu and Robinson 2000). This is to say that the maturity of a technology may not be an inherent property of the technology per se, but an artifact of the accumulation of regulatory barriers and protections sought by the industry in order to limit competition and secure rents (Stigler 1971), as well as the restrictions that have been permitted to amass by those seeking to control the technology for other purposes (Smith 2007; Taylor 2016). The idealized discussion of "permissionless innovation" (Thierer 2016) compared to the problems of technologies born into extant regulatory barriers illustrates this point.

Industrial sectors that receive the most innovation policy support are often the ones with the greatest accumulation of enemies. In Australia, for instance, until recently when the automotive manufacturing industry shut down, it was the single largest beneficiary of support through R & D tax credits and direct government transfers for particular innovation-focused government coinvestment. But the products this industry produces are very heavily regulated and controlled (e.g., for consumer safety features), which makes innovation difficult (e.g., developing driverless cars, alternative drivetrains, etc.). The same point can be made about healthcare, education, and other so-called mature sectors that receive large levels of innovation policy support, but, at the same time, little public policy support in engaging the enemies of innovation in those same sectors. This is because enemies of innovation do not present themselves as "enemies" but as having concerns with safety, sustainability, tradition, fairness, and justice, with concern for the future, harm minimization, risk management, managing transitions, and other such nostrums to elicit sympathetic concern. These actions impose costs on innovation, shifting the margins of its activities.

What of the prospect of a grand Coasean bargain between the friends and enemies of innovation to get the enemies of innovation to stand down? Such bargains are almost impossible to make without government intervention (Twight 1994). Such a bargain would be attractive to a benevolent dictator, but is unlikely in a multiparty democracy because the coalitions needed would be unstable.

9.3 Against Innovation: Theory

Who is against innovation, and why? The idea that to be a friend of commerce and the innovation it brings is socially respectable is a modern idea that emerged from the commercial societies of the Enlightenment, as Deirdre McCloskey (2006, 2010, 2016) explains in her *Bourgeois* trilogy. It was not always thus. These days, friends of innovation tend to paint its enemies as culturally primitive, intellectually unsophisticated, or simply ignorant: as against progress, as clinging to the past, as emotional and fear-ridden—as "them," not "us" (Hartley and Potts 2014). This is unhelpful.[3] As Juma (2016, 183) explains, "Technological controversies often arise from the tensions between the need to innovate and the pressure to maintain social order, continuity and stability," a point that Schumpeter (1912, 87) was also acutely aware of. So in one sense this is about weighing the *social* costs and benefits of two courses of action—change or no change—and recognizing there are *individual* utility consequences that accrue from changes in relative prices, from market revaluations of assets and shifted choice sets, and from nonmarket externalities. Friends and enemies of innovation, in this view, are simply two-sides of an ex ante Coasean bargaining process intermediated by government.[4]

The heat in these debates doesn't come from the distributional calculus alone. Friends of innovation are often accused of starry-eyed optimism. Yet the historical record supports that position; for the most part innovation really does make things better overall (Postrel 1998; Mokyr 2002, 2009; Ridley 2010; Deaton 2013). Rather, the enemies of innovation tend to suffer specific biases and logical fallacies that lead to overestimating the costs and hazards of innovation, particularly with respect to the assessment of risk.

First, there are strong instinctual (i.e., evolved psychological) aversions that are standard in the human behavioral repertoire, such as fear, disgust, and phobias that can be triggered by novel technologies or ways of doing things. Often these can be overcome through exposure and be entrained by other more powerful instincts (e.g., through social learning, group identity, and so on). But only a small percentage of humans consistently actively seek innovative novelty; most are resistant (Rogers 2005; Witt 2009). For enemies of innovation these instinctive emotional responses are usually easy to harness. Fear of the unknown can be used to conjure hazards from pure imagination, and contrasted with the safety of doing nothing. "Much of the concern," Juma (2016, 11) observes, "is driven by perceptions of loss, not necessarily by concrete evidence of loss." Novelty can be framed as an invasion (fear), as unnatural (disgust), as uncontrolled (avoidable hazard), as from outsiders (in-group preference), all of which facilitate emotional prejudice that can render evidence irrelevant (Kahneman 2011; Hartley and Potts 2014). There are also strong status quo biases, loss aversion, and endowment effects at work in skewing the behavioral assessment of the costs and benefits of change that will tend to assign a zero measure to the costs of not changing, but a positive value to the costs of changing (Potts 2017).

Second, these social cost-benefit arguments earmarked with appeals to the public losses and exposed hazards that buttress the costs of change can provide cover for a pure play of vested interests. In the early stages of any innovation there is in most cases greater value tied up in the status quo than in change.[5] Where these assets (and not just physical assets, but also including jobs and human capital) are highly fungible, or when the benefits of the change are large and evenly distributed, we expect little resistance. Yet these conditions rarely hold in practice. The real factors determining the measure and extent of resistance will be a function of the scale of the losses (i.e., the rents under protection), which is itself a function of the fungibility of investments, and also the ability of the affected parties to mobilize and coordinate their actions. The case studies Juma (2016) documents overwhelmingly show the ability to organize is a significant determining factor in the effectiveness of resistance.

Third, intellectual arguments matter too—particularly around the morality of the particular innovation—and these defensive arguments against change often come from high-status individuals or sociocultural institutions, further impacting the complex psychological calculus that allocates friends and enemies of innovation. Juma (2016) illustrates this with the centuries-long and largely religious opposition to coffee that was only overcome when the head of the Catholic Church shifted position on the morality of coffee consumption. Similar debates are currently playing out in genetically modified organisms and synthetic biology, and in artificial intelligence and its applications, such as in autonomous vehicles. In the case of new technologies such as CRISPR,[6] the enemies of innovation gather around moral and philosophical arguments about how this technology could fundamentally change what it means to be human. Serious, intelligent, and well-informed people can disagree about such deep questions, and there is significant public value in having these debates. But enormous harm comes from allowing these discussions to be dominated by incumbent positions or hijacked by vested interests, sometimes as cover for other political causes or private agendas. For example, by protesting GMOs (i.e., being an enemy of that particular innovation) a person can signal his morality of concern for unspecified others to attain a private reputational benefit without bearing the cost that opposition imposes on specific others, such as the potential consumers of the new technology (i.e., the forgone benefits of lower prices or enhanced quality of food). Society can find itself in a bad equilibrium where specific innovations have too many enemies (because the private costs of being an enemy are low, whereas the private benefits are high) and too few friends (because the private costs are high, and the benefits are mostly public). There is an opportunity for government to provide a public good by engaging the enemies.

9.4 A Better Approach to Innovation Policy

The "friends and enemies" view suggests a further reinterpretation of the "innovation problem." When defined a priori as a market failure (Arrow 1962b) or systems failure (Nelson 1993) problem, then any solution must address private investment or institutions—that is, it must resolve a problem of constrained resources, demand, or infrastructure. There is no way to solve the innovation problem without "helping friends" by transferring resources or rents to them, whether to individuals, organizations, or sectors. The incentive alignment with a political economy model in which friends of innovation form an organized interest group to lobby for innovation support (Mokyr 1994; Goolsbee 1998; Taylor 2016) is simply a happy accident.

Viewing the innovation problem from the "friends and enemies" perspective gives us a different perspective on the mechanisms at work. Rather than an exclusively production cost-centered view (from which innovation policy targets production costs, whether by creating rents or transferring resources), the "friends and enemies" view of innovation as an economic problem seeks to minimize the sum of production costs *and transaction costs*. Transaction costs matter because no innovation is just a technology; new technologies always come embedded in a sociocultural web of institutions (Dopfer and Potts 2008). For a new technology to be adopted and retained (as useful knowledge) these rules and institutions also need to adapt. That requires collective action and social learning: both are processes shaped by transaction costs.

Enemies of innovation have their effect by raising the transaction costs on innovation. When the friends of an innovation fail, it often has less to do with missing the mark on technological development (which is usually well incentivized by global Schumpeterian competition), than with failing to overcome some governance or collective action problem due to high transaction costs (Acemoglu and Robinson 2006). This is likely in early-stage new technologies before organized lobby groups or industry associations have formed, because sufficient Schumpeterian rents have not yet accrued to fund such collective action, and the industry itself may not yet exist or may be still nascent (Foster and Heeks 2013; Feldman and Tavassoli 2015). Innovations can fail not only for production cost reasons but also for transaction cost reasons, and yet the mainstream innovation policy model is configured to support innovation problems as if they were exclusively production cost problems.

An alternative approach to innovation policy is to focus on minimizing the transaction costs to innovation (rather than minimizing production costs). This approach seeks to engage with the enemies of innovation, who seek to raise transaction costs, and to work toward finding ways to lower those transaction costs. This solves what for the friends of innovation is a pure collective action problem (and thus subject to a tragedy-of-the-commons social dilemma). It is perhaps useful to see this from the perspective of the friends of innovation (as in figure 9.2), who have a choice about whether to engage government (to lobby for production cost support), or to engage with enemies (to obtain lowered transaction costs). Under reasonable assumptions about risk preferences and capabilities of innovators, lobbying government will be preferable to engaging enemies. Risks are fewer and more manageable, and rewards are greater and potentially long-lasting.

Yet who will engage the enemies? Or rather, who will solve the transaction cost version of the innovation problem to overcome psychological, behavioral, sociocultural, and institutional resistance? This is a collective action problem: the costs to the action are borne individually, and may involve costs in both resources and reputation. But the benefits accrue as an industry-specific public

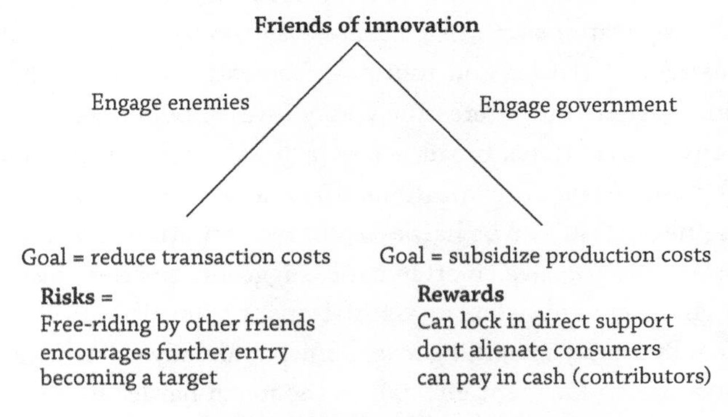

Figure 9.2 Why friends of innovation prefer to engage government

good and are available to all who follow. Indeed, the provision of this public good is likely to lead to increased entry and therefore competition.

So unless there is some mechanism for the first mover to capture those benefits, we would not expect to observe private provision of this public good (Bergstrom et al. 1986). An example of such a mechanism is a platform monopoly (Weyl and White 2014), as evidence of the recent willingness of Uber, a private company, to take on the enemies of innovation in ride-sharing, namely the incumbent taxi industry and its political beneficiaries, by funding a massive global public relations campaign. Another such mechanism Schumpeter (1942) alluded to when an existing monopolist is able to leverage rents from a previous innovation to lobby for regulatory exemptions to enable it to develop new technologies, much as Google, an information technology conglomerate, has leveraged rents from search technologies to bridge to AI and autonomous vehicles, or Monsanto has leveraged rents from agrochemicals to bridge into biotechnology, in both cases maintaining significant incumbent advantages.

In the expectation that private orderings are unlikely to effectively coordinate to solve this problem except in special circumstances, there is a distinct role for government action. Consider three basic principles for overcoming innovation resistance, approximately in order of significance.

Facilitate Collective Learning

First, the vocal, protesting, or otherwise self-identified enemies of innovation are usually the tip of a much larger population of those who are undecided about the new technology, but by default are weakly opposed or skeptical until persuaded otherwise. While "engage the enemies" innovation policy will need to engage with the vocal 10 percent, the more important target is the weakly undecided 90 percent in order to help them through a process of collective learning and familiarization. Much of this will involve demystifying a technology and moving it out of the realms of something that only experts understand to things that, for instance, children can use and that are part of ordinary life (Heiskanen et al. 2010). Key stations on this path are easy-to-use prototypes and integration into existing activities and routines. Domestication is the basic logic of inclusive innovation, and interestingly may involve public media and cultural organizations (e.g., national broadcasters or public arts organizations) at least as much as public science organizations. The role of seeding and prompting collective imagination can also be harnessed to redirect attention away from *unintended risks* and hazards, which often easily suggest themselves by analogy with previous high-salience disasters or associations (e.g., nuclear power and nuclear weaponry) or by simply imagining losses of what already exists (thus triggering loss aversion and endowment effects); to the much harder to imagine context of *unintended benefits*, where people will usually need help to make connections to benefits from adoption of the new technology that might not be at first obvious or immediately salient, or may only accumulate slowly (Juma 2014). For example, the benefits of mobile phones as safety devices for communication during emergencies or as geolocation devices were unintended and very difficult to intuit early on.

Build Innovation Commons

Overcoming innovation resistance by "engaging the enemy" suggests confrontation in which the technology is developed and then enemies are dealt with, in sequence. But key lessons from previous successful adoption of radical new technologies emphasizes the importance of codevelopment of the technology itself along with the institutional framework by which the innovation is both accessed and evaluated, particularly in relation to risks and the domain of uses (Marchant et al. 2013; Juma 2016). In short, the more inclusive the development of the technology, the more permissive the institutional framework will tend to be that regulates the technology. The technology and the rules governing the technology, in other words, need to coevolve. This is best achieved by creating a large and inclusive pool of participatory stakeholders, each vested with the development of the technology and its institutional framework. In such a situation, with a consensus created by open access, and conflict resolution mechanisms already in place, cooperation becomes the default behavioral setting. A technology or innovation that develops in such an institutional context can adapt to new information about the uses, costs, or benefits through rule-governed, consensus decision-making, which affords the process legitimacy (Lopez-Berzosa and Gawer 2014).

This innovation-commons model of technology governance rules intended to minimize innovation resistance is almost the opposite of an expert-driven, top-down model of technology regulation that has relatively minimal involvement of, or attempt to induct or construct a community of, users in the governance process. But that is also unsurprising, as the regulatory model was never intended to minimize innovation resistance, but rather to achieve the twin goals of maximizing political involvement and political rents by providing rules that the enemies of the innovation wanted (to raise transaction costs) or the rules that the friends wanted (to offset production costs, including those rules that raise the costs of subsequent entry), and often both sorts of rules at once. Examples of the inclusive community-led, innovation commons model of engagement in rule-building and rule-making, and therefore in consensus, are in collaborative innovation such as open-source software, or in technologies that have emerged from hackerspaces, such as 3D printing and cryptocurrencies. An innovation commons can facilitate engagement with the enemies of innovation, and transform them into participatory stakeholders, by co-opting them in the process of developing not just the technology and innovation, but the institutional rules by which it is used and accessed. This is likely to lead to a more adaptive framework of technology governance that is able to change as more information comes in.

Minimize Innovation Rent-Seeking

The economic problem of engaging with the enemies of innovation (to minimize transaction costs) sits on top of a deeper problem that arises when political actors benefit by supporting *either* enemies *or* friends of innovation. The political problem to be solved is to ensure that engaging with the enemies of innovation has a higher political payoff than seeking to provide benefits to either enemies or supporters of innovation. Political insiders can increase their own payoff to helping friends (the right-hand path in figure 9.2) by working to increase the transaction costs[7] to engaging in political bargaining, both by raising information costs about what is going on, and by raising the agreement and enforcement costs of political action to undo the benefits bestowed. The policy objective must be to minimize opportunities for insiders to raise the transaction costs associated with political bargaining over innovation policy spending, technology regulation, and other forms of political rent creation.

In order to shift the political calculus away from supporting friends (*or* appeasing enemies) of innovation and toward incentivizing engaging enemies (*and* friends), two things must happen. First, the costs of political action to support interest groups need to be raised above their manifest benefits. Second, the benefits from brokering Coasean bargains, in order to unwind political inefficiency (MacDonald 2016), need to be raised above their manifest costs. This can be achieved through a combination of political bargaining and direct action to shift perceptions of the costs and benefits of a new technology. This suggests a new public choice logic to innovation policy in which the economic efficiency of "engaging the enemy" accrues from the unwinding of political transaction-cost inefficiencies (and their impact on innovation/market exchanges) created by interventionist innovation policy aimed at correcting market and systems failures. That is to say, there may be something of a discord between interventionist innovation policy (whether helping friends or appeasing enemies) and an inclusive innovation policy of engagement: transaction-cost impediments to bargaining often accrue as an unintended consequence of otherwise well-meaning policy interventions.

While regulation and legislation within a nation-state are prime instances of Coasean bargains that can potentially be made, a further example of Coasean bargaining to facilitate the stand-down of the enemies of innovation, and thus to lower the transaction costs to innovation, is costs imported through global treaties (e.g., bilateral trade agreements that require harmonization with technology bans or regulations made in one nation to satisfy domestic lobbies).

Efforts to contain the spread of these rents across national boundaries contribute to minimizing transaction costs of innovation.

Examples: Uber and Bitcoin

Uber, a private US technology company, is notable for the absence of government funding directed toward the development of its innovative ridesharing platform based on software and the mass adoption of smartphones. Uber is also a good example of creative destruction in the transport service industry, disrupting the rents that have long existed in the licensed taxi industry. The enemies of innovation here are not consumers, most of whom are happy users of the product and appreciate its many unintended benefits. Rather, the enemy is the taxi industry, and particular the owners of taxi licenses, and the local governments who administer and control this system and who benefit from the sale of taxi licenses. Because governments benefit from the incumbent system, they are among the enemies of this particular innovation. Uber has therefore taken it upon itself to engage with this enemy in a global campaign, fought on at least three fronts—public relations, law, and politics—to engage a collective learning process as to the personal, social, and economic benefits of this new technology and way of producing transport services.

The curious thing about the Uber case is that this is precisely the sort of activity that a government should be doing, rather than a private company, which is in effect providing a public good. Instead, the reason governments are not engaged in this process, or take the side of the enemies of innovation, is because of the extent to which local governments institutionally embed themselves in particular technological solutions. This aspect is often overlooked in innovation policy discussion when we fail to connect it to a further instance of government failure through innovation planning (viz., picking winners). The regulation of a particular industry involves not just social control of business, but implicit selection of technological platforms, business models, and associated institutions. Invariably, there will be winners (usually concentrated) and losers (usually diffuse) as a result of the choice of any particular technological/institutional matrix, and so the social costs of these political choices can be hard to identify.

Uber is engaged in picking apart the skein of costs imposed on society in order to release the benefits of a new technology through Coasean bargaining at the level of public persuasion, coalition formation, side payments and exchanges, and legal challenges. This "networked political entrepreneurship," however, is really what elected officials should have been doing all along, were they disinterested guardians of the public welfare.

Another example can be found in the new crypto-economy technologies of bitcoin and blockchain. Again, this new technology and platform did not emerge from conventional innovation policy (i.e., supporting friends), but arose from private citizens and innovation commons communities (hackers), and was immediately a direct challenge to existing government-supported technologies, such as government-issued money and government-regulated payments and banking systems. Governments once again found themselves supporting the enemies of innovation.

So who would engage the enemies and deliver the public good? What emerged in the crypto-economy space, largely from the innovation commons, are organizations such as Bitcoin Embassy[8] and Coin Centre,[9] which are devoted to assuaging enemies. Another example is the Muskoka Group,[10] an open-platform organization that campaigns "to fight misconceptions about the [blockchain] technology, which they say is unfairly perceived as insecure and susceptible to criminal activity." In both cases these organizations are not lobbying for government funding, that is, seeking to engage government as a friend of innovation. Rather, they are trying to change restrictive policy in order to "help accelerate and drive the progress of blockchain technology." These are private entities driving public innovation policy. That this is necessary points to the failure of public innovation policy to engage with the enemies of innovation.

9.5 Inclusive Innovation: A New Social Contract

A new approach to innovation policy shifts government's role from supporting those engaged in innovation—whether by transferring resources or creating rents through political exchange, something we have characterized as "helping friends" of innovations—to a very different role in which the task of innovation policy is to let innovators get on with their business, but to direct government energy and resources to a different task—namely "engaging enemies" of innovation. In other words, we think that modern innovation policy spends too much time doing the easy vote-winning things, and not enough time engaging with the hard problem that blocks innovation, namely that many people, whether for good or bad reasons, resist innovation. That resistance matters because in the long run it has a large social cost: it makes us all poorer. But there is no easy constituency to solve this problem. It is a collective action problem, yet one that governments, because of their own self-interest as vote-maximizing agents, as public choice theory has long understood, tend to make worse.

We need a renewed conversation about what innovation policy ought to be. The main task of innovation policy should be to solve a collective action problem that arises when new technologies create losers (and not just winners). Those losers have the means and motive to block, retard, or distort the new technologies, often, at least in the short run, successfully. The innovation problem is not market failure in private investment in R & D. The innovation problem, in my view, is the collective action problem in engaging in Coasean political bargaining to induce the enemies of innovation to stand down.

This new approach to innovation policy implies an attempt to rewrite the "social contract" (or perhaps better, the "political bargain") about technological innovation. McCloskey's (2006, 2010, 2016) *Bourgeois* trilogy claims that the modern era of growth—the Great Enrichment—got started not when we discovered coal or invented steam engines and factories, but rather when talk of trade and commerce became respectable. The great enrichment wasn't an industrial revolution as much as an ethical and rhetorical product of the Enlightenment (Mokyr 2009). This shift came packaged with what McCloskey calls the "bourgeois deal," a three-act play: in the first act, the bourgeois are permitted to have a go; in the second act, if they succeed under competition, they keep their profits; and in the third act, everyone benefits from those improvements. The essence of the act 1 deal (the freedom to engage in life-bettering trade and commerce) is what happens in the third act, which is that everyone benefits as a market outworking of natural equality and social justice.[11] McCloskey's point is that this is an inclusive deal: it only works if there is a third act.

Most modern innovation policy is first-act and second-act policy, but inclusive innovation is third-act innovation policy. It seeks to address the issues of risks, harms, and exclusion that innovation brings in order to build the type of society that conditions innovation on the understanding—the new social contract—that the third act will be honored: that no one will be left behind or excluded (which is not the same as saying that no one will bear any cost). The construction of this institutional, political, and sociocultural consensus is the goal of innovation policy, in my view. Many good writers and thinkers have proposed closely related ideas in which policy should seek to unleash entrepreneurial and innovative forces in society: for instance, Postrel's (1998) dynamism, Atkinson's (2004) Schumpeterian innovative society, Baumol's (2001) free-market innovation machine, Phelps's (2012) mass flourishing, and Thierer's (2016) permissionless innovation.

However, unleashing or celebrating the entrepreneurs and innovators in order to create a society based on or organized around them—that is, an entrepreneurial culture, or an innovative society, or a creative economy, and so on—should not actually be the goal. Rather, the goal should be to create a society that *tolerates* innovation, which is different to *supporting* it. Tolerance means you don't prejudge, and you don't stand in the way of innovation. You accept that this may actually impose immediate costs on you, as well as future benefits (that you might not be able to see yet). But it doesn't mean that you are uninterested or uninvested or uninvolved. Tolerance means that you approach matters rationally, understand risk, and are open to evidence. The objective is to create a social contract, culture, and institutional system that are tolerant of innovation, and for the most part that means engaging with the enemies of innovation, not boosting its supporters.

Another important consideration is the role of governmental leadership, particularly with respect to the prestigious expert adviser roles in modern innovation policy, such as chief scientist. In the "help your friends" mode, these roles are largely that of "chief friend," as someone who is deeply respected in the scientific or technology community and can act as czar, or a high-level interface between government and the science, technology, and innovation industries. In my view, this function would be differently configured as an emissary or even front-line combat role. The job of chief scientist in government is different from the role of a head scientist in industry or academia, which is to lead research. But in the context of innovation policy a chief scientist should identify and defuse threats to innovation, frame the public debate about the risks, hazards, costs, and benefits of innovation, and work to broker inclusive innovation.

Top-down leadership needs to be complemented with bottom-up organization, which is the role of emergent communities and organizations that furnish what is in effect a local or technology-specific public good by engaging with the enemies of innovation, seeking to turn them from resisters into tolerators, and in so doing, lowering the transaction costs of innovation. The basic economic problem is where the organization and resources for this undertaking come from. One prospect is that they come from civil society through the innovation commons (Allen and Potts 2016) in the form of the surplus resources of technology enthusiasts, organized in the form of a club good. Another possibility is these resources are furnished by mature industry associations in order to benefit their members as they collectively adopt new technology. Such organizations (effectively private clubs) will often have accumulated political capital they can exploit and effective governance to overcome social dilemmas. The problem in both cases, however, is that these constituencies are naturally limited.

We need an innovation policy model intended to create a fully inclusive constituency, giving everyone what Matt Ridley above called "a stake in the new." This is an idea from development economics, where the policy goal of inclusive economic development (Chataway et al. 2014; Papaioannou 2014) is not a distributional goal per se, but a way of creating a sociopolitical consensus about collective pooling of both risks and benefits. "People are more likely to accept the risks of new technologies if they have been part of the process of deciding on their use," Calestos Juma explained in a press interview. This consensus-building process, and an understanding that both costs and benefits will be shared, is particularly important for controversial new technologies, especially those heavy with emotional and ideological freight (e.g., genetic engineering, nuclear technologies, robotic substitution, and so on). The task here is not simply that of educating the public. Ignorance is rarely the main barrier to overcome. The broader and more salient task is to develop inclusive strategies to establish the legitimacy and quality of risk assessment, to manage risk perception, and to foster a spirit of inquiry and trust with respect to any new technology or innovative practice.

A friends-and-enemies classification of the innovation problem therefore suggests a different approach to innovation policy. It is less focused on transferring resources to solve market failure problems or on high-level planning to resolve systems failure problems, than on solving sociobehavioral and political resistance problems. This is a different sort of policy—possibly harder, and with fewer opportunities for rent creation. It will likely require a different sort of policymaker. But an economy that can solve this problem effectively may be at a substantial innovation advantage over economies that fail to solve it.

In recent years economists have noted a global slowdown in economic growth, concentrated at the frontier (Gordon 2016). Many explanations have been offered, including running out of ideas (Cowen 2011). But an alternative hypothesis is that the slowdown is due to the gradual rise in the transaction costs of innovation due to the increasing success of the enemies of innovation. If that is the case, long-run economic growth will depend on a new course for innovation policy to solve this collective action problem.

Notes

1. "I hope future policymakers will pay greater attention to the disjuncture between rapid technological innovation and the slow pace of institutional adjustment" (Juma 2016, 263).
2. Note that the Olsonian logic (Olson 1965) of collective action for the friends of innovation to seek concentrated benefits (innovation rents) and impose disperse costs (on taxpayers) is symmetrical for the enemies of innovation. Persuading politicians to enact their preferred policy to block an innovation creates concentrated benefits (by staving off the expected concentrated costs) and dispersed costs by preventing at the margin innovation, growth, and prosperity. This is why it is easy for enemies of innovation to successfully lobby (Becker 1983) and hard for individual citizens to organize to stop or engage them. Both friends and enemies of innovation are acting in a symmetrical (but inverted) Olsonian logic. This is why it should fall to government to undertake the role of engaging the enemies.
3. There is a rich literature in science and technology studies on the sociology of technological resistance; see for example, Bauer 1997.
4. It should be emphasized that the two sides are populated by rational agents; some people will have made capital investments (asset specificity, including in human capital) that will be devalued by innovation. Ex post, these will turn out to be mistaken investments ("malinvestments," in Austrian capital theory), but these ex ante investments were made from behind a veil of uncertainty.
5. This is why large changes in technological infrastructure and industrial structure are often only possible after an exogenous destruction of capital value, for example, a war or a severe economic collapse (Olson 1982).
6. Clustered Regularly Interspaced Short Palindromic Repeats, an editing technology of genetic engineering.
7. It is useful to distinguish between natural and *contrived transaction costs* (Twight 1988, 1994). Natural transaction costs are those that exist even when all political actors cooperate to minimize impediments to political exchange in an optimal Coasean bargaining between

friends and enemies of innovation. Contrived transaction costs are those that exist because they are in the self-interest of those doing the bargaining, and so deliberately created to benefit political insiders. They are broadly composed of "perception costs" and "action costs."

8. "By encouraging dialogue between businesses, banks, the media, and regulators, The Bitcoin Embassy aims to provide guidelines about compliance with Dutch and European laws when dealing with cryptocurrencies" (Amsterdam bitcoin embassy).
9. http://coincenter.org/entry/what-coin-center-believes-in-and-what-we-do. "Coin Center is the only organization in the US dedicated exclusively to the policy and regulatory issues affecting open permissionless decentralized-cryptocurrency networks and decentralized-computing platforms like Bitcoin and Ethereum."
10. http://www.muskokagroup.org/.
11. See Wilkinson 2016, https://niskanencenter.org/blog/the-great-enrichment-and-social-justice/.

10

Conclusion

The evolutionarily rational response to uncertainty is cooperation, forming a group to pool information to reduce uncertainty. This is also the evolutionary origin of innovation.

The innovation commons is a positive response to uncertainty by group formation through institutional means to pool information for entrepreneurial discovery.[1] Uncertainty about entrepreneurial prospects is not resolved in firms or in markets, but rather in the commons, from which firms and markets subsequently emerge. The innovation commons are rules for cooperation to pool information for the mutual purpose of prospective opportunity discovery. This emergent institutional form is the true origin of entrepreneurship and the innovative firms and new industries of the Schumpeterian canon.

The innovation commons is not a new economy, or a fundamental break in human nature and economic institutions from those of the market economy (cf. Bauwens 2005; Bollier 2014; Kostakis and Bauwens 2014; Benkler 2006). Novelty, newness, and discovery are all economic goods that, under particular behavioral, institutional, and environmental circumstances, are efficiently and effectively jointly produced through cooperation in the commons. The innovation commons—including the adaptive behaviors and the institutions that compose it—are in this fundamental sense a natural part of an open, evolving, market economy. They are not prima facie evidence of an emerging turn to a new type of more cooperative economic society. Rather, innovation commons have always been with us. But their apparent rise in recent times is associated with the growing demand for their services due to increased dynamics and complexity and lower transaction costs of coordination, a trend likely to continue (Munger 2018). As market economies grow and become more complex, we will see a greater role for innovation commons.

10.1 The Institutional Origin of Innovation

The standard approach to innovation economics is based on market failure, corrected by government intervention. The innovation commons approach emphasizes a collective action problem, with a governance solution.

Governance and *government* look like similar words, but a wide blue ocean of meaning separates these two approaches to the same problem. The key insight of the governance approach, or the *innovation commons* approach, to the innovation problem is that it is solved with *institutions*. The ambition of this book has been to open a new frontier in new institutional economics over a space traditionally occupied by Schumpeterian or evolutionary economics, or more generally by innovation economics. Institutions coordinate human actions, including economic actions, and of those, actions pertaining to the production and use of new ideas—technological discovery and innovation—are certainly within that remit. Institutions incentivize individual behavior, but they also make communities and govern groups.

Indeed, missing from the standard innovation story is the role of something approximated by the notion of a community or a group. Now perhaps "group" sounds sociological. But if I sharpen it up and say *effectively self-governed community*, we're closer to the mark. A firm, for example, in the sense of the Marshallian/Penrosian innovating firm at the core of the Schumpeterian model is an instance of an effectively self-governed community. But so are groups of people coming together to pool resources to create new ideas and explore the opportunities of a new technology, as in Eric von Hippel's "user communities" (Gambardella et al. 2017) or the networks of "open innovation" that Henry Chesbrough (2003a, 2003b) writes about.

I have sought to develop a general theory of innovation communities, or innovation in groups that have as their end state monopolistic firms in mature industries. Prior to that, as the Schumpeterian research program has explored, there is a phase of creative destruction in which new firms displace old firms, as a new technology displaces extant technologies and ways of doing things. At the beginning of that process, according to Schumpeter (and now every business school) is the entrepreneur. The modern theory of innovation-driven economic growth and development thus begins with the entrepreneurial firm. More sophisticated models will add supporting accoutrements such as venture finance, intellectual property protection, innovation management, and public support via the panoply of innovation policy infrastructures. This is phase 1 of the standard Schumpeterian model, consisting of a new idea and the entrepreneurial firm seeking to exploit and develop it.

But the origin of innovation is not the entrepreneur. The origin of innovation is not creative genius. The origin of new industries is not a government program.

The true origin of innovation is neither innovative firms, nor free markets, nor dynamic economies, nor competitive societies, nor creative cultures. These are emergent consequences. These innovative individuals, firms, markets, industries, economies, cultures, and societies are what you get, not what you start with.

Nor is the true origin of innovation found in the new technology or the new idea itself. It is not in the patent, nor in the engineered prototype, and if you stumbled upon one lying on the sidewalk, you would no more have originated the innovation than the creative genius. This is an elusive concept to apprehend because it seems so obvious that innovation begins with a new valuable invention, from a creative entrepreneurial person, organized by a competitive innovative firm. This is the Schumpeterian canon. But that's what we see *once we know the outcome*. To understand the true origin of innovation, we need to bring into view the events that prefigure the calculated entrepreneurial actions of firms in markets.

The surprising truth about these events is that they don't look like innovation. For a start, they're a lot more cooperative than you might expect. There's a lot of sharing going on, without contracted reciprocation. There's also fewer entrepreneurs than you might expect. In fact, there are possibly none. But there is also more order than at first seems, with many of the community's rules revealing themselves only when you break them. Indeed, there is a distinct community, and it matters whether you are inside or outside it. The very early stage of innovation is distinctly club-like, a spontaneous product of civil society, a group of people who form a rule-governed group to enable them to pool resources and share information, and so to create a common-pool resource—what I have called an "innovation commons."

The innovation commons is the true origin of innovation. It is the source from which the subsequent markers of innovation emerge—the entrepreneurial actors, the innovating firms, the new markets, and so on. But the innovation commons will often not appear to be part of the same innovation process because a "fundamental transformation," in the Oliver Williamson (1979) sense, occurs when the institutions of innovation shift from the early phase of the innovation commons to organizations and markets in subsequent and more conventionally understood phases of the innovation trajectory.

This book has sought to show how this first fundamental phase of innovation works. We began by recognizing that the first problem to be solved, the foundation of the innovation problem, is a collective action problem of how a group of people come together to share information, the purpose and value of which is contemporaneously unclear. That's a governance problem of collective action under uncertainty for the purpose of pooling resources for the discovery of entrepreneurial opportunities. This is the fundamental innovation problem, and it is a problem of economic organization and incentives. What is surprising is that this has been almost entirely overlooked as a problem that can be understood from within the domain of economic analysis.

10.2 Implications for Economic Theory

The main implication of the argument developed in this book is to extend the domain of economic theory and analysis further back to the origin of innovation. This space has hitherto been occupied by the study of creativity, imagination, invention, genius, insight, alertness, and other ways of saying that the origin of novelty and innovation is a product of the human mind. The microfoundations of innovation economics, and the search for the true origin of innovation, would then be properly located within the domains of psychology, neuroscience, and the study of human brains and behavior, including their interactions with the world. But I have argued that this is wrong.

The deep origin of innovation, and therefore of economic growth, is a question for economics—not psychology or neuroscience—because the discovery of opportunity is itself an economic process. It requires coordination and incentives set up through institutional governance. It is a production process that combines inputs in order to create value by using a technology. But that technology is a governance or institutional technology—a social technology. And the production process, using the institutional technology, creates a common-pool resource. That common-pool resource is an input into entrepreneurial action. Such entrepreneurial action has been understood ever since Schumpeter as the origin of innovation, but it is not. It is, rather, the origin of rational individual entrepreneurial action. Yet that in itself is not the origin of the innovation process.

The theory I have proposed shifts the economics of innovation further back in space and time, positing a "zeroth phase" of the trajectory that precedes the standard Schumpeterian (or meso) trajectory. This extension of the economic model of innovation has the benefit of explaining how the conditions and opportunities for entrepreneurial action arise without relying on an exogenous explanation (creativity/imagination/alertness). Rather, it relies on a previous phase of economic production (creating a common-pool resource in information about a new technology) that requires solving a problem of cooperation under uncertainty: this is a governance problem, and it is solved with the economic institutions of the innovation commons.

The origins of innovation, and therefore of economic growth, begin with the emergence of governance technologies to create common-pool resources in information about opportunities. The role of governance technologies in the economics of innovation has been utterly dominated by the hierarchical organization—the firm—which, as emphasized, is often an efficient governance technology for the coordination of economic activity only once an entrepreneurial opportunity has been created or discovered (which is at phase 1 of the conventional Schumpeterian technological trajectory).

However, the institutions of the commons—as studied by Elinor Ostrom and others—are an economic solution to the governance and coordination problem of pooling resources under uncertainty to create value. Different technologies of governance and coordination are required along the path of an innovation trajectory, and at the very beginning, when uncertainty is highest, those institutions need to incentivize maximum cooperation to pool resources. Economic theory, and particularly evolutionary microeconomics, needs an integrated model of the evolution of governance along an innovation trajectory. A consequence of this theoretical insight is to diminish the role of policy (planning) and to emphasize instead emergent private orderings arising from effective communities and the social technologies of governance.

10.3 The Innovation-Sharing Economy

The sharing economy is part of the digital zeitgeist, a combination of ubiquitous internet, smartphone saturation, and the cultural mores of open-source software, Wikipedia, BitTorrent, and consumer rating systems.[2] The rise of the sharing economy is sometimes attributed to a kind of moral progress, where a new generation of economic citizens, born of long-lasting peace and wealthy societies, are now rediscovering the lost virtues of trust and cooperation. It's socialism writ small and networked, living in a world that software has already eaten (Andreessen 2011).

But the innovation economy is the original sharing economy. This is not because of proto-socialism or atavistic communitarian loveliness among early stage innovators, but because of institutional economic efficiency. If you trace back to the beginning of almost any innovation process, you will observe the same economic coordination problem being solved in the same way: namely, a group of people with a shared enthusiasm for a new technology pooling and sharing "innovation resources"—data, information, know-how, equipment, material, access, connections, and so on—under a commons-like institutional governance structure. Observe that this sharing economy is not a free-for-all—it is not a public good. There are rules about what you give and what you take, and there are consequences for breaking those rules, the most significant being exclusion from the shared innovation resources, that is, banishment from the innovation commons, and therefore from access to the resources it contains. But these rules are ad hoc, adapted to local circumstances, and both made by, and enforced by, the community itself. These rules are, because of that process, legitimate. The core of the innovation-sharing economy does not reside in the kindness of people, but in the effectiveness of rules. It exists not in the behaviors of people, but in the institutions that govern them.

The crucial part of this story, however, is why this innovation-sharing economy exists at all. It is not because early-stage innovators are naturally more cooperative people. They may have all sorts of special characteristics, and entrepreneurship research has long sought to discover the psychobehavioral or sociodynamic equivalent of the entrepreneurial gene: for example, different theories propose they are more risk-loving, less concerned with material payoffs, younger, more experienced, outsiders, more creative, more open to experience, the youngest sibling, and so on. I made no such claim here because after a time, as we repeatedly observe, most such people in the innovation commons stop their cooperative sharing behaviors and shift to more overtly competitive behavior (starting firms, for instance). The Homebrew Computer Club we met in chapter 1 eventually collapsed because the early members started firms or worked for firms building on the innovations that emerged from Homebrew. Indeed, my general theory is that most innovation commons will collapse when they've achieved their purpose, which is to pool distributed innovation resources to reveal entrepreneurial opportunities. Innovation commons don't collapse when they fail; they collapse when they succeed.

This point of collapse that gives rise to the emergence of first entrepreneurs and then firms usually marks the beginning of an innovation trajectory. From the perspective of the state, the innovation trajectory begins here, because that is where the official data trail begins, with first intellectual property, or first registered company, or first employment contracts.

In innovation theory, this identifies phase 1 of a three-phase innovation trajectory, with phase 2 being the adoption-diffusion phase, and phase 3 as institutional embedding (Dopfer and Potts 2008; Dopfer 2012). But what we see here is a prior phase—a zeroth phase to create a commons of innovation resources—that is institutionally different from the subsequent three phases, which are all in the realm of firms, markets, and governments, because it is a private ordering of rules. This is the true origin of innovation.

Notes

1. The standard formulation of uncertainty in economic action is uncovered risk over a distribution of outcomes, suggesting a reciprocally contracted pooling equilibrium in a context in which markets already exist. Similarly, the strategic model of real options (Dixit and Pindyk 1994) also supposes that markets exist to cover these forward options. In both cases, trivially, markets already exist. From a different starting point, institutional and behavioral economics argues that the positive consequence of uncertainty is the use of decision rules (Simon 1955; Cyert and March 1963); the consequence of such heuristics for innovation is that economies are stabilized and that evolution is path dependent.

2. Founding texts are by Benkler (2006), Leadbeater (2008) and Shirky (2008), who emphasized the path from open-source movement and the rise of the possibility of peer-to-peer consumption (aka collaborative consumption [Botsman and Roos 2010]), particularly to release value in underutilized assets. This is better described as a "platform economy," as the transactions are not sharing (i.e., unreciprocated transfers) but intermediation in a two-sided market exchange. Munger (2015a) explains this in Coasian terms as a transaction cost revolution.

REFERENCES

Acemoglu, D., Robinson, J. (2000). "Political losers as a barrier to economic development." *American Economic Review*, 90(2), 126–130.

Acemoglu, D., Robinson, J. (2006). "Economic backwardness in political perspective." *American Political Science Review*, 100(1), 115–131.

Acemoglu, D., Robinson, J. (2012). *Why Nations Fail.* New York: Crown Business.

Aghion, P., Bloom, N., Blundell, R., Griffith, R., Howitt, R. (2005). "Competition and innovation: An inverted-U relationship." *Quarterly Journal of Economics*, 120(2), 701–728.

Aghion, P., David, P., Foray, D. (2009). "Science, technology and innovation for economic growth: Linking policy research and practice in STIG systems." *Research Policy*, 38, 681–693.

Aghion, P., Tirole, J. (1994). "The management of innovation." *Quarterly Journal of Economics*, *109*(4), 1185–1210.

Agrawal, A. (2002). "Common resources and institutional sustainability." In E. Ostrom, T. Dietz, N. Dolšak, P., Stern, S. Stovich, E., Weber, U. (eds.), *The Drama of the Commons.* Washington, DC: National Academy Press. Pp. 41–86.

Ainsworth, S., Sened, I. (1993). "The role of lobbyists: Entrepreneurs with two audiences." *American Journal of Political Science*, 37(3), 834–866.

Akcigit U., Lui Q. (2016). "The role of information in innovation and competition." *Journal of the European Economic Association*, 14(4), 828–870.

Akerlof, G. (1970). "The market for lemons: Quality uncertainty and the market mechanism." *Quarterly Journal of Economics*, 84(3), 488–500.

Alchian, A. (1950). "Uncertainty, evolution, and economic theory." *Journal of Political Economy*, 58(3), 211–221.

Alchian, A., Demsetz, H. (1972). "Production, information costs, and economic organization." *American Economic Review*, 62(5), 777–795.

Aldrich, H., Fiol, M. (1994). "Fools rush in? The institutional context of industry creation." *Academy of Management*, 19(4), 645–670.

Aligica, P., Boettke, P. (2009). *Challenging Institutional Analysis and Development: The Bloomington School.* New York: Routledge.

Aligica, P., Tarko, V. (2012). "Polycentricity: From Polanyi to Ostrom, and Beyond." *Governance*, 25(2), 237–262.

Allen, D.W. (2011). *The Institutional Revolution.* Chicago: University of Chicago Press.

Allen, D.A. (2016). "Hackerspaces as entrepreneurial anarchy." SSRN: http://papers.ssrn.com/sol3/papers.cfm?abstract_id=2749016.

Allen, D. (2017). "The private governance of entrepreneurship: An institutional approach to entrepreneurial discovery." PhD thesis, RMIT University.

Allen, D.A., Potts, J. (2016). "How innovation commons contribute to discovering and developing new technologies." *International Journal of the Commons*, 10(2), 1035–1054.

Allen, R. (1983). "Collective invention." *Journal of Economic Behavior and Organization*, 4, 1–24.

Alvarez, S., Barney, J. (2007). "Discovery and creation: Alternative theories of engtrepreneurial action." *Strategic Entrepreneurship Journal*, 1(1–2), 11–26.

Anderson, B. (1991). *Imagined Communities*. London: Verso.

Andersson, Å. E., Andersson, D. (2015). "Creative cities and the new global hierarchy." *Applied Spatial Analysis and Policy*, 8, 181–198.

Andersson, D. Andersson, Å. E. (eds.) (2011). *Handbook of Creative Cities*. Cheltenham: Edward Elgar.

Andreessen, M. (2011). "Why software is eating the world." *Wall Street Journal*, August 20, 2011. http://www.wsj.com/articles/SB10001424053111903480904576512250915629460.

Aoki, M. (2007). "Endogenizing institutions and institutional changes." *Journal of Institutional Economics*, 3(1), 1–31.

Arora, A., Fosfuri, A., Gambardella, A. (2001). *Markets for Technology: The Economics of Innovation and Corporate Strategy*. Cambridge, MA: MIT Press.

Arrow, K. (1962a). "The economic implications of learning by doing." *Review of Economic Studies*, *29*(3), 155–173.

Arrow, K. (1962b). "Economic welfare and the allocation of resources for innovation." In Richard R. Nelson (ed.), *The Rate and Direction of Inventive Activity*. Princeton, NJ: Princeton University Press. Pp. 609–626.

Arrow, K. (1974). "Limited knowledge and economic analysis." *American Economic Review*, 64(1), 1–10.

Arthur, W. B. (2009). *The Nature of Technology*. New York: Oxford University Press.

Atkinson, R. (2004). *The Past and Future of America's Economy*. Cheltenham: Edward Elgar.

Audretsch, D., Feldman, M. (1996). "R&D spillovers and the geography of innovation and production." *American Economic Review*, 86(3), 630–640.

Axelrod, R. (1984). *The Evolution of Cooperation*. New York: Basic Books.

Axelrod, R., Hamilton, W. (1981). "The evolution of cooperation." *Science*, 211, 1390–1396.

Axtell, R., Epstein, J. (1996). *Growing Artificial Societies: Social Science from the Bottom Up*. Cambridge, MA: MIT Press.

Bak, P., Tang, C., Wiesenfeld, K. (1987). "Self-organized criticality: An explanation of the 1/f noise." *Physical Review Letters*, 59(4), 381.

Baker, W., Bulkley, N. (2014). "Paying it forward or rewarding reputation: Mechanisms of generalized reciprocity." *Organization Science*, 25(5), 1493–1510.

Bakhshi, H., Freeman, A., Potts, J. (2011). *State of Uncertainty: Innovation Policy through Experimentation*. NESTA Provocation 14. London: NESTA.

Baldwin, C., von Hippel, E. (2011). "Modelling a paradigm shift: From producer innovation to user and open collaborative innovation." *Organization Science*, 22(6), 1399–1417.

Barnett, W., Mischke, G., Ocasio, W. (2000). "The evolution of collective strategies among organizations." *Organization Studies*, 21(2), 325–354.

Basalla, G. (1988). *The Evolution of New Technology*. New York: Cambridge University Press.

Bass, F. (1969). "A new product growth model for consumer durables." *Management Science*, 15, 215–227.

Bator, F. (1958). "The anatomy of market failure." *Quarterly Journal of Economics*, 72(3), 351–379.

Bauer, J., Franke, N., Tuertscher, P. (2016). "Intellectual property norms in online communities: How user-organized intellectual property regulation supports innovation." *Information Systems Research*, 27(4), 724–750.

Bauer, M. (ed.) (1997). *Resistance to New Technology: Nuclear Power, Information Technology and Biotechnology*. New York: Cambridge University Press.

Baumol, W. (1990). "Entrepreneurship: Productive, unproductive and destructive." *Journal of Political Economy*, 98(5), 893–921.

Baumol, W. (2001). *The Free Market Innovation Machine*. Princeton, NJ: Princeton University Press.

Bauwens, M. (2005). "The political economy of peer production." https://journals.uvic.ca/index.php/ctheory/article/view/14464/5306>.

Beck, N. (2018). *Hayek and the Evolution of Capitalism*. Chicago: University of Chicago Press.

Becker, G. (1983). "A theory of competition among pressure groups for political influence." *Quarterly Journal of Economics*, 98, 371–400.

Benkler, Y. (2006). *The Wealth of Networks: How Social Production Transforms Markets and Freedom*. New Haven: Yale University Press.

Benkler, Y., Nissenbaum, H. (2006). "Commons-based peer production and virtue." *Journal of Political Philosophy*, 14, 394–419.

Benner, C. (2003). "Learning communities in a learning region: The soft infrastructure of cross-firm learning networks in Silicon Valley." *Environment and Planning A*, 35(10), 1809–1830.

Bergstrom, T. (2002). "Evolution of social behavior: Individual and group selection." *Journal of Economic Perspectives*, 16(2), 67–88.

Bergstrom, T., Blume, L., Varian, H. (1986). "On the private provision of public goods." *Journal of Public Economics*, 29(1), 25–49.

Bertacchini, E., Bravo, G., Marrelli, M., Santagata, W. (2012). *Cultural Commons: A New Perspective on the Production and Evolution of Cultures*. Cheltenham: Edward Elgar.

Bessen, J., Meurer, M., Ford, J. (2011). "The private and social costs of patent trolls." Boston University School of Law, Law and Economics Research Paper No. 11-45.

Bhide, A. (2010). *The Venturesome Economy*. Princeton: Princeton University Press.

Bleda, M., del Rio, P. (2013). "The market failure and the systemic failure rationales in technological innovation systems." *Research Policy*, 42, 1039–1052.

Boehm, C. (2012). *Moral Origins*. New York: Basic Books.

Boettke, P. (2012). *Living Economics*. Oakland, CA: Independent Institute.

Boettke, P., Coyne, C. (2005). "Methodological individualism, spontaneous order and the research program of the Workshop in Political Theory and Policy Analysis." *Journal of Economic Behavior and Organization*, 57(2), 145–158.

Boettke, P., Coyne, C., Leeson, P., Sautet, F. (2005). "The new comparative political economy." *Review of Austrian Economics*, 18(3–4), 281–304.

Boettke, P., Coyne, C., Leeson, P. (2007). "Saving government failure theory from itself: Recasting political economy from an Austrian perspective" *Constitutional Political Economy*, 18(1), 127–143.

Boldrin, M., Levine, D. (2002). "The case against intellectual property." *American Economic Review*, 92, 209–212.

Boldrin, M., Levine, D. (2004). "Rent-seeking and innovation." *Journal of Monetary Economics*, 51, 127–160.

Boldrin, M., Levine, D. (2007). *Against Intellectual Monopoly*. New York: Cambridge University Press.

Bollier, D. (2013). *Think Like a Commoner*. www.thinklikeacommoner.com.

Bonvillian, W. (2014). "The new model innovation agencies: An overview." *Science and Public Policy*, 41, 425–437.

Bostaph, S. (2013). "Driving the market process: Alertness versus innovation and creative destruction." *Quarterly Journal of Austrian Economics*, 16(4), 421–458.

Botsman, R. (2010). *What's Mine Is Yours: How Collaborative Consumption Is Changing the Way We Live*. London: HarperCollins.

Bowles, S. (2004). *Microeconomics: Behavior, Institutions, and Evolution*. Princeton, NJ: Princeton University Press.

Bowles, S., Choi, K. (2013). "Coevolution of farming and private property during the early Holocene." *Proceedings of the National Academy of Sciences*, 110, 8830–8835.

Bowles, S., Choi, K., Hopfensitz, A. (2003). "The coevolution of individual behavior and social institutions." *Journal of Theoretical Biology*, 223(2), 135–147.

Bowles, S. Gintis, H. (2005). "Can self-interest explain cooperation?" *Evolutionary and Institutional Economic Review*, 2(1), 21–41.

Bowles, S., Gintis, H. (2011). *A Cooperative Species: Human Reciprocity and Its Evolution*. Princeton, NJ: Princeton University Press.

Box, S. (2009). "OECD work on innovation: A stocktaking of existing work." STI Working Paper No. 2009/2.

Boyd, R., Richerson, P. (1992). "Punishment allows the evolution of cooperation (or anything else) in sizable groups." *Ethology and Sociobiology*, 13, 171–195.

Boyd, R., Richerson, P., Henrich, J. (2011). "The cultural niche: Why social learning is essential for human adaptation." *Proceedings of the National Academy of Sciences*, 108(2), 10918–10925.

Boyle, J. (2008). *The Public Domain*. New Haven: Yale University Press.
Breznitz, D. (2007). *Innovation and the State*. New Haven: Yale University Press
Buchanan, J. (1965). "An economic theory of clubs." *Economica*, 32, 1–14.
Buchanan, J. (1975). "A contractarian paradigm for applying economic theory." *American Economic Review*, 65(2), 225–230.
Buchanan, J. (1990). "The domain of constitutional economics." *Constitutional Political Economy*, 1(1), 1–18.
Buchanan, J., Tullock, G. (1962). *The Calculus of Consent*. Ann Arbor: University of Michigan Press.
Buchanan, J., Vanberg, V. (1991). "The market as a creative process." *Economics and Philosophy*, 7(2), 167–186.
Buenstorf, G. (2003). "Designing clunkers: Demand side innovation and the early history of the mountain-bike." In J. Metcalfe, U. Cantner (eds.), *Change, Transformation and Development*. Heidelberg: Springer. Pp. 53–70.
Bush, V. (1945). *Science: The Endless Frontier*. Washington, DC: US Govt. Printing Office.
Buss, D., Haselton, M., Shackelford, T., Bleske, A., Wakefield, J. (1998). "Adaptations, exaptations, and spandrels." *American Psychologist*, 53(5), 533–542.
Cavazos, D., Szyliowicz, C. (2011). "How industry associations suppress threatening innovation: The case of the US recording industry." *Technology Analysis and Strategic Management*, 23(5), 473–487.
Chataway, J., Hanlin, R., Kaplinsky, R. (2014). "Inclusive innovation: An architecture for policy development." *Innovation and Development*, 4(1), 33–54.
Chesbrough, H. (2003a). *Open Innovation: The New Imperative for Creating and Profiting from Technology*. Boston: Harvard Business Press.
Chesbrough, H. (2003b). "The era of open innovation." *MIT Sloan Management Review*, 44 (3), 35–41.
Chesbrough, H., Birkinshaw, J., Teubal, M. (2006). "Introduction to the *Research Policy* 20th anniversary special issue of the publication of 'Profiting from Innovation' by David J. Teece." *Research Policy*, 35, 1091–1099.
Coase, R. (1937). "The nature of the firm." *Economica*, 4(16), 386–405.
Coase, R. (1960). "The problem of social cost." *Journal of Law and Economics*, 3(1), 414–440.
Coase, R. (1974). "The market for goods and the market for ideas." *American Economic Review*, 64(2), 384–391.
Colander, D., Kupers, R. (2014). *Complexity and the Art of Public Policy*. Princeton: Princeton University Press.
Congleton, R. (2010). *Perfectinng Parliament*. Cambridge: Cambridge University Press.
Congleton, R., Vanberg, V. (2001). "Help, harm or avoid? On the personal advantage of dispositions to cooperate and punish in multilateral PD games with exit." *Journal of Economic Behavior & Organization*, 44(2), 145–167.
Cowen, T. (ed) (1992). *Public Goods and Market Failures*. New Brunswick: Transaction Publishers.
Cowen, T. (2011). *The Great Stagnation*. Penguin ebook.
Cowen, T. (2017). *The Complacent Class*. New York: St Martin's Press.
Cox, M., Arnold, G., Villamayor Tomás, S. (2010). "A review of design principles for community-based natural resource management." *Ecology and Society*, 15(4), 38.
Coyne, C. (2008). *After War: The Political Economy of Exporting Democracy*. Stanford, CA: Stanford University Press.
Cyert, R., March, J. (1963). *A Behavioral Theory of the Firm*. Englewood Cliffs, NJ: Prentice Hall.
Dahlander, L., Gann, D. (2010). "How open is innovation?" *Research Policy*, 39, 699–709.
Dahlman, C. (1979). "The problem of externalities." *Journal of Law and Economics*, 22(1), 141–162.
Dalziel, M. (2006). "The impact of industry associations: Evidence from Statistics Canada data." *Innovation: Management, Policy & Practice*, 8(3), 296–306.
Damsgaard, J., Lyytinen, K. (2001). "The role of intermediating institutions in the diffusion of Electronic Data Interchange (EDI): How industry associations intervened in Denmark, Finland, and Hong Kong." *Information Society*, 17(3), 195–210.
Dasgupta, P., David, P. (1994). "Toward a new economics of science." *Research Policy*, 23, 487–521.

David, P. (1998). "Common agency contracting and the emergence of open science institutions." *American Economic Review*, 88(2), 15–21.

David, P. (2001). "Tragedy of the public knowledge 'commons'? Global science, intellectual property and the digital technology boomerang." Research Memorandum No. 3. Maastricht University, Maastricht Economic Research Institute on Innovation and Technology.

David, P. (2004). "Understanding the emergence of 'open science' institutions." *Industrial and Corporate Change*, 13(4), 571–589.

David, P. (2008). "The historical origins of 'open science': An essay on patronage, reputation and common agency contracting in the scientific revolution." *Capitalism and Society*, 3(2), 1–103.

David, P. (2015). "Zvi Grilliches and the economics of technology diffusion." http://siepr.stanford.edu/sites/default/files/publications/15-005_0.pdf.

David, P., Hall, B., Toole, A. (2000). "Is public R&D a complement or substitute for private R&D? A review of the econometric evidence." *Research Policy*, 29(4–5), 497–523.

Davidson, S., de Filippi, P., Potts J. (2018). "Blockchains and the economic institutions of capitalism." *Journal of Institutional Economics*, 14(4), 639–658.

Davidson, S., Potts, J. (2016a). "A new institutional approach to innovation policy." *Australian Economic Review*, 49(2), 200–207.

Davidson, S., Potts, J. (2016b). "The stationary bandit model of intellectual property." *Cato Journal*, 37(1), 69–88.

Davidson, S., Potts, J. (2016c). "Social costs and the institutions of innovation policy." *Economic Affairs*, 36(3), 282–293.

Davidson, S., Spong, H. (2010). "Positive externalities and R&D: Two conflicting traditions in economic theory." *Review of Political Economy*, 22 (3), 355–372.

Davis, L., North, D. (1971). *Institutional Change and American Economic Growth*. New York: Cambridge University Press.

Dawes, R. (1980). "Social dilemmas." *Annual Review of Psychology*, 31, 169–193.

Dawes, R., John, M., Alphons van de Kragt (1986). "Organizing groups for collective action." *American Political Science Review*, 80(4), 1171–1185.

Dawkins, R. (1976). *The Selfish Gene*. Oxford: Oxford University Press.

Deaton, A. (2013). *The Great Escape*. Princeton, NJ: Princeton University Press.

Dekker, E. (2016). *The Viennese Students of Civilization*. New York: Cambridge University Press.

Demsetz, H. (1968). "The costs of transacting." *Quarterly Journal of Economics*, 82, 33–53.

Demsetz, H. (1969). "Information and efficiency: Another viewpoint." *Journal of Law and Economics*, 12(1), 1–22.

Diamond, A., Jr. (2006). "The relative success of private funders and government funders in funding important science." *European Journal of Law and Economics*, 21, 149–161.

Dietz, T., Ostrom, E. Stern, P. (2003). "The struggle to govern the commons." *Science* 302(5652), 1907–1912.

Dixit, A., Pindyck, R. (1994). *Investment under Uncertainty*. Princeton, NJ: Princeton University Press.

Djankov, S., Glaeser, E., La Porta, R., Lopez de Silanes, F., Shleifer, A. (2003). "The new comparative economics." *Journal of Comparative Economics*, 31(4), 595–616.

Dodgson, M., Hughes, A., Foster, J., Metcalfe, S. (2011). "Systems thinking, market failure, and the development of innovation policy: The case of Australia." *Research Policy*, 40, 1145–1156.

Doner, R., Schneider, B. (2000). "Business associations and economic development: Why some associations contribute more than others." *Business and Politics*, 2(3), 261–288.

Dopfer, K. (2004). "The economic agent as rule maker and rule user: Homo sapiens oeconomicus." *Journal of Evolutionary Economics*, 14(2), 177–195.

Dopfer, K. (2012). "The origins of meso economics: Schumpeter's legacy and beyond." *Journal of Evolutionary Economics*, 22(1), 133–160.

Dopfer, K., Foster, J., Potts, J. (2004). "Micro, meso, macro." *Journal of Evolutionary Economics*, 14, 263–279.

Dopfer, K., Potts, J. (2008). *The General Theory of Economic Evolution*. London: Routledge.

Dopfer, K., Pyka, A., Potts, J. (2016). "Upward and downward complementarity: The meso core of evolutionary growth theory." *Journal of Evolutionary Economics*, 26(4), 753–763.

Dosi, G. (1982). "Technological paradigms and technological trajectories." *Research Policy*, 11(3), 147–162.

Dosi, G., Nelson, R. (2010). "Technological change and industrial dynamics as evolutionary processes." In B. Hall, N. Rosenberg (eds.), *Handbook on the Economics of Innovation*, Vol. 1. Amsterdam: Elsevier. Pp. 51–127.

Dourado, E., Tabarrok, A. (2015). "Public choice perspectives on intellectual property." *Public Choice*, 163(1–2), 129–151.

Dreber, A., Rand, D., Fudenberg, D., Nowak, M. (2008). "Winners don't punish." *Nature*, 452(7185), 348–351.

Dunbar, R. (2003). "The social brain: Mind, language, and society in evolutionary perspective." *Annual Review of Anthropology*, pp. 163–181.

Durkheim, E. (1933). *The Division of Labor in Society*. New York: Macmillan.

Earl, P. (2003). "The entrepreneur as a constructor of connections." *Advances in Austrian Economics*, 6, 113–130.

Earl, P., Potts, J. (2011). "A Nobel Prize for governance and institutions: Oliver Williamson and Elinor Ostrom." *Review of Political Economy*, 23(1), 1–24.

Earl, P., Potts, J. (2013). "The creative instability hypothesis." *Journal of Cultural Economics*, 37, 153–173.

Earl, P., Potts, J. (2015). "The management of creative vision and the economics of creative cycles." *Managerial & Decision Economics*, 37(7), 474–484.

Ebner, A. (2006). "Institutions, entrepreneurship, and the rationale of government: An outline of the Schumpeterian theory of the state." *Journal of Economic Behavior & Organization*, 59(4), 497–515.

Eckhardt, J., Shane, S. (2003). "Opportunities and entrepreneurship." *Journal of Management*, 29(3), 333–349.

Eisenberg, R., Nelson, R. (2002). "Public vs. proprietary science: A fruitful tension?" *Daedalus*, 131(2), 89–101.

Eliasson, G. (1991). "Modelling the experimentally organized economy." *Journal of Economic Behavior and Organization*, 16(1–2), 153–182.

Epstein, J. (2006). *Generative Social Science*. Princeton, NJ: Princeton University Press.

Epstein, J. (2014). *Agent Zero: Toward Neurocognitive Foundations for Generative Social Science*. Princeton, NJ: Princeton University Press.

Evans, D., Schmalensee, R. (2016). *Matchmakers: The new economics of multisided platforms*. Cambridge, MA: HBR Press.

Fauchart, E., von Hippel, E. (2008). "Norms-based intellectual property systems: The case of French chefs." *Organization Science*, 19(2), 187–201.

Fehr, E., Fischbacher, U. (2003). "The nature of human altruism." *Nature*, 425(6960), 785–791.

Fehr, E., Gächter, S. (2000). "Cooperation and punishment." *American Economic Review*, 90, 980–994.

Fehr, E., Gächter, S. (2002). "Altruistic punishment in humans." *Nature*, 415(6868), 137–140.

Feldman, M., Tavassoli, S. (2015). "Something new: Where do new industries come from?" In D. Audretsch, A. Link (eds.), *Oxford Handbook of Local Competitiveness*. New York: Oxford University Press. Pp. 125–141.

Felin, T., Zenger, T. (2009). "Entrepreneurs as theorists: On the origins of collective beliefs and novel strategies." *Strategic Entrepreneurship Journal*, 3, 127–146.

Flowers, S. (2008). "Harnessing the hackers: The emergence and exploitation of outlaw innovation." *Research Policy*, 37:177–193.

Foray, D. (2003). "On the provision of industry-specific public goods: Revisiting a policy process." In A. Geuna, A. Salter, W. Steinmueller (eds.), *Science and Innovation*. Cheltenham: Edward Elgar. Pp. 79–94.

Foray, D., David, P., Hall, B. (2009). "Smart specialisation: The concept." In *Knowledge for Growth: Prospects for Science, Technology and Innovation*. Report EUR 24047. European Union. Pp. 25–29.

Foss, K., Foss, N. (2005). "Resources and transactions costs: How property rights economics furthers the resource-based view." *Strategic Management Journal*, 26, 541–553.

Foss, K., Foss, N., Klein, P., Klein, S. (2007). "The entrepreneurial organization of heterogeneous capital." *Journal of Management Studies*, 44(7), 1165–1186.

Foss, N., Klein, P. (2012). *Organizing Entrepreneurial Judgment: A New Approach to the Firm*. New York: Cambridge University Press.

Foster, C., Heeks, R. (2013). "Conceptualising inclusive innovation: Modifying systems of innovation frameworks to understand diffusion of new technology to low-income consumers." *European Journal of Development Research*, 25, 333–348.

Foster, J. (2005). "From simplistic to complex adaptive systems in economics." *Cambridge Journal of Economics*, 29, 873–892.

Foster, S. (2011). "Collective action and the urban commons." *Notre Dame Law Review*, 87(1), 57–134.

Franke, N., Shah, S. (2003). "How communities support innovative activities: An exploration of assistance and sharing among end-users." *Research Policy*, 32(1), 157–178.

Franzoni, C., Sauermann, H. (2014). "Crowd science: The organization of scientific research in open collaborative projects." *Research Policy*, 43(1), 1–20.

Freeman, C. (1991). "Networks of innovators: A synthesis of research issues." *Research Policy*, 20(5), 499–514.

Freeman, C. (1995). "The national system of innovation in economic perspective." *Cambridge Journal of Economics*, 19(1), 5–24.

Freeman, C. (2002). "Continental, national and sub-national innovation systems: Complementarity and economic growth." *Research Policy*, 31, 191–211.

Freeman, C., Louca, F. (2001). *As Time Goes By: The Information Revolution and Industrial Revolutions in Historical Perspective*. New York: Oxford University Press.

Freiberger, P., Swaine, M. (1984). *Fire in the Valley: The Making of the Personal Computer*. New York: McGraw-Hill.

Frenken, K., Nuvolari, A. (2004). "The early development of the steam engine: An evolutionary interpretation using complexity theory." *Industrial and Corporate Change*, 13, 419–450.

Frijters, P., Foster, G. (2013). *An Economic Theory of Greed, Love, Groups and Networks*. New York: Cambridge University Press.

Frischmann, B. (2012). *Infrastructure: The Social Value of Shared Resources*. New York: Oxford University Press.

Frischmann, B., Madison, M., Strandburg, K. (eds.) (2014a). *Governing Knowledge Commons*. New York: Oxford University Press.

Frishmann, B., Madison, M., Strandburg, K. (2014b). "Governing knowledge commons." In B. Frischmann et al. (eds.), *Governing Knowledge Commons*. New York: Oxford University Press. Pp. 1–43.

Fudenberg, D., Gilbert, R., Stiglitz, J., Tirole, J. (1983). "Preemption, leapfrogging and competition in patent races." *European Economic Review*, 22(1), 3–31.

Gächter, S., von Krogh, G., Haefliger, S. (2010). "Initiating private-collective innovation: The fragility of knowledge sharing." *Research Policy*, 39(7), 893–906.

Gaglio, C., Katz, J. (2001). "The psychological basis of opportunity identification: Entrepreneurial alertness." *Small Business Economics*, 16(2), 95–111.

Galenson, D. (2007). *Old Masters and Young Geniuses*. Princeton, NJ: Princeton University Press.

Galor, O., Moav, O. (2002). "Natural selection and the origin of economic growth." *Quarterly Journal of Economics*, 117, 1133–1191.

Gambardella, A., Raasch, C., von Hippel, E. (2017). "The user innovation paradigm: Impacts on markets and welfare." *Management Science*, 63(5), 1450–1468.

Gans, J., Hsu, D., Stern, S. (2002). "When does start up innovation spur the gale of creative destruction?" RAND Journal of Economics, 33(4), 571–586.

Gans, J., Stern, S. (2003). "The product market and the market for 'ideas': Commercialization strategies for technology entrepreneurs." *Research Policy*, 32(2), 333–350.

Gans, J., Stern, S. (2010). "Is there a market for ideas?" *Industrial and Corporate Change*, 19 (3), 805–837.

Gaspart, F., Seki, E. (2003). "Cooperation, status seeking and competitive behaviour: Theory and evidence." *Journal of Economic Behavior and Organization*, 51(1), 51–77.

Gennaioli, N., La Porta, R., Lopez-de-Silanes, F., Shleifer, A. (2013). "Human capital and regional development." *Quarterly Journal of Economics*, 128(1), 105–164.

Georgescu-Roegen, N. (1971). *The Entropy Law and the Economic Process*. Cambridge, MA: Harvard University Press.

Geroski, P. (2000). "Models of technology diffusion." *Research Policy*, 29, 603–625.

Gibson, C., McKean, M., Ostrom, E. (eds.) (2000). *People and Forests: Communities, Institutions and Governance*. Cambridge, MA: MIT Press.

Gintis, H. "Strong reciprocity and human sociality." *Journal of Theoretical Biology*, 206(2), 169–179.

Gintis, H., Smith, E., Bowles, S. (2001). "Costly signaling and cooperation." *Journal of Theoretical Biology*, 213(1), 103–119.

Gintis, H., Van Schaik, C., Boehm, C. (2015). "Zoon politikon: The evolutionary origins of human political systems." *Current Anthropology*, 56(3), 327–353. doi:10.1086/681217.

Giroux, H. (2007). *University in Chains: Confronting the Military-Industrial-Academic Complex*. Boulder, CO: Paradigm Publishers.

Gladwell, M. (2000). *The Tipping Point*. New York: Little, Brown.

Glaeser, E., Porta, R.L., de Silanes, F., Shleifer, A. (2004). "Do institutions cause growth?" *Journal of Economic Growth*, 9(3), 271–303.

Globerman, S. (1980). "Markets, hierarchies, and innovation." *Journal of Economic Issues*: 977–998.

Goolsbee, A. (1998). "Does government R&D policy mainly benefit scientists and engineers?" *American Economic Review*, 88(2), 298–302.

Goolsbee, A., Klenow, P. (2006). "Valuing consumer products by the time spend using them: Application to the internet." *American Economic Review*, 96, 108–113.

Gordon, H. (1954). "The economic theory of a common-property resource: The fishery." *Journal of Political Economy*, 62(2),124–142.

Gordon, R. (2016). *The Rise and Fall of American Growth*. Princeton, NJ: Princeton University Press.

Gort, M., Klepper, S. (1982). "Time paths in the diffusion of product innovation." *Economic Journal*, 92(367), 630–653.

Graham, P. (2004). *Hackers and Painters*. Palo Alto, CA: O'Reilly Media.

Granovetter, M. (1985). "Economic action and social structure: The problem of embeddedness." *American Journal of Sociology*, 91(3), 481–510.

Granovetter, M. (1995). "Coase revisited: Business groups in the modern economy." *Industrial and Corporate Change*, 4(1), 93–130.

Greenberg, D. (2001). *Science, Money and Politics: Political Triumph and Ethical Erosion*. Chicago: University of Chicago Press.

Greenstein, S. (2015). *How the Internet Became Commercial*. Princeton: Princeton University Press.

Griliches, Z. (1957). "Hybrid corn: An exploration in the economics of new technology." *Econometrica*, 48, 501–522.

Gunningham, N., Rees, J. (1997). "Industry self-regulation: An institutional perspective." *Law and Policy*, 19(4), 363–414.

Gurri, M. (2014). *The Revolt of the Public and the Crisis of Authority in the New Millennium*. Amazon Digital Services.

Haeussler, C. (2010). "Information-sharing in academia and industry: A comparative study." *Research Policy*, 40(1), 105–122.

Haidt, J. (2012). *The Righteous Mind*. New York: Vintage.

Hall, P., Soskice, D. (2001). *Varieties of Capitalism*. New York: Oxford University Press.

Hamari, J., Sjöklint, M., Ukkonen, A. (2015). "The sharing economy: Why people participate in collaborative consumption." *Journal of the Association for Information Science and Technology*, 67(9), 2047–2059.

Hamilton, W. (1963). "The evolution of altruistic behavior." *American Naturalist*, 97 (896), 354–356.

Hamilton, W. (1964). "The genetical theory of social behavior." *Journal of Theoretical Biology*, 7, 1–16.

Hannan, M., Freeman, J. (1989). *Organisational Ecology*. Cambridge, MA: Harvard University Press.

Hanusch, H., Pyka, A. (eds) (2007). *The Elgar Companion to Neo-Schumpeterian Economics*. Cheltenham: Edward Elgar.

Hansen, J. (1991). "Choosing sides." *Studies in American Political Development* 2, 183–229.

Hardin, G. (1968). "The tragedy of the commons." *Science*, 162(3859), 1243–1248.

Harhoff, D., Henkel, J., von Hippel, E. (2003). "Profiting from voluntary information spillovers: How users benefit by freely revealing their innovations." *Research Policy*, 32 (10), 1753–1769.

Harhoff, D., Lakhani, K. (eds.) (2016). *Revolutionizing Innovation: Users, Communities, and Open Innovation*. Cambridge, MA: MIT Press.

Harper, D., Endres, A. (2010). "Capital as a layer-cake: A systems approach to capital and its multi-level structure." *Journal of Economic Behavior and Organization*, 74(1–2), 31–40.

Harsanyi, J. (1962). "Bargaining in ignorance of the opponents utility function." *Journal of Conflict Resolution*, 6(1), 29–38.

Harsanyi, J. (1967). "Games with incomplete information played by Bayesian players." *Management Science*, 14(3), 159–182.

Hart, O., Moore, J. (2008). "Contracts as reference points." *Quarterly Journal of Economics*, 123(1), 1–48.

Hartley, J., Potts, J. (2014). *Cultural Science: A Natural History of Stories, Demes, Knowledge and Innovation*. New York: Bloomsbury.

Harvey, M., McMeekin, A. (2007). *Public or Private Economies of Knowledge*. Cheltenham: Edward Elgar.

Harvey, M., McMeekin, A. (2009). "Public or private economies of knowledge: The economics of diffusion and appropriation of bioinformatics tools." *International Journal of the Commons*, 4(1),481–506.

Harvey, M., Metcalfe, J. S. (2004). "The ordering of change: Polanyi, Schumpeter and the nature of the market mechanism." *Journal des economistes et des etudes humaines*, 4, 87–114.

Hausmann, R., Rodrik, D. (2003). "Economic development and self-discovery." *Journal of Development Economics*, 72(2), 603–633.

Hayek, F. (1937). "Economics and knowledge." *Economica* n.s. 4, 33–54.

Hayek, F. ([1941] 2007). *The Pure Theory of Capital*. Chicago: University of Chicago Press.

Hayek, F. (1945). "The use of knowledge in society." *American Economic Review*, 35, 519–530.

Hayek, F. (1960). *The Constitution of Liberty*. Chicago: University of Chicago Press.

Hayek, F. (1967). "Notes on the evolution of systems of rules of conduct." In F. Hayek (ed.), *Studies in Philosophy, Politics and Economics*. Chicago: University of Chicago Press. Pp. 66–81.

Hayek, F. (1968). "Competition as a discovery procedure." (trans. M. Snow), republished in *Quarterly Journal of Austrian Economics* (2002). 5(3), 9–23.

Hayek, F. (1973). *Law, Legislation and Liberty*, vol. 1: *Rules and Order*. Chicago: University of Chicago Press.

Hayek, F. (1988). *The Fatal Conceit*. Chicago: University of Chicago Press.

Heiner, R. (1983). "The origin of predictable behavior." *American Economic Review*, 73(4), 560–595.

Heiskanen, E., Hyysalo, S., Kotro, T., Repo, P. (2010). "Constructing innovative users and user-inclusive innovation communities." *Technology Analysis & Strategic Management*, 22(4), 495–511.

Henrich, J. (2004). "Cultural group selection, coevolutionary processes and large-scale cooperation." *Journal of Economic Behavior and Organization*, 53, 3–35.

Henrich, J. (2015). *The Secret of Our Success*. Princeton, NJ: Princeton University Press.

Henrich, J., Gil-White, F. (2001). "The evolution of prestige: Freely conferred deference as a mechanism for enhancing the benefits of cultural transmission." *Evolution and Human Behavior*, 22(3), 165–196.

Herrmann, E., Call, J., Hernández-Lloreda, M., Hare, B., Tomasello, M. (2007). "Humans have evolved specialized skills of social cognition: The cultural intelligence hypothesis." *Science*, 317(5843), 1360–1366.

Hess, C. (2008). "Mapping the New Commons." SSRN: https://ssrn.com/abstract=1356835.

Hess, C. (2012). "Constructing a new research agenda for cultural commons." In E. Bertacchini et al. (eds.), *Cultural Commons: A New Perspective on Production and Evolution of Cultures*. Cheltenham: Edward Elgar. Pp. 23–34.

Hess, C., Ostrom, E. (2003). "Ideas, artefacts, and facilities: Information as a common-pool resource." *Law and Contemporary Problems*, 66(1–2), 111–146.

Hess, C., Ostrom, E. (eds.) (2006). *Understanding Knowledge as a Commons: From Theory to Practice*. Cheltenham: Edward Elgar.

Hienerth, C., von Hippel, E., Jensen, M. (2014). "User community vs. producer innovation development efficiency: A first empirical study." *Research Policy*, 43(1), 190–201.

Hillman, A., Keim, G., Schuler, D. (2004). "Corporate political activity: A review and research agenda." *Journal of Management*, 30(6), 837–857.

Hirschman, A. (1970). *Exit, Voice and Loyalty*. Cambridge, MA: Harvard University Press.

Hirschman, A., Lindblom, C. (1962). "Economic development, research and development, policy making: Some converging views." *Behavioral Science*, 7(2), 211–222.

Hodgson, G. (1993). *Economics and Evolution: Bringing Life back into economics*. Cambridge: Polity Press.

Hodgson, G. (2015). *Conceptualizing Capitalism*. Chicago: University of Chicago Press.

Hodgson, G., Knudsen, T. (2010). *Darwin's Conjecture*. Chicago: University of Chicago Press.

Holcombe, R. (2003). "The origin of entrepreneurial opportunities." *Review of Austrian Economics*, 16(1), 25–43.

Holmstrom, B. (1989). "Agency costs and innovation." *Journal of Economic Behavior and Organization*, 12(3), 305–327.

Howes, A. (2016). "The improving mentality: Innovation during the British Industrial Revolution." 1651–1851.

Hwang, V. (2012). *The Rainforest*. Los Altos Hills, CA: Regenwald.

Ikeda, S. (1990). "Market-process theory and 'dynamic' theories of the market." *Southern Economic Journal*, 57(1), 75–92.

James, F., English, J. (2009). *The Economy of Prestige: Prizes, Awards, and the Circulation of Cultural Value*. Cambridge, MA: Harvard University Press.

Jaumotte, F., Pain, N. (2005). "An overview of public policies to support innovation." OECD Economics Department, Working Paper No. 456. Paris: OECD.

Jones, C. (2010). "Intermediate goods, weak links, and superstars: A theory of economic development." NBER papers.

Jones, C., Williams, J. (1998). "Measuring the social return to R&D." *Quarterly Journal of Economics*, 113(4), 1119–1135.

Jones, G. (2012). "The O-ring sector and the foolproof sector: An explanation for skill externalities." *Journal of Economic Behavior and Organization*, 85(1), 1–10.

Jones, G. (2015). *Hive Mind*. Palo Alto: Stanford Economics and Finance.

Juma, C. (2014). *The Gene Hunters: Biotechnology and the Scramble for Seeds*. Princeton, NJ: Princeton University Press.

Juma, C. (2016). *Innovation and Its Enemies: Why People Resist New Technologies*. New York: Oxford University Press.

Kahneman, D. (2011). *Thinking, Fast and Slow*. New York: Farrar, Straus and Giroux.

Kealey, T. (1996). *The Economic Laws of Scientific Research*. London: Macmillan.

Kealey, T., Ricketts, M. (2014). "Modelling science as a contribution good." *Research Policy*, 43(6), 1014–1024.

Kelly, K. (2010). *What Technology Wants*. New York: Viking Press.

Kelly, C. (1979). "Clunkers among the hills." *Bicycling* (January), 40–42. See http://sonic.net/~ckelly/Seekay/clunker.htm.

King, A., Lenox, M. (2000). "Industry self-regulation without sanctions: The chemical industry's Responsible Care Program." *Academy of Management Journal*, 43(4), 698–716.

Kirzner, I. (1973). *Competition and Entrepreneurship*. Chicago: University of Chicago Press.

Kirzner, I. (1997). "Entrepreneurial discovery and the competitive market process: An Austrian approach." *Journal of Economic Literature*, 35(1), 60–85.

Klein, B., Crawford, R., Alchian, A. (1978). "Vertical integration, appropriable rents, and the competitive contracting process." *Journal of Law and Economics*, 21(2), 297–326.

Klein, D. (2013). *Knowledge and Coordination*. New York: Oxford University Press.

Klepper, S., Graddy, E. (1990). "The evolution of new industries and the determinants of market structure." *RAND Journal of Economics*, 21(1), 27–44.

Knight, F. (1921). *Risk, Uncertainty and Profit*. Boston: Houghton Mifflin.

Knoke, D. (1986). "Associations and interest groups." *Annual Review of Sociology*, 12, 1–21.

Kollock, P. (1998). "Social dilemmas: The anatomy of cooperation." *Annual Review of Sociology*, 24(1), 183–214.

Koppl, R., Kauffman, S., Felin, T., Longo, G. (2015). "Economics for a creative world." *Journal of Institutional Economics*, 11(1), 1–31.

Kostakis, V., Bauwens, M. (2014). *Network Society and Future Scenarios for a Collaborative Economy*. Basingstoke: Palgrave Macmillan.

Kostakis, V., Nairos, V., Giotitsas, C. (2014). "Production and governance in hackerspaces: A manifestation of commons-based peer production in the physical realm?" *International Journal of Cultural Studies*, 18(5), 555–573.

Kremer, M. (1993a). "Population growth and technological change: One million B.C. to 1990." *Quarterly Journal of Economics*, 108(4), 681–716.

Kremer, M. (1993b). "The O-ring theory of economic development." *Quarterly Journal of Economics*, 108(3), 551–575.

Kremer, M. (1998). "Patent buy-outs: A mechanism for encouraging innovation." *Quarterly Journal of Economics*, 113(4), 1137–1167.

Krueger, A. (1974). "The political economy of the rent-seeking society." *American Economic Review*, 64(3), 291–303.

Lachmann, L. (1956). *Capital and Its Structure*. Kansas City: Sheed Andrews.

Lachmann, L. (1976). "From Mises to Shackle: An essay on Austrian economics and the kaleidic society." *Journal of Economic Literature*, 14(1), 54–62.

Lachmann, L. (1994). "Expectations and the meaning of institutions." In D. Lavoie (ed.), *Expectations and the Meaning of Institutions*. London: Routledge.

Lakhani, K., von Hippel, E. (2003). "How open source software works: Free user-to-user assistance." *Research Policy*, 32(6), 923–943.

Lakhani, K., Panetta, J. (2007). "The principles of distributed innovation." *Innovations*, 2(3), 97–112.

Lakhani, K., Wolf, R. (2005). "Why hackers do what they do: Understanding motivation and effort in OSS projects." In J. Feller et al. (eds.), *Perspectives on Free and Open Source Software*. Cambridge, MA: MIT Press. Pp. 3–22.

Laland, K., Matthews, B., Feldman, M. (2016). "An introduction to niche construction theory." *Evolutionary Ecology*, 30(2), 191–202.

Langlois, R. (2018). "Fission, forking and fine-tuning" *Journal of Institutional Economics*, 14(6), 1049–1070.

Langlois, R., Foss, N. (1999). "Capabilities and governance: The rebirth of production in the theory of economic production." *Kyklos*, 52(2), 351–385.

Langlois, R., Garzarelli, G. (2008). "Of hackers and hairdressers: Modularity and the organizational economics of open-source collaboration." *Industry and Innovation*, 15(2), 125–143.

Lanham, R. (2006). *The Economics of Attention*. Chicago: University of Chicago Press.

Latour, B. (2007). *Reassembling the Social*. New York: Oxford University Press.

Lavoie D. (1994). "Introduction." In D. Lavoie (ed.), *Expectations and The Meaning of Institutions: Essays in Economics by Ludwig Lachmann*. London: Routledge. Pp. 1–19.

Lavoie, D. (2001). "Subjective orientation and objective wealth: Entrepreneurship and the evolution of the structure of the 'text'." Working paper, School of Public Policy, George Mason University.

Lavoie, D. (2004). "Subjectivism, entrepreneurship, and the convergence of groupware and hypertext." In J. Birner, P. Garrouste (eds.), *Markets, Information, and Communication*. New York: Routledge. Pp. 33–52.

Lavoie, D., Prychitko, D. (1995). "The market as a procedure for the discovery and conveyance of inarticulate knowledge." *Advances in Austrian Economics*, 13, 115–137.

Leadbeater, C. (2008). *We Think*. London: Allen & Unwin.

Lee, G., Cole, R. (2003). "From a firm-based to a community-based model of knowledge creation: The case of the Linux kernel development." *Organizational Science*, 14(6), 633–649.

Leeson, P. (2014). *Anarchy Unbound: Why Self-Governance Works Better than You Think*. New York: Cambridge University Press.

Lerner, J., Tirole, J. (2002). "Some simple economics of open source." *Journal of Industrial Economics*, 50, 197–234.

Lerner, J., Tirole, J. (2004). "Efficient patent pools." *American Economic Review*, 94(3), 691–711.

Lerner, J., Tirole, J. (2005). "The economics of technology sharing: Open source and beyond." *Journal of Economic Perspectives*, 19(2), 99–120.

Lessig, L. (2001). *The Future of Ideas: The Fate of the Commons in a Connected World*. New York: Random House.

Lessig, L. (2004a). "The Creative Commons." *Montana Law Review*, 65(1), 1–14.

Lessig, L. (2004b). *Free Culture*. Creative Commons. http://www.free-culture.cc/freeculture.pdf.

Lindsay, C., Dougan, W. (2013). "Efficiency in the provision of pure public goods by private citizens." *Public Choice*, 156, 31–43.

Lippman, S., Rumelt., R. (2003). "A bargaining perspective on resource advantage." *Strategic Management Journal*, 24(11), 1069–1086.

List, F. (1856). *National System of Political Economy*. Philadelphia: J.B. Lippincott.

Loasby, B. (1999). *Knowledge, Instittuions, and Evolution in Economics*. London: Routledge.

Lohmann, S. (1995). "A signaling model of competitive political pressures." *Economics and Politics*, 7(3), 181–206.

Lopez-Berzosa, D., Gawer, A. (2014). "Innovation policy within private collectives: Evidence on 3GPP's regulation mechanisms to facilitate collective innovation." *Technovation*, 34, 734–745.

Lotman, Y. (2009). *Culture and Explosion*. Berlin: de Gruyter.

Louca, F. (1997). *Turbulence in Economics*. Cheltenham: Edward Elgar.

Louca, F., Freeman, C. (2001). *As Time Goes By*. New York: Oxford University Press.

Loury, G. (1979). "Market structure and innovation." *Quarterly Journal of Economics*, 93(3), 395–410.

Lucas, R. (1988). "On the mechanics of economic development." *Journal of Monetary Economics*, 22, 3–42.

Lucas, R. (2009). "Ideas and growth." *Economica*, 76(301), 1–19.

Luksha, P. (2008). "Niche construction: The process of opportunity creation in the environment." *Strategic Entrepreneurship Journal*, 2(4), 269–283.

Lundvall, B.-Å. (ed.). (1992). *National Systems of Innovation: An Analytical Framework*. London: Pinter.

Lundvall, B.-Å., Borras, S. (2004). "Science, technology, and innovation policy." In J. Fagerberg et al. (eds.), *The Oxford Handbook of Innovation*. New York: Oxford University Press. Pp. 599–631.

Luppi, B., Parisi, F. (2011). "Toward an asymmetric Coase theorem." *European Journal of Law and Economics*, 31, 111–122.

Lüthje, C., Herstatt, C., von Hippel., E. (2005). "User-innovators and 'local' information: The case of mountain biking." *Research Policy*, 34(6), 951–965.

Lyons, J. (2013). *The Society for Useful Knowledge*. New York: Bloomsbury.

MacDonald, T. (2015). Theory of non-territorial internal Exit." SSRN: https://ssrn.com/abstract=2661226.

MacDonald, T. (2016). "The political-jurisdictional Coase theorem." SSRN: http://ssrn.com/abstract=2815765.

Madison, M., Frischmann, B., Strandburg, K. (2010a). "Constructing commons in the cultural environment." *Cornell Law Review*, 95(4), 657–710.

Madison, M., Frischmann, B., Strandburg, K. (2010b). "The complexity of commons." *Cornell Law Review*, 95(4), 839–850.

Mansfield, E. (1961). "Technical change and the rate of imitation." *Econometrica*, 29, 741–766.

Mansfield, E. (1963). "The speed of response of firms to new technologies." *Quarterly Journal of Economics*, 77, 290–311.

Marchant, G., Abbot, K., Allenby, B. (eds.) (2013). *Innovative Governance Models for Emerging Technologies*. Cheltenham: Edward Elgar.

Marsden, D., Canibano, C. (2010). "An economic perspective on employee participation." In A. Wilkinson, P. Gollan, M. Marchington, D. Lewin (eds.), *The Oxford Handbook of Participation in Organizations*. New York: Oxford University Press.

Martimort, D. (1999). "The life cycle of regulatory agencies." *Review of Economic Studies*, 66(4), 929–947.

Martin, S., Scott, J. (2000). "The nature of innovation market failure and the design of public support for private innovation." *Research Policy*, 29, 437–447.

Maskus, K. (2000). *Intellectual Property Rights in the Global Economy*. Washington, DC: Institute for International Economics.

Maurseth, P., Verspargen, B. (1999) . "Europe: One or several systems of innovation? An analysis based on patent citations." In J. Fagerberg et al. (eds.), *The Economic Challenge for Europe*. Cheltenham: Edward Elgar. pp. 173–186.

May, T. (1994). The Cyphernomicon. http://www.cypherpunks.to/faq/cyphernomicron/cyphernomicon.txt.

Maynard Smith, J. (1972). *On Evolution*. Edinburgh: Edinburgh University Press.

Maynard Smith, J. (1976). "Evolution and the theory of games." *American Scientist*, 61, 41–45.

Mazzucato, M. (2013). *The Entrepreneurial State*. London: Anthem Press.

McCloskey, D. (2006). *The Bourgeois Virtues*. Chicago: University of Chicago Press.

McCloskey, D. (2010). *Bourgeois Dignity: Why Economics Can't Explain the Modern World*. Chicago: Chicago: University of Chicago Press.

McCloskey, D. (2016). *Bourgeois Equality: How ideas, not capital or institutions, enriched the world*. Chicago: University of Chicago Press.

McCraw, T. (2009). *Prophet of Innovation: Joseph Schumpeter and Creative Destruction*. Cambridge, MA: Belknap Press.

McIntyre, J., Mitchell, R., Boyle, B., Ryan, S. (2013). "We used to get and give a lot of help: Networking, cooperation and knowledge flow in the Hunter Valley wine cluster." *Australian Economic History Review*, 53(3), 247–267.

Merton, R. (1973). *The Sociology of Science*. Chicago: University of Chicago Press.

Mesoudi, A. (2011). *Cultural Evolution*. Chicago: University of Chicago Press.

Mesoudi, A., Chang, L., Dall, S., Thornton, R. (2016). "The evolution of individual and cultural variation in social learning." *Trends in Ecology & Evolution*, 31(3), 215–225.

Mesoudi, A., Whiten, A., Laland, K. (2006). "Towards a unified science of cultural evolution." *Behavioral and Brain Sciences*, 29(4), 329–347.

Metcalfe, J. S. (1998). *Evolutionary Economics and Creative Destruction*. London: Routledge.

Metcalfe, J. S. (2004). "The entrepreneur and the style of modern economics." *Journal of Evolutionary Economics*, 14, 157–175.

Meyer, P. (2003). "Episodes of collective invention." US Bureau of Labor Statistics Working Paper No. 368.

Milgrom, P., Stokey, N. (1982). "Information, trade and common knowledge." *Journal of Economic Theory*, 26, 17–27.

Miller, G. (2000). *The Mating Mind*. New York: Anchor.

Mirowski, P. (1989). *More Heat than Light*. New York: Cambridge University Press.

Mirowski, P. (2001). *Machine Dreams: Economics Becomes a Cyborg Science*. New York: Cambridge University Press.

Mises, L. (1949). *Human Action: A Treatise on Economics*. New Haven: Yale University Press.

Moilanen, J., Daly, A., Lobato, R., Allen, D. (2014). "Cultures of sharing in 3D printing: What can we learn from the license choices of Thingiverse users?" *Journal of Peer Production*, 6, 1–9.

Mokyr, J. (1990). *The Lever of Riches: Technological Creativity and Economic Progress*. New York: Oxford University Press.

Mokyr, J. (1994). "Cardwell's Law and the political economy of technological progress." *Research Policy*, 23(5), 561–574.

Mokyr, J. (2002). *The Gifts of Athena: Historical Origins of the Knowledge Economy*. Princeton, NJ: Princeton University Press.

Mokyr, J. (2009). *The Enlightened Economy: An Economic History of Britain, 1700–1850*. New Haven: Yale University Press.

Mokyr, J. (2016a). "Institutions and the origins of the great enrichment." *Atlantic Economic Journal*, 44, 243–259.

Mokyr, J. (2016b). *A Culture of Growth: Origins of the Modern Economy*. Princeton, NJ: Princeton University Press.

Mokyr, J., Voth, H. (2010). "Understanding growth in Europe, 1700–1870: theory and evidence." In S. Broadberry, K. O'Rourke (eds.), *Cambridge Economic History of Modern Europe*. Cambridge: Cambridge University Press. Pp. 7–42.

Molloy, J. (2011). "The Open Knowledge Foundation: Open data means better science." *PLoS Biol*, 9(12), e1001195.

Monteverde, K., Teece, D. (1982). "Supplier switching costs and vertical integration in the automobile industry." *Bell Journal of Economics*, 13(1), 206–213.

Moser, P. (2005). "How do patent laws influence innovation? Evidence from nineteenth-century world's fair." *American Economic Review*, 95(4), 1214–1236.

Moser, P. (2012). "Innovation without patents: Evidence from world's fairs." *Journal of Law and Economics*, 55(1), 43–74.

Munger, M. (2015a) . "Coase and the 'sharing economy.'" In *Forever Contemporary: The Economics of Ronald Coase*. London: IEA. pp. 187–208.

Munger, M. (2015b). *The Thing Itself: Essays on Academics, Economics, and Policy*. N.p.: Mungerella Publishing.

Munger, M. (2018). *Tomorrow 3.0: Transactions Costs and the Sharing Economy*. New York: Cambridge University Press.

Muthukrishna, M., Heinrich, J. (2016). "Innovation in the collective brain." *Philosophical Transactions of the Royal Society B*, 371, 20150192.

Narula, R., Zanfei, A. (2004). "Globalisation of innovation: The role of multinational enterprises." In J. Fagerberg et al. (eds.), *Handbook of Innovation*. New York: Oxford University Press. Pp. 157–182.

Nelson, R. (1959). "The simple economics of basic scientific research." *Journal of Political Economy*, 67, 296–307.

Nelson, R. (ed.) (1993). *National Innovation Systems*. New York: Oxford University Press.

Nelson, R. (2004). "The market economy and the scientific commons." *Research Policy*, 33, 455–471.

Nelson, R., Winter, S. (1982). *An Economic Theory of Economic Change*. Cambridge, MA: Harvard University Press.

Nielsen, M. (2011). *Reinventing Discovery: The New Era of Networked Science*. Princeton, NJ: Princeton University Press.

Niosi, J. (2010). *Building National and Regional Innovation Systems*. Cheltenham: Edward Elgar.

Nordhaus, W. (2004). "Schumpeterian profits in the American economy: Theory and measurement." NBER Working Paper No. 10433.

Nordhaus, W. (2015). "Climate clubs: Overcoming free-riding in international climate policy." *American Economic Review*, 105(4), 1339–1370.

North, D. (1990). *Institutions, Institutional Change and Economic Performance*. New York: Cambridge University Press.

North, D. (2005). *Understanding the Process of Economic Change*. Princeton: Princeton University Press.

Novak, M., Davidson, S., Potts, J. (2018). "The cost of trust: A pilot study." SSRN: https://papers.ssrn.com/sol3/papers.cfm?abstract_id=3218761.

Nowak, M. (2011) *Supercooperators: Altruism, Evolution, and why we need each other to succeed*. New York: Free Press.

Nowak, M. (2006a). *Evolutionary Dynamics: Exploring the Equations of Life*. Cambridge, MA: Harvard University Press.

Nowak, M. (2006b). "Five rules for the evolution of cooperation." *Science*, 314(5805), 1560–1563.

Nowak, M., Sigmund, K. (1998). "Evolution of indirect reciprocity by image scoring." *Nature*, 393(6685), 573–577.

Nowak, M., Tarnita, C., Wilson, E. O. (2010). "The evolution of eusociality." *Nature*, 466(7310), 1057–1062.

Nuvolari, A. (2004). "Collective invention during the British Industrial Revolution: The case of the Cornish pumping engine." *Cambridge Journal of Economics*, 28, 347–363.

Nuvolari, A. (2005). "Open source software development: Some historical perspectives." *First Monday*, 10(1), 30.

Oates, W. (2006). "The many faces of the Tiebout model." In W. Fischel (ed.), *The Tiebout Model at Fifty*. Cambridge, MA: Lincoln Institute of Land Policy.

O'Mahony, S. (2003). "Guarding the commons: How open source contributors protect their work." *Research Policy*, 32(7), 1179–1198.

O'Mahony, S. (2007). "The governance of open source initiatives: What does it mean to be community managed?" *Journal of Management and Governance*, 11(2), 139–150.

O'Mahony, S., Ferraro, F. (2007). "The emergence of governance in an open source community." *Academy of Management Journal*, 50(5), 1079–106.

Organization for Economic Cooperation and Development (OECD) (2003). *The Sources of Economic Growth in OECD Countries*. OECD: Paris.

Organization for Economic Cooperation and Development (OECD) (2013). *Innovation Driven Growth in Regions: The Role of Smart Specialization*. OECD: Paris.

Ogus, A. (2000). Self-Regulation. In B. Bouckaert, G. De Geest (eds.), *Encyclopedia of Law and Economics*, vol. 5: *The Economics of Crime and Litigation*. Cheltenham: Edward Elgar. Pp. 587–602.

Oliveira, P., von Hippel, E. (2011). "Users as service innovators: The case of banking services." *Research Policy*, 40(6), 806–818.

Olson, M. (1965). *The Logic of Collective Action*. Cambridge, MA: Harvard University Press.

Olson, M. (1982). *The Rise and Decline of Nations*. New Haven: Yale University Press.

Osborn, R., Hagedoorn, J. (1997). "The institutionalization and evolutionary dynamics of interorganizational alliances and networks." *Academy of Management Journal*, 40(2), 261–278.

Osterloh, M., Rota, S. (2007). "Open source software development: Just another case of collective invention?" *Research Policy*, 36(2), 157–171.

Ostrom, E. (1990). *Governing the Commons: The Evolution of Institutions for Collective Action*. Cambridge: Cambridge University Press.

Ostrom, E. (1999a). "Coping with tragedies of the commons." *American Review of Political Science*, 2, 493–535.

Ostrom, E. (1999b). "Polycentricity, complexity, and the commons." *Good Society*, 9(2), 37–41.

Ostrom, E. (2000). "Collective action and the evolution of social norms." *Journal of Economic Perspectives*, 14(3), 137–158.

Ostrom, E. (2005). *Understanding Institutional Diversity*. Princeton, NJ: Princeton University Press.

Ostrom, E. (2009). "A general framework for analyzing sustainability of social-ecological systems." *Science*, 325(5939), 419–422.

Ostrom, E. (2010). "Beyond markets and states: Polycentric governance of complex economic systems." *American Economic Review*, 100(3), 641–672.

Ostrom, E., Chang, C., Pennington, M., Tarko, V. (2012). "The future of the commons." London: Institute of Public Affairs.

Ostrom, E., Hess, C. (2006a). "A framework for analyzing the knowledge commons." In C. Hess, E. Ostrom (eds.), *Understanding Knowledge as a Commons*. Cheltenham: Edward Elgar. Pp. 41–82.

Ostrom, E., Hess, C. (eds.). (2006b). *Understanding Knowledge as a Commons: From Theory to Practice*. Cheltenham: Edward Elgar.

Ostrom, E., Janssen, M., Andries, R. (2007). "A diagnostic approach for going beyond panaceas." *Proceedings of the National Academy of Sciences*, 104(39), 15181–15187.

Ostrom, E., Walker, J., Gardner, R. (1992). "Covenants with and without a sword: Self-governance is possible." *American Political Science Review*, 86, 404–417.

Ostrom, V., Ostrom E. (1999). "Public goods and public choices." In M. D. McGinnis (ed.), *Polycentricity and Local Public Economies: Readings from the Workshop in Political Theory and Policy Analysis*. Ann Arbor: University of Michigan Press. Pp. 75–103.

Ostrom, V., Tiebout, C., Warren, R. (1961). "The organization of government in metropolitan areas: A theoretical inquiry." *American Political Science Review*, 55(4), 831–842.

Pagel, M. (2012). *Wired for Culture*. New York: Norton.

Papaioannou, T. (2014). "How inclusive can innovation and development be in the twenty-first century?" *Innovation and Development*, 4(2), 187–202.

Papaioannou, T., Dinar, K., Mugwagwa, J., Watkins, A. (2014). "The role of industry associations in health innovation and politics of development: The case of South Africa and India" Presented at the 15th International Schumpeter Society Conference 2014.

Parente, S., Prescott. E. (1994). "Barriers to technology adoption and development." *Journal of Political Economy*, 102(2), 298–321.

Pelikan, P., Wegner, G. (eds.) (2003). *The Evolutionary Analysis of Economic Policy*. Cheltenham: Edward Elgar.

Penrose, E. (1959). *The Theory of the Growth of the Firm*. New York: Oxford University Press.

Perez, C. (2002). *Technological Revolutions and Financial Capital: The Dynamics of Bubbles and Golden Ages*. Cheltenham: Edward Elgar.

Phelps, E. (2013). *Mass Flourishing*. Princeton, NJ: Princeton University Press.

Pinker, S. (2012). *The Better Angels of Our Nature*. New York: Penguin.

Popper, K. (1972). *Objective Knowledge: An Evolutionary Approach*. New York: Oxford University Press.

Popper, N. (2015). *Digital Gold: The Untold Story of Bitcoin*. London: Penguin.

Postrel, V. (1998). *The Future and its Enemies*. New York: Free Press.

Poteete, A., Janssen, M., Ostrom, E. (2010). *Working Together: Collective Action, the Commons, and Multiple Methods in Practice*. Princeton, NJ: Princeton University Press.

Potter, J., Sloof, R. (1996). "Interest groups: A survey of empirical models that try to assess their influence." *European Journal of Political Economy*, 12, 403–442.

Potts, J. (2000). *The New Evolutionary Microeconomics*. Cheltenham: Edward Elgar.

Potts, J. (2012). "Novelty-bundling markets." In D. E. Andersson (ed.), *The Spatial Market Process*. Bingley: Emerald. Pp. 291–312.

Potts, J. (2014). "Innovation is a spontaneous order." *Cosmos and Taxis*, 1(2), 1–10.

Potts, J. (2016). "Innovation policy in a global economy." *Journal of Entrepreneurship and Public Policy*, 5(3), 308–324.

Potts, J. (2017). "Behavioral innovation economics." In R. Frantz (ed.), *Routledge Handbook on Behavioral Economics*. New York: Routledge. Pp. 392–404.

Potts, J. (2018). "Governing the innovation commons." *Journal of Institutional Economics*, 14(6), 1025–1047.

Potts, J., Almudi, I., Fatas-Villafranca, F., Izquierdo, L. (2017a). "Economics of utopia: A co-evolutionary model of ideas, citizenship, and socio-political change." *Journal of Evolutionary Economics*, 27(4), 629–662.

Potts, J., Almudi, I., Fatas-Villafranca, F. (2017b). "Utopia competition: A new approach to the micro-foundations of sustainability transitions." *Journal of Bioeconomics*, 19(1), 165–185.

Potts, J., Hartley, J. (2015). "How the social economy produces innovation." *Review of Social Economy*, 73(3), 263–282.

Potts, J., Hartley, J., Montgomery, L., Neylon, C., Rennie, E. (2018). "A journal is a club: A new model for scholarly publishing." *Prometheus*, 35(1), 75–92.

Potts, J., Roe, G. (2016). "Detecting new industry emergence using government data." *Innovation: Management, Practice and Policy*, 18(3), 373–388.

Potts, J., Thomas, S. (2018). "How industry competition ruined windsurfing." *Sport, Business, and Management* (forthcoming).

Potts, J., Waters-Lynch, J. (2017). "Social economy of a coworking space: A focal point model of coordination." *Review of Social Economy*, 75(4), 417–433.

Powell, W., Koput, K., Smith-Doerr, L. (1996). "Interorganizational collaboration and the locus of innovation: Networks of learning in biotechnology." *Administrative Science Quarterly*, 41, 116–145.

Price, G. (1972). "Fisher's 'fundamental theorem' made clear." *Annals of Human Genetics*, 36(2), 129–140.

Price, D. de Solla (1963). *Big Science, Little Science*. New York: Columbia University Press.

Raine, A., Foster, J., Potts, J. (2006). "The new entropy law and the economic process." *Ecological Complexity*, 3(4), 354–360.

Ramo, J. (2016). *The Seventh Sense: Power, Fortune and Survival in the Age of Networks*. New York: Little, Brown.

Raustiala, K., Sprigman, C. (2006). "The piracy paradox: Innovation and intellectual property in fashion design." *Virginia Law Review*, 86, 1687–777.

Rawls, J. (1972). *A Theory of Justice*. Cambridge, MA: Harvard University Press.

Raymond, E. (1999). "The cathedral and the bazaar." *Knowledge, Technology & Policy*, 12(3), 23–49.

Richardson, G. (1972). "The organisation of industry." *Economic Journal*, 82(327), 883–896.

Richardson, G. (1990). *Information and Investment*. New York: Oxford University Press.

Richerson, P., Boyd, B. (2006). *Not by Genes Alone*. Chicago: University of Chicago Press.

Richerson, P., Boyd, R., Henrich, J. (2003). "The cultural evolution of human cooperation." In P. Hammerstein (ed.), *The Genetic and Cultural Evolution of Cooperation*. Cambridge, MA: MIT Press. Pp. 357–388.

Rid, T. (2016). *Rise of the Machines: The lost history of cybernetics*. New York: Norton.

Ridley, M. (2010). *The Rational Optimist*. New York: HarperCollins.

Riker, W., Sened, I. (1991). "A political theory of the origin of property rights." *American Journal of Political Science*, 35, 951–969.

Robertson, P., Langlois, R. (1995). "Innovation, networks, and vertical integration." *Research Policy*, 24, 543–562.

Rochet, J., Tirole, J. (2003). "Platform competition in two-sided markets." *Journal of the European Economic Association*, 1(4), 990–1029.

Rodrik, D. (2004). "Industrial policy for the 21st century." John F. Kennedy School of Government, Harvard University, Cambridge, MA.

Rodrik, D. (2007a). *One Economics, Many Lessons*. Princeton, NJ: Princeton University Press.

Rodrik, D. (2007b). "Normalizing industrial policy." John F. Kennedy School of Government, Harvard University, Cambridge, MA.

Rogers, E. (1962/2005). *Diffusion of Innovations*. 5th ed. New York: Free Press.

Romano, R. (1989). "Aspects of R&D subsidization." *Quarterly Journal of Economics*, 104(4), 863–873.

Romer, P. (1990). "Endogenous technological change." *Journal of Political Economy*, 98(2), S71–S102.

Rose, C. (2008). "Big roads, big rights: Public infrastructure and environmental consequences." *Arizona Law Review*, 50, 408–456.

Rosenberg, N. (1982). *Inside the Black Box: Technology and Economics*. Cambridge: Cambridge University Press.

Ruef, M. (2009). *The Entrepreneurial Group: Social Identities, Networks, and Collective Action*. Princeton, NJ: Princeton University Press.

Sako, M. (1996). "Suppliers' associations in the Japanese automobile industry: Collective action for technology diffusion." *Cambridge Journal of Economics*, 20(6), 651–671.

Salerno, J. (2008). "The entrepreneur: Real and imagined." *Quarterly Journal of Austrian Economics*, 11(3–4), 188–207.

Salisbury, R. (1969). "An exchange theory of interest groups." *Midwest Journal of Political Science*, 13(1), 1–32.

Samuelson, P. (1954). "The pure theory of public expenditure." *Review of Economics and Statistics*, 36(4), 387–389.

Sandler, T., Tschirhart, J. (1980). "The Economic theory of Clubs: An Evaluative Survey'" *Journal of Economic Literature*, 18 (4), 1481–1521.

Sarasvathy, S. (2008). *Effectuation*. Cheltenham: Edward Elgar.

Saxenian, A. L. (1994). *Regional Advantage*. Cambridge, MA: Harvard University Press.

Schelling, T. (1960). *The Strategy of Conflict*. Cambridge, MA: Harvard University Press.

Schelling, T. (1978). *Micromotives and Macrobehaviour*. New York: Norton.

Schneider, M., Teske, P. (1992). "Toward a theory of the political entrepreneur: Evidence from local government." *American Political Science Review*, 86(3), 737–747.

Schultz, M. (2006). "Fear and norms and rock & roll: What jambands can teach us about teaching people to obey copyright law." *Berkeley Technology and Law Journal*, 21, 651–679.

Schumpeter, J. ([1912] 1934). *The Theory of Economic Development*. Cambridge, MA: Harvard University Press.

Schumpeter, J. (1939). *Business Cycles: A Theoretical, Historical and Statistical Analysis*. 2 vols. New York: McGraw Hill.

Schumpeter, J. (1942). *Capitalism, Socialism and Democracy*. New York: Harper & Row.

Schumpeter, J. (1947). "The creative response in economic history." *Journal of Economic History*, 7, 149–159.

Scott, J. (1998). *Seeing Like a State*. New Haven: Yale University Press.

Scott, J. (2009). *The Art of Not Being Governed*. New Haven: Yale University Press.

Scranton, P. (1997). *Endless Novelty*. Princeton: Princeton University Press.

Seabright, P. (2004). *The Company of Strangers*. Princeton: Princeton University Press.

Selton, R. (1975). "A reexaminiation of the perfectness concept for equilibrium points in extensive games." *International Journal of Game Theory*, 4(1), 25–55.

Shackle, G. L. S. (1972). *Epistemics and Economics*. London: Transaction Publishers.

Shah, S. (2000). "Sources and patterns of innovation in a consumer products field: Innovations in sporting equipment." WP-4105, Sloan School of Management, Massachusetts Institute of Technology, Cambridge, MA.

Shah, S. (2005). "From innovation to firm formation in the windsurfing, skateboarding and snowboarding industries." University of Illinois Working Paper No. 05-0107.

Shah, S. (2006). "From innovation to firm formation: Contributions by sports enthusiasts to the windsurfing, snowboarding & skateboarding industries." *Engineering of Sport*, 6, 29–34.

Shah, S., Tripas, M. (2007). "The accidental entrepreneur: The emergent and collective process of user entrepreneurship." *Strategic Entrepreneurship Journal*, 1, 123–140.

Shaked, A., Sutton, J. (1981). "The self-regulating profession." *Review of Economic Studies*, 48, 217–234.

Shane, S. (2000a). *A General Theory of Entrepreneurship: The Individual-Opportunity Nexus*. Cheltenham: Edward Elgar.

Shane, S. (2000b). "Prior knowledge and the discovery of entrepreneurial opportunity." *Organizational Science*, 11(4), 448–469.

Shane, S. (2001). "Technological opportunities and new firm creation." *Management Science*, 47(2), 205–220.

Shirky, C. (2008). *Here Comes Everybody*. New York: Penguin.

Shirky, C. (2010). *Cognitive Surplus*. New York: Penguin.

Simon, H. (1955). "A behavioral model of rational choice." *Quarterly Journal of Economics*, 96(1), 99–118.

Simon, H. (2005). "Darwinism, altruism and economics." In K. Dopfer (ed.), *The Evolutionary Foundations of Economics*. New York: Cambridge University Press. Pp. 89–104.

Simonton, D. (1999). *Origins of Genius: Darwinian Perspectives on Creativity*. New York: Oxford University Press.

Singh, R. (1998). *Entrepreneurial Opportunity Recognition through Social Networks*. New York: Garland.

Skyrms, B. (2003). *The Stag Hunt and the Evolution of Social Structure*. New York: Cambridge University Press.

Slack, P. (2014). *The Invention of Improvement*. New York: Oxford University Press.

Smith, A. (1759). *Theory of Moral Sentiments*. Originally printed for A. Kincaid and J. Bell, Edinburgh. (Gutenburg Publishers ed. 2011).

Smith, V. (2003). "Constructivist and ecological rationality in economics." *American Economic Review*, 93(3), 465–508.

Smith, D. (2007). "The politics of innovation: Why innovations need a godfather." *Technovation*, 27(3), 95–104.

Sober, E., Wilson, D. S. (1994). "Reintroducing group selection to the human behavioral sciences." *Behavior and Brain Sciences*, 17, 585–654.

Sober, E., Wilson, D. S. (1998). *Unto Others*. Cambridge, MA: Harvard University Press.

Soete, L., Freeman, C. (1995). *Economics of Industrial Innovation*. London: Routledge.
Solow, R. (1956). "A contribution to the theory of economic growth." *Quarterly Journal of Economics*, 70, 65–94.
Spence, A. M. (1973). "Job market signalling." *Quarterly Journal of Economics*, 87, 355–374.
Squicciarini, M., Voigtländer, N. (2014). "Human capital and industrialisation: Evidence from the Age of Enlightenment." NBER Working Paper No. 20219.
Stephan, P. (1996). "The economics of science." *Journal of Economic Literature*, 34, 1199–1235.
Stern, P. (2011). "Design principles for global commons: Natural resources and emerging technologies." *International Journal of the Commons*, 5(2), 213–232.
Stephenson, N. (1999). *Cryptonomicon*. New York: Avon Books.
Stigler, G. (1961). "The Economics of information." *Journal of Political Economy*, 69(3), 213–225.
Stigler, G. (1971). "The theory of economic regulation." *Bell Journal of Economics*, 2(1), 3–21.
Stiglitz, J. (1975). "The theory of screening, education, and the distribution of income." *American Economic Review*, 65(3), 283–300.
Stiglitz, J. (1999). "Knowledge as a global public good." In I. Kaul et al. (eds.), *Global Public Goods*. New York: Oxford University Press. Pp. 308–325.
Stiglitz, J. (2006). "Global public goods and global finance: Does global governance ensure that the global public interest is served?" In J. Touffut (ed.), *Advancing Public Goods*. Cheltenham: Edward Elgar. Pp. 149–164.
Storper, M. (1996). "Systems of innovation as collective action: Conventions, products and technologies." *Industrial and Corporate Change*, 5(3), 1–30.
Stringham, E. (2015). *Private Governance*. New York: Oxford University Press.
Sugden, R. (1995). "A theory of focal points." *Economic Journal*, 105, 533–550.
Sundararajun, A. (2016). *The Sharing Economy*. Cambridge, MA: MIT Press.
Swan, J., Newell, S. (1995). "The role of professional associations in technology diffusion." *Organization Studies*, 16(5), 847–874.
Swann, P. (2014). *Common Innovation*. Cheltenham: Edward Elgar.
Tarko, V. (2016). *Elinor Ostrom: An Intellectual Biography*. New York: Rowman & Littlefield.
Tassey, G. (2013). "Beyond the business cycle: The need for a technology based growth strategy." *Science and Public Policy*, 40(3), 293–315.
Taylor, M. Z. (2016). *The Politics of Innovation*. New York: Oxford University Press.
Teece, D. (1986a). "Profiting from technological innovation: Implications for integration, collaboration, licensing and public policy." *Research Policy*, 15, 285–303.
Teece, D. (1986b). "Transaction cost economics and the multinational enterprise." *Journal of Economic Behavior and Organization*, 7, 21–45.
Teece, D. (1992). "Competition, cooperation, and innovation: Organizational arrangements for regimes of rapid technological progress." *Journal of Economic Behavior and Organization*, 18(1), 1–25.
Teece, D. (1996). "Firm organization, industrial structure and technological innovation." *Journal of Economic Behavior and Organization*, 31, 193–224.
Thierer, A. (2016). *Permissionless Innovation*. Arlington, VA: Mercatus Centre.
Thomas, S., Potts J. (2018). "The role of industry associations in coordinating technological change." Paper presented at International Joseph A. Schumpeter Society Conference, Seoul, 2018.
Tocqueville, A. (1840/2000). *Democracy in America* (republished). Chicago: University of Chicago Press.
Tomasello, M. (2009). *Why We Cooperate*. Cambridge, MA: MIT Press.
Tomasi, J. (2012). *Free Market Fairness*. Princeton: Princeton University Press.
Trajtenberg, M. (2012). "Can the Nelson-Arrow paradigm still be the beacon of innovation policy?" In J. Lerner, S. Stern (eds.), *The Rate and Direction of Inventive Activity Revisited*. Chicago: University of Chicago Press. Pp. 679–684.
Traulsen, A., Nowak, M. (2006). "Evolution of cooperation by multilevel selection." *Proceedings of the National Academy of Sciences*, 103(29), 10952–10955.
Trivers, R. (1971). "The evolution of reciprocal altruism." *Quarterly Review of Biology*, 46, 35–57.
Trivers, R. (2011). *The Folly of Fools: The Logic of Deceit and Self-Deception in Human Life*. New York: Basic Books.

Tullock, G. (1959). "Problems of majority voting." *Journal of Political Economy*, 69, 200–203.
Turchin, P. (2007). *War and Peace and War*. New York: Plume.
Turchin, P. (2015). *Ultrasociety*. Peter Turchin Publishing.
Twight, C. (1988). "Government manipulation of constitution-level transactions costs: A general theory of transaction cost augmentation and the growth of government." *Public Choice*, 56, 131–152.
Twight, C. (1994). "Political transaction cost manipulation." *Journal of Theoretical Politics*, 6(2), 189–216.
Usher, D. (1964). "The welfare economics of invention." *Economica*, 31(123), 279–287.
Vanberg, V. (1986). "Spontaneous market order and social rules: A critique of F.A. Hayek's theory of cultural evolution." *Economics and Philosophy*, 2, 75–100.
Van Vugt, M. (2006). "Evolutionary origins of leadership and followership." *Personality and Social Psychology Review*, 10, 354–371.
Van Winden, F. (1999). "On the economic theory of interest groups: Toward a group frame of reference in political economics." *Public Choice*, 100(1–2), 1–29.
Verspagen, B., Werker, C. (2003). "The invisible college of the economics of innovatiuon and technological change." MERIT Research Report 008.
Vigna, P., Case, M. (2015). *The Age of Cryptocurrency*. New York: Gildad Media.
Vincenti, W. (1990). *What Engineers Know and How They Know It*. Baltimore: Johns Hopkins University Press.
von Hippel, E. (1986). "Lead users: A source of novel product concepts." *Management Science*, 32(7), 791–805.
von Hippel, E. (1987). "Cooperation between rivals: Informal know-how trading." *Research Policy*, 16, 291–302.
von Hippel, E. (1994). "Sticky information and the locus of problem solving." *Management Science*, 40(4), 429–439.
von Hippel, E. (1998). "Economics of product development by users: The impact of 'sticky' local information." *Management Science*, 44(5), 629–641.
von Hippel, E. (2005). *Democratizing Innovation*. Cambridge, MA: MIT Press.
von Hippel, E. (2007). "Horizontal innovation networks: By and for users." *Industrial and Corporate Change*, 16(2), 293–315.
von Hippel, E., von Krogh, G. (2003). "Open source software development and the private-collective innovation model: Issues for organization science." *Organization Science*, 14(2), 208–223.
von Hippel, E., von Krogh, G. (2006). "Free revealing and the private-collective model for innovation incentives." *R&D Management*, 36(3), 295–306.
von Krogh, G., Haefliger, S., Spaeth, S., Wallin, M. (2012). "Carrots and rainbows: Motivation and social practice in open source software development." *MIS Quarterly*, 36, 649–676.
von Krogh, G., Spaeth, S., Lakhani, K. (2003). "Community, joining, and specialization in open source software innovation: A case study." *Research Policy*, 32(7), 1217–1241.
Waguespack, D., Fleming, L. (2009). "Scanning the commons: Evidence on the benefits to startups participating in open standards development." *Management Science*, 55, 210–223.
Wallis, J., North, D. (1986). "Measuring the transactional sector of the American economy 1870–1970." In S. Engerman and R. Gallman (eds.), *Long Term Factors in American Economic Growth*, NBER, Chicago: University of Chicago Press. Pp.95–162.
Watts, D., Strogatz, S. (1998). "Collective dynamics of 'small world' networks." *Nature*, 393, 440–442.
Wegner, G. (1997). "Economic policy from an evolutionary perspective: A new approach." *Journal of Institutional and Theoretical Economics*, 153(3), 485–509.
West, J., Lakhani, K. (2008). "Getting clear about communities in open innovation." *Industry and Innovation*, 15(2), 223–231.
Weyl, G., White, A. (2014). "Let the right 'one' win: Policy lessons from the new economics of platforms." University of Chicago Coase-Sandor Institute for Law & Economics Research Paper, 709–818.
Williams, G. (1966). *Adaptation and Natural Selection*. Princeton, NJ: Princeton University Press.

Williams, M., Hall, J. (2015). "Hackerspaces: A case study in the creation and management of a common pool resource." *Journal of Institutional Economics*, 11(4), 769–781.

Williamson, O. (1975). *Markets and Hierarchies: Analysis and Antitrust Implications*. New York: Free Press.

Williamson, O. (1979). "Transaction cost economics: The governance of contractual relations." *Journal of Law and Economics*, 22(2), 233–261.

Williamson, O. (1985a). *The Economic Institutions of Capitalism*. New York: Free Press.

Williamson, O. (1985b). "Employee ownership and internal governance: A perspective." *Journal of Economic Organization and Behavior*, 6, 243–256.

Williamson, O. (1996). *Mechanisms of Governance*. New York: Oxford University Press.

Williamson, O. (2000). "The new institutional economics: Taking stock, looking ahead." *Journal of Economic Literature*, 38, 595–613.

Williamson, O. (2002). "The lens of contract: Private ordering." *American Economic Review*, 92(2), 438–443.

Williamson, O. (2005). "The economics of governance." *American Economic Review*, 95(2), 1–18.

Wilkinson, W. (2016). "The great enrichment and social justice." https://niskanencenter.org/blog/the-great-enrichment-and-social-justice/

Wilson, D. S., Kniffin, K. (1999). "Multilevel selection and the social transmission of behavior." *Human Nature*, 10(3), 291–310.

Wilson, D. S., Ostrom, E., Cox, R. (2013). "Generalizing the core design principles for the efficacy of groups." *Journal of Economic Behavior and Organization*, 90: S21–S32.

Wilson, D. S., Sober, E. (1994). "Reintroducing group selection to the human behavioral sciences." *Behavioral and Brain Sciences*, 17, 585–654.

Wilson, D. S., Wilson, E. O. (2007). "Rethinking the theoretical foundation of sociobiology." *Quarterly Review of Biology*, 82(4), 327–348.

Wilson, D. S., Wilson, E. O. (2008). "Evolution for the good of the group." *American Scientist*, 96(5), 380–389.

Winter, S. (1984). "Schumpeterian competition in alternative technological regimes." *Journal of Economic Behavior and Organization*, 5(3–4), 287–320.

Witt, U. (2003). "Economic policy making in evolutionary perspective." *Journal of Evolutionary Economics*, 13(1), 77–94.

Witt, U. (2009). "Propositions about novelty." *Journal of Economic Behavior and Organization*, 70(1), 311–320.

Wolf, C. (1979). "A theory of non-market failure." *Journal of Law and Economics*, 22(1), 107–139.

Wright, R. (2001). "The man who invented the web." *Time*, June 24, 2001. http://content.time.com/time/magazine/article/0,9171,137689,00.html.

Wu, T. (2006). "Intellectual property, innovation, and decentralised decisions." *Virginia Law Review*, 92, 123–147.

Wuchty, S., Jones, B., Uzzi, B. (2007). "The increasing dominance of teams in production of knowledge." *Science*, 316, 1036–1039.

Zerbe, R., McCurdy, H. (1999). "The failure of market failure." *Journal of Policy Analysis and Management*, 18(4), 558–578.

Ziman, J. (ed.) (2000). *Technological Innovation as an Evolutionary Process*. New York: Cambridge University Press.

Zywicki, T. (2000). "Was Hayek right about group selection after all?' Review essay of Unto Others: The evolution and psychology of unselfish behavior, by Elliott Sober and David Sloan Wilson." *Review of Austraian Economics*, 13(1), 81–95.

INDEX

Tables and figures are indicated by an italic *t*, and *f*, respectively, following the page number.